GCSE
INTEGRATED HUMANITIES

N E GUIDES

Jonathon Hickman
David Walker

Longman

LONGMAN REVISE GUIDES

SERIES EDITORS:
Geoff Black and Stuart Wall

TITLES AVAILABLE:
Art and Design
Biology
British and European History
Business Studies
CDT: – Design and Realisation
Chemistry
Computer Studies
Economics
English
English Literature
French
Geography
German
Home Economics
Integrated Humanities
Mathematics
Mathematics: Higher Level and Extension
Physics
Religious Studies
Science
Social and Economic History
Typewriting and Keyboarding Applications
World History

FORTHCOMING:
CDT: – Technology
Human Biology
Music

Longman Group UK Limited
*Longman House, Burnt Mill, Harlow,
Essex CM20 2JE, England
and Associated Companies throughout the world.*

First published 1989

British Library Cataloguing in Publication Data

Hickman, Jonathon
    Integrated humanities.
    1. England. Secondary schools. Curriculum subjects:
    Humanities. Integrated studies
    I. Title   II. Walker, David
    001.3′07′1242

    ISBN 0-582-04031-0

Produced by The Pen and Ink Book Company,
Huntingdon, Cambridgeshire

Set in 10/12pt Century Old Style

Printed and bound in Great Britain by
William Clowes Limited, Beccles and London

CONTENTS

EDITORS' PREFACE

Longman Revise Guides are written by experienced examiners and teachers, and aim to give you the best possible foundation for success in examinations and other modes of assessment. Examiners are well aware that the performance of many candidates falls well short of their true potential, and this series of books aims to remedy this, by encouraging thorough study and a full understanding of the concepts involved. The Revise Guides should be seen as course companions and study aids to be used throughout the year, not just for last minute revision.

Examiners are in no doubt that a structured approach in preparing for examinations and in presenting coursework can, together with hard work and diligent application, substantially improve performance.

The largely self-contained nature of each chapter gives the book a useful degree of flexibility. After starting with the opening general chapters on the background to the GCSE, and the syllabus coverage, all other chapters can be read selectively, in any order appropriate to the stage you have reached in your course.

We believe that this book, and the series as a whole, will help you establish a solid platform of basic knowledge and examination technique on which to build.

Geoff Black and Stuart Wall

ACKNOWLEDGEMENTS

We are grateful to colleagues in Northamptonshire schools, with special thanks to the members of the Humanities Departments of Kingsthorpe Upper School and Montsaye School, Rothwell; to all students who have contributed to the guide, with special thanks to Nicola Denham, Neil Stone, Amanda Greatbach, Yvonne Labruyere, Kathryn Stephenson, Lisa Hirst, Katie Furniss and Vicki McKnight; Nicki Little, Assistant Secretary, Midland Examining Group, with special responsibility for Integrated Humanities; and Pat Watkin, Resources Department, Montsaye School. Thanks to Tracy for the photographs.

Thanks also go to Southwold School, Nottinghamshire, Hind Leys School, Leicestershire, Dartmouth High School, Birmingham, King Edward VII Upper School, Melton Mowbray, and John Turner, Chief Examiner, Midland Examining Group Integrated Humanities. We acknowledge the help of the Northern Examining Association, the Southern Examining Group and the Midland Examining Group, especially for the use of their Integrated Humanities coursework booklet.

Finally, a big thank you to Jane, Amy, Rona and Hanna, for their patience.

INTRODUCING INTEGRATED HUMANITIES

GCSE AND INTEGRATED HUMANITIES

WHAT IS INTEGRATED HUMANITIES?

THE KEY FEATURES OF INTEGRATED HUMANITIES

THE AIMS OF YOUR COURSE

ASSESSMENT OBJECTIVES

CONTENT

TYPES OF ASSESSMENT TASK

EXAMINATION GROUP REQUIREMENTS

MARKING YOUR WORK

GETTING STARTED

To understand a particular topic or issue as fully as possible we will frequently need to draw on a *number* of Humanities subjects. Integrated Humanities is not itself a discipline, such as History, Geography or Economics, etc. It borrows a variety of methods and ideas from these subjects in order to study particular issues and themes. In this way it *integrates* what each subject can tell us into the study of the whole topic under consideration.

Of course, for a given issue the approach of some Humanities subjects will be more relevant than others. You have freedom to use the ideas and methods of *particular subjects* when they are useful and appropriate. However, over the course as a whole, you will be required to demonstrate that in your work you have used the ideas and methods of the *full range* of Humanities subjects.

In this chapter we look at:

- the key features of Integrated Humanities;
- the aims of your course;
- the assessment of objectives;
- the content of your course;
- what you are required to do during your course;
- how your work is marked.

ESSENTIAL PRINCIPLES

1 ⟩ GCSE AND INTEGRATED HUMANITIES

The successful introduction of the GCSE has brought about important changes in the way in which young people are assessed at the end of their period of compulsory education. In particular, GCSE has introduced three key features for all 16+ examinations.

Positive achievement

❝ Assessing what you know, understand and *can* do ❞

In GCSE examinations, students have the opportunity to be assessed on what they know, understand and *can* do. This represents a move away from a system of examination which depended largely on your ability to recall facts which had been learned and which resulted in a 'pass' or a 'fail'. Instead, the GCSE offers a way of assessing and rewarding you according to how well you can achieve particular tasks. To enable this to take place, the GCSE has written into each subject exactly what the *objectives* of that subject are – that is, the range of skills, understanding and knowledge which is considered relevant to that subject. The grades which you will obtain in your GCSE are designed to record the *extent* to which you are able to demonstrate your ability to meet these objectives. Grades are therefore *positive descriptions* of what you are able to achieve in a particular subject. They are no longer designed merely to record whether you have passed or failed, or to enable comparison between your performance and that of other students. Grades become, in effect, statements of *your own* achievements.

Differentiation

❝ In Integrated Humanities, most assessment tasks are designed to be attempted by everyone. ❞

The GCSE is an examination which aims to give everyone a chance to show what they can achieve. *Differentiation* is the term used to describe the means by which all students are given that chance. For Integrated Humanities, differentiation is achieved mainly by *outcome*. This means that all students will attempt *similar tasks*, but the tasks will be designed to enable each student to show his or her ability, from brief, simple responses to more extended and involved ones. This is unlike some GCSE courses, which give the more able students *different tasks* from those set for the less able.

Coursework

❝ Coursework assesses your achievements throughout your course. ❞

Coursework is work which is assessed and counts as part of your final examination grade but is produced by you during your course and not at the end of it. This is, in fact, nothing new! Coursework has always provided an alternative to the *end-of-course examination* – that is, an examination which you take on a particular day, for a few hours, which gives you your only opportunity to demonstrate your achievements over two years of study. Coursework means that your achievements are rewarded over a longer period of time, that the work you produce during your course counts for something. This can provide an incentive and increase your motivation, because the rewards of examination success are no longer dependent on a distant, two-hour examination but on the work which you produce while you are in the process of learning. Coursework can reward you for *applying* your skills and knowledge to the everyday world outside the classroom. This helps your subject to come alive, as you see its relevance to real-life situations.

The GCSE emphasises the importance of coursework by making it a *requirement* in the examination of most subjects (with the exception of foreign languages) and by making it worth *at least* 20% of the final mark. Integrated Humanities is one of a few subjects which go still further, with coursework being worth 100% of your final examination mark.

Although the GCSE has introduced real and significant changes, for many Humanities subjects these have not been too dramatic. This is because the GCSE has grown out of, and extended, many of the developments that were already taking place. It should be seen as part of a continuous process of improving the methods of examination and making assessment more relevant to the aims of the subject, thus raising standards.

2 ⟩ WHAT IS INTEGRATED HUMANITIES?

Humanities is the title usually given to those subjects which study how human beings behave, the things they experience, and how they make sense of those experiences. Exploring human behaviour and experiences, and so understanding the human condition, involves asking a number of questions about human beings, questions such as:

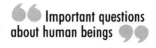
Important questions about human beings 99

- Where are they located?
- How do they interact with their environment?
- How, and where, are decisions made that affect human beings and their environment?
- What happened in the past, how does this affect the present and influence the future?
- How do human beings make use of the scarce resources available to them?
- How do their beliefs help them to make sense of their experiences, and how do these beliefs influence their behaviour?

The subjects which make up Humanities have each developed their own skills, concepts and methods to answer some of these questions. For example, *Geography* is concerned with spatial location and with patterns of distribution. It involves developing graphic and data-handling skills, as well as the skills needed for fieldwork enquiry. *History* is concerned with the re-creation of the past and involves the understanding of key concepts such as continuity and change, cause and consequence, similarity and difference. You must also develop the skills which are necessary for studying the variety of available historical evidence. *Social Science* is concerned with developing an awareness, knowledge and understanding of how people behave, as individuals and as groups. It involves using a range of methods for collecting, analysing and interpreting data about society.

Each Humanities subject contributes in its own way to our understanding of human behaviour and experience, but although each has its own area, many overlap, and you find similar things being talked about in different subject lessons.

Consider this example of a conversation in a History lesson.

The teacher is giving a lesson on the conflict in the Middle East with the help of a map of the area.

Teacher: What is that piece of land there, marked 'B'?
Pupil A : The Gaza Strip?
Teacher: That's right. And what about the area marked 'F'? What's that?
Pupil B : That must be the West Bank.
Teacher: Yes. Now, look at the shape of the State of Israel as it was after the end of the war in 1949. You see it's in several sections – a coastal strip and an inland area near a lake. What lake is that, by the way?
Pupil C : The Sea of Galilee?
Teacher: Right. Now, the third area is this southern triangle, reaching down to the Gulf of Aqaba. This was land held by Israel after winning a war, so we can assume that it was largely what the Israelis wanted. But why did they want these three areas in particular? Let's start with the coast strip. What advantages did control of that strip have for Israel?
Pupil B : The coast was fertile.
Pupil C : There would have been trade with the West going on from coastal ports.
Teacher: Yes.
Pupil D : Tel Aviv is on the coast, and that had become the main Israeli city.
Teacher: That's right. There seems to be plenty of worthwhile reasons for wanting to control the Mediterranean coast.

66 **A full understanding may involve *several* Humanities subjects.** 99

This dialogue might be taken from a *History* lesson, but the teacher can teach about the course of warfare in the Middle East only by using knowledge and ideas taken from *Geography*. In the same way, when talking about, say, the location of industry in *Geography*, you need to understand the *economic* factors and the *historical* reasons that led to certain industries being located in certain regions.

Therefore, to understand a particular topic or issue as fully as possible, we will frequently need to draw on a *number* of Humanities subjects. If you try 'brainstorming' – that is, quickly writing down all the areas which may be relevant to the understanding of an issue, such as famine in Ethiopia, you will end up with a 'topic web' (see Fig 1.1).

Each Humanities subject has developed and refined the skills and concepts needed to understand the questions raised in studying that subject. However, you will develop a full understanding of many issues only when you *bring together* the skills learned in *all* the separate subject areas.

So, as you can see, Integrated Humanities is unlike other Humanities subjects. It is not a discipline in itself, but borrows a variety of methods and ideas from other subjects in order to study particular issues and themes. In this way it *integrates* what each subject can tell us into the study of the whole topic under consideration. This is not to say that *each* study and

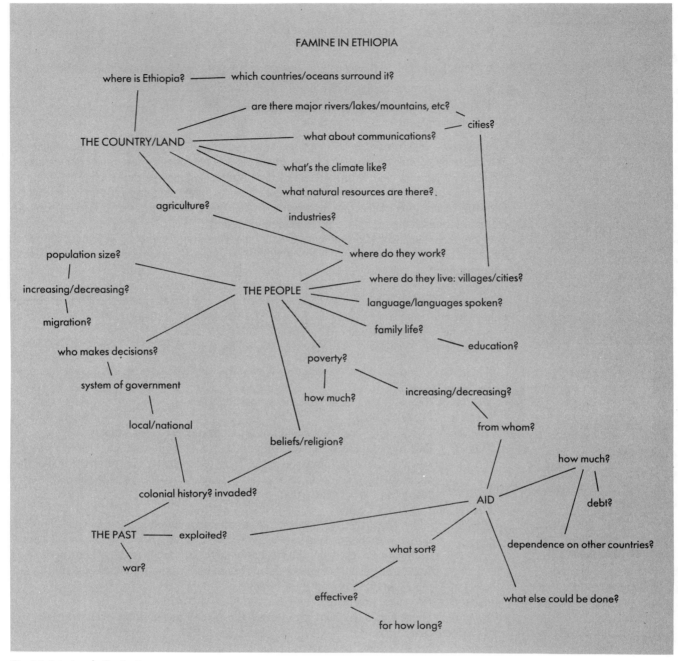

Fig. 1.1 A topic web: Famine in Ethiopia.

piece of work you do must involve a balance of *all* the Humanities subjects. For a given issue, the approach of some Humanities subjects will be more relevant than others. You have the freedom to use the ideas and methods of particular subjects when they are useful and appropriate. However, over the course as a whole, you will be required to demonstrate that in your work you have used the ideas and methods of the full range of Humanities subjects.

WHICH SUBJECTS CAN MAKE UP INTEGRATED HUMANITIES?

In your Integrated Humanities course you can expect to use the ideas and methods of the main Humanities subjects:

- History
- Geography
- Social Science, or the subjects which make up the Social Sciences – namely:
  - Economics
  - Sociology
  - Politics
  - Religious Studies

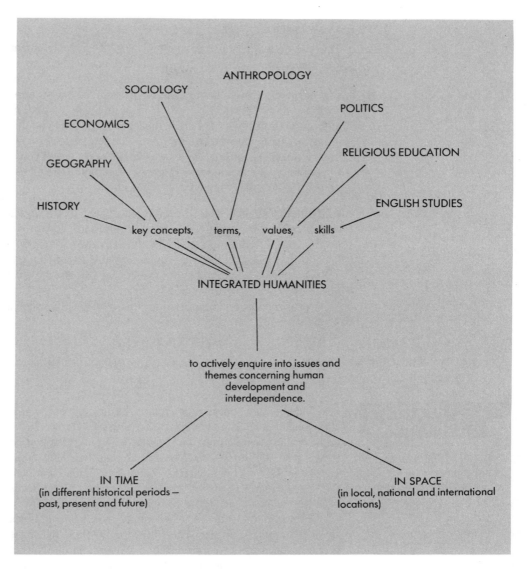

Fig. 1.2 The subjects involved in Integrated Humanities.

In addition, Integrated Humanities courses may make use of subjects which are not normally found in Humanities departments:

- English – issues can be approached through literature and your work might involve communicating effectively and responding imaginatively in a variety of media;
- Expressive Arts – issues can be explored through drama and music;
- CDT – your work may involve designing, making and evaluating artefacts.

3 ▷ THE KEY FEATURES OF INTEGRATED HUMANITIES

Learning through doing

Enquiry-based learning

Integrated Humanities is concerned less with your ability to remember and recall what you have learned and more with your ability to apply and use your knowledge, skills and techniques. This means that the emphasis is on finding and handling data, on solving problems and drawing your own conclusions. What is important is the *way* in which you go about learning. The objectives of Integrated Humanities – enquiry, analysis, interpretation, communication, etc. – involve the various *means* by which the process of your learning can be advanced.

Content

The list of possible topics and issues which could be studied in a GCSE Integrated Humanities course is enormous. The precise choice of the content of the course is left to your teacher, who, in consultation with the examination board, must ensure that it is coherent and allows you to experience the methods of a range of Humanities subjects. The flexibility of the course should enable issues and topics which are of current relevance and interest to be chosen for study.

Assessment

There is no external examination for any Integrated Humanities syllabus. All assessments are under the control of the teacher, who, within the requirements of the particular syllabus, is able to devise the kinds of assessment tasks which are most appropriate. This also means that assessment can take place at the most appropriate time during the course, such as when a particular topic or issue is being studied. Your teacher should be able to monitor your progress towards a final grade, helping you to identify your strengths and the areas in which you need to improve. Continuous assessment means that you will need to keep a careful record of those assessed projects which you complete. You will then be able to spot any gaps in your coverage of assessment objectives and ensure that they are filled before the final deadline for the assessment.

Integrated Humanities is, therefore, designed to be as flexible as possible. It avoids an end-of-course, externally set examination, and allows the individual school to select, in accordance with the regulations set down by the examination board, appropriate issues and assessment tasks. In this way courses can be designed to fit the requirements of individual schools, teachers and students. The course can also be changed from year to year so that new issues and concerns can be studied.

At present three examination groups offer GCSE syllabuses in Integrated Humanities. These are:

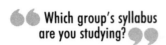
Which group's syllabus are you studying?

- Midland Examining Group (MEG)
- Northern Examining Association (NEA)
- Southern Examining Group (SEG)

4 ▷ THE AIMS OF YOUR COURSE

The *National Criteria* set out standards for a subject which every syllabus must meet.

The 'aims' of any course of study are, basically, a list of goals for the student – what he or she should gain from covering the course. These may involve learning a number of important facts, understanding how or why things happen, and developing a range of skills.

Many GCSE courses have to ensure that their aims comply with those set out for their subject in the 'National Criteria' documents. These state what students should gain from a GCSE course in that subject. Every syllabus for GCSE Biology, for example, must comply with the aims set out in the National Criteria for Biology.

For 'integrated' courses, where more than one traditional subject is involved, there are *no* set National Criteria. When drawing up their syllabuses, however, the examination groups must take into consideration the aims in the National Criteria for *all* the subjects which contribute to the integrated course. For Integrated Humanities, therefore, the aims of each syllabus will reflect those which have been established for all *Humanities* subjects. You could, of course, look all these up, but this is not really necessary. Each of the integrated Humanities syllabuses sets out its main aims at the beginning of its syllabus document.

MEG

1 To stimulate an interest in, and understanding of the issues that affect human societies.
2 To create an awareness that alternative solutions may exist to problems facing contemporary societies.
3 To develop the ability to use different types of information and to recognise the influence of differing values and perspectives in forming reasoned judgements about contemporary issues.
4 To encourage personal and collaborative investigation of issues, and the development of enquiry and decision-making skills.
5 To encourage responsible participation in a multi-cultural society by developing the student's sensitivity and empathy towards people living in a different context from their own.

NEA

. . . the syllabus is intended to encourage courses which will develop the individual's understanding and awareness of:

a) the social and historical nature of society and the implications of social, technological and cultural change;
b) the diversity, abundance and validity of different human values which are derived from a whole range of historical, socio-economic, cultural, political and geographical contexts;

c) the social, economic, political and cultural matrix within which choices, decisions and judgements can be made at the personal, local, national and international levels;
d) the benefits of personal initiative and self-activity being brought to bear on the learning process in order that students can take a responsible and meaningful part in the design, progression and overall direction of their work.

SEG

1 An understanding of human societies which will enable informed and reasoned judgements to be made about significant contemporary issues.
2 An understanding of the social and cultural context of life in modern society, and the range of possible personal futures in a world of rapid technological and cultural change.
3 An awareness of the meaning and diversity of human values, a sensitivity and empathy towards people living within different spatial, temporal, socio-economic and cultural contexts, and thus a preparation for responsible participation in a multi-cultural society.
4 Social, economic and political literacy, which will enable reasoned predictions to be made about the locus and likely consequences of decisions taken at individual, community, national and global levels.
5 Active and collaborative involvement in the learning process, which will enable candidates to develop decision-making skills and responsibility for the planning, direction and monitoring of their work.

As you can see, there is a considerable divergence in the way the aims are phrased and worded by each examination group. However, this does not mean that their aims are different. The aims can, in fact, be summed up in the following way:

The focus of study

 **The common aims of Integrated Humanities syllabuses**

The *focus* of study will be *human societies*. To understand human behaviour at any level (individual, local community, national or global), an understanding of the *variety* of values, beliefs and perspectives in existence is necessary. These, in turn, can only be understood through the consideration of a wide range of *contexts* – geographical, historical, social, economic, cultural, political, etc.

The process of study

The actual *process* of learning is an important factor. You will be encouraged to learn through *experience*, developing the range of skills appropriate to the subject-matter and applying them to your own studies. As well as taking responsibility for your own work, you will be encouraged to work collaboratively – that is, co-operate with others, sharing ideas in order to solve problems.

Personal development

The *skills* you develop during the course (that is, techniques and methods you learn to use in your studies) will be of lasting relevance to you as an active participant in a changing world.

5 ⟩ ASSESSMENT OBJECTIVES

Every GCSE syllabus outlines its *assessment objectives* – a list of the skills and abilities which the student is expected to develop, which should be seen in his or her work and which can, therefore, be assessed.

In the past, examinations have often concentrated on the candidate's ability to recall a body of facts learned during the course. The emphasis is now more on skills, and on letting each candidate show what they can do, so that facts and memory play a much less important role.

As we have seen, in *Integrated Humanities* your work is assessed throughout the course, in a range of tasks which require a range of skills, abilities and knowledge to be shown. It is, therefore, very important for you to know and understand clearly the assessment objectives, as they tell you what is expected of you and what the examination boards are looking for in your work (the variety and number of tasks required of you will be discussed later in this chapter). Remember, whatever the task, it will have been designed by your teacher to enable you to *show* the abilities and skills you have developed.

The assessment objectives of the three syllabuses available are shown in detail in Figure 1.3. As you can see, the ways in which they are phrased and grouped vary, but each examination board is looking for a number of common skills and abilities:

ASSESSMENT OBJECTIVES

MIDLANDS EXAMINING GROUP	NORTHERN EXAMINING ASSOCIATION	SOUTHERN EXAMINING GROUP
There are 9 objectives grouped in 3 domains	The scheme of study should allow the candidate to demonstrate the following:	The examination will assess a candidate's ability to:

MIDLANDS EXAMINING GROUP

1 *Understanding and Communication*
This area is concerned with candidates' ability to communicate clearly in more than one medium and to demonstrate their understanding of those terms, concepts and generalizations appropriate to the study of a given situation.

Candidates should be able
a) to understand and use appropriate concepts, terms and generalisations.
b) to present a coherent narrative or description.
c) to demonstrate empathy towards people living within a different cultural, geographical or historical context.

2 *Enquiry*
This area is concerned with the skills and techniques candidates will need to employ in gathering and recording evidence:

Candidates should be able:
a) to locate and select relevant material
b) to derive relevant information from a range of materials and record findings in a coherent and purposeful form.
c) to identify and explain the results of research and deficiencies within it.

NORTHERN EXAMINING ASSOCIATION

a) *Understanding and Knowledge*
The ability to comprehend
i) the terminology involved;
ii) the main generalisations made, stressing the inter-relationships and inter-dependence of factors from individual humanities subjects;
iii) the concepts used, including those of cause and consequence, continuity and change, similarity and difference;
iv) specific examples on which the generalisations and concepts are based, reflecting a local, national, international and worldwide scale;
v) the sources of information which are available, the methodology of investigation and the criteria for the evaluation of evidence used;
vi) contending approaches to and wider perspectives of, the topics studied.

b) *Investigation*
I The ability to identify the possible sources of primary and secondary data relevant to any investigation. These possible sources should include the use of:
  i) books, newspapers, periodicals and other forms of written material in a discriminating manner;
  ii) media resources,
  iii) maps and other diagrammatical representations,
  iv) numerical and statistical data,
  v) general libraries, museums, resource centres and the community at large;
  vi) questionnaires, participant observation, surveys and other appropriate techniques of social investigation.
II The ability to locate and select primary and secondary evidence relevant to any investigation from given stimulus material.

SOUTHERN EXAMINING GROUP

1 *Understand* the disciplines, concepts and methods applicable to the topics being studied including:
a) the relevant disciplines;
b) the terminology involved in the study of the topics;
c) the main concepts used;
d) specific examples on which generalisations and concepts are based;
e) the sources of information which are available;
f) the methods of investigation which are available;
g) competing viewpoints and perspectives, demonstrating empathy with these;
h) the criteria for evaluation of evidence used.

2 *Enquire* critically and purposefully from a variety of information sources:
a) identify and discriminate between the possible sources of knowledge, both primary and secondary;
b) selectively use and interpret books, maps and numerical or quantitative material;
c) draw critically from experiences and encounters within the community;
d) use resources outside the classroom – e.g. resource centres, libraries, museums, workplaces and external agencies;
e) construct and conduct questionnaires and surveys;
f) carry out other fieldwork – e.g. observation and recording;
g) use imagination to develop hypotheses.

ASSESSMENT OBJECTIVES		
MIDLANDS EXAMINING GROUP	NORTHERN EXAMINING ASSOCIATION	SOUTHERN EXAMINING GROUP

3 *Interpretation and Evaluation* This area is concerned with candidates' ability to use evidence in relation to particular problems or issues.
 	
Candidates should be able.
a) to organise and compare different types of evidence, including an awareness of the uses which can be made of such information.
b) to assess the reliability and limitations of evidence, including an awareness of bias.
c) to reach reasoned conclusions based on evidence.
	c) *Interpretation & Evaluation of Argument* The ability to
	  i) formulate initial hypotheses,
	  ii) interpret the available information and in so doing, distinguish probable cause and effect, identify the subjective and objective nature of evidence and expose bias, prejudice, irrationality and taken-for-granted assumptions,
	  iii) formulate conclusions and assess the ethical implications of these on one's own personal views,
	  iv) confirm, reject or modify (in the light of (ii) and (iii) above) original hypotheses,
	  v) empathise with the context of people's lives by informed evaluation from various points of view.
	
	d) *Transmission & Presentation of Argument* The ability to
	  i) offer organised, coherent and rational explanations,
	  ii) communicate these in a clear, relevant and logical manner by the use of a variety of written, oral, visual, numerical and statistical techniques.
		3 *Analyse and Evaluate* material:
		  a) organise information;
		  b) summarise findings;
		  c) draw conclusions;
		  d) test hypotheses;
		  e) identify cause and effect;
		  f) distinguish between fact and opinion, and detect bias;
		  g) make ethical decisions relating to own personal life.
		
		4 *Communicate* effectively in enquiry analysis and presentation of material:
		  a) use inter-personal and collaborative skills;
		  b) demonstrate creativity;
		  c) select and recognise appropriate techniques of presentation;
		  d) demonstrate a range of writing styles;
		  e) present information visually and numerically;
		  f) demonstrate graphicacy.

Fig. 1.3

UNDERSTANDING

The three syllabuses cover similar areas in terms of *understanding*. Being familiar with a number of key words will be useful.

- **Disciplines**
  These are the various *subjects* which make up Integrated Humanities. Each discipline, or subject, has its own way of operating, its own 'tools for the job'.

- **Concepts**
  These are the main *ideas* which recur within a subject. For example, historians use the concepts of cause and consequence, similarity and difference; geographers use the concepts of spatial location, distribution, etc.

- **Terms**
  These are part of the *terminology* associated with a subject – that is, the words used to describe particular things to do with that subject. You will already have come across many of them. Sometimes two subjects use the same term, but not always with the same meaning! For example, the term 'solution' means something very different to a chemist and to a mathematician.

- **Generalisations**
  These are statements that are *broadly* true. Making generalisations means looking at a *particular* case and assessing all the evidence available, before deciding whether or not what has been found in one case is likely to be true for others generally. To enable you to do this you must be aware of whether the particular case studied is representative or not, and if not, why not.

■ **Empathy**

The ability to empathise with people of different societies, times, cultures, etc. means being able to understand how situations appear to other people. This requires not only imagination but also a knowledge and understanding of the variety of influences affecting people – the historical, geographical, cultural, socio-economic and political contexts in which they live or lived. Empathy implies an awareness of, and sensitivity towards, the views and perspectives of other people. You must appreciate the factors which have helped shape those views and perspectives if you are to be able to understand specific behaviour and responses to certain problems and issues.

ENQUIRY/INVESTIGATION

Whichever syllabus you are following, during your course you will conduct some form of *enquiry* or *investigation*. This means producing one or more pieces of research about a particular question or issue, demonstrating your ability to find and select relevant evidence either by yourself or from stimulus material you are provided with.

❝ Evidence can be in the form of *primary* and *secondary* information. ❞

Where you take responsibility for finding out about a topic yourself, you will need to show that you know where to find, or *locate*, different sorts of information or evidence for different purposes. You need to be able to make full use of your school and public libraries, and to know which public or private institutions could supply you with particular sorts of information. This involves the sort of enquiry material which has been written and published *by others* (secondary information). Your job is to find such material, then select what is relevant and discard what is not. Gathering evidence can also involve generating your *own* information (primary information). This may involve going out to study a geographical or historical site, conducting surveys of your locality, perhaps interviewing people, using questionnaires, or simply making observations.

So, the evidence you collect can be in very different *forms* – from printed books, magazines and newspaper articles to personal documents, diaries and letters; from maps and graphs to photographs and illustrations; from interviews with people to radio or TV broadcasts. You should try to show that you have sought out a *wide range of information*, or data, in a *variety of forms*, and that you have *selected* those items which are most relevant and appropriate to the task in hand.

EVALUATION AND INTERPRETATION OF EVIDENCE

The need for the wide range of information will become obvious as you become more practised in *using* evidence. A source of information might seem straightforward, but you will need to analyse and evaluate it:

■ is it *primary* or *secondary* material?
■ is it *fact* or *opinion*?
■ is there evidence of *bias*?
■ are all the available facts presented, or just some?
■ is the opinion expressed valid and reasoned, or is it formed out of prejudice and misunderstanding?

Answering such questions will be easier if you have a *range* of information and evidence, so that you can *compare* what is stated and make reasoned judgements. You will be expected to *interpret* the evidence you have gathered (or which has been given to you) – that is, state clearly what it means and decide for yourself which elements of it are important to your study (saying why). Demonstrating that you *have* evaluated and interpreted the information will give weight to the conclusions you come to in your work. These must be firmly based on the evidence used and on your analysis of it.

COMMUNICATION

The ability to *communicate* to others is important throughout the course. It is no good understanding issues, and being able to analyse and interpret material, if you cannot communicate your conclusions. As an assessment objective, communication of your views, ideas and comprehension involves two main areas:

■ the ability to express yourself in a *logical* and *coherent* way so that your ideas, explanations or descriptions are *easily understandable* to the reader;
■ the ability to express yourself in a *variety of ways*: by writing narrative/description; by

graphic representation (illustrations, maps, graphs, etc.); by presenting information in numerical or statistical form; by using a variety of media which might include audio- and video-recordings, etc. Here the examiner will be looking for an ability to use *different forms* of presentation and to select the *most appropriate form* according to what it is that you are trying to communicate.

THE WEIGHTING OF ASSESSMENT OBJECTIVES

The *weighting* of the assessment objectives simply means the degree of importance given to each; this is usually expressed in terms of the percentage of the total marks given to each. Exact comparisons between the various syllabuses is difficult because of the way each examination group places the various objectives under different headings. MEG, for example, combines 'understanding' with 'communication', whilst the other two syllabuses keep these separate. Moreover, the NEA syllabus allows the school some degree of flexibility in the weighting of assessment objectives, by setting a *range* of percentage marks for each heading (20% to 30% for each of the four) instead of a fixed percentage for each. Nevertheless, to give you some idea of the relative importance attached to each assessment objective, the following table may be useful.

Assessment Objective	MEG	NEA	SEG
Understanding and Knowledge	33·3%	20–30%	25%
Communication		20–30%	20%
Investigation and Enquiry	33·3%	20–30%	25%
Evaluation and Interpretation	33.3%	20–30%	30%

6 > CONTENT

All Integrated Humanities syllabuses allow the teacher considerable freedom in deciding on the issues and topics selected for study. Each examination group does, however, impose certain restrictions. These are to ensure that your studies will involve a broad range of key Humanities concepts, and that you will use a variety of methods found in Humanities subjects.

MEG

MEG Integrated Humanities requires all the content to relate to five 'organizing perspectives'. These are *broad themes* which, between them, cover the main Humanities concepts. Four of these organising perspectives are *set by the examination group*.

Organising Perspective	Examples of Some Possible Content
Continuity and Change	Change in the community; growth of village/urban area; changes in family size and lifestyle; changing patterns of migration; changing roles of women; effects of the technological revolution.
Freedom and Constraint	Norms, rules and laws; the organisation of law and justice; examination of totalitarian regimes; growth of democracy; political parties and parliament.
Conflict and Co-operation	Local issue – for example, planning of a new by-pass; pressure-group campaigns, etc.; case study of conflict – for example, Northern Ireland, Middle East, etc.; political and economic co-operation between states – for example, United Nations, European Community, etc.
Equality and Inequality	Analysis of information and indicators of poverty; access to housing; distribution of social services; growth of the education system; case study of a developing country.

A fifth organising perspective is required, and this is to be devised *by the school*. The syllabus offers some examples:

- Development and Decline
- Capital and Labour
- Conservation and Exploitation.

EQUALITY AND INEQUALITY

INPUT	ACTIVITY	POSSIBLE OUTPUT
Concept: Equality Literary extract: *The Chironians*	Reading and class discussion Simulation and group discussion Enactment and class discussion	Own piece of sci-fi writing Written report on apparent mechanics of equality/inequality
Concept: Poverty Drama role-play: *The Scrurridges, The Sommersbys* Booklet: *Breadline Britain*	Analysis of information and isolation of indicators of poverty; group discussion Class discussion and analysis Notes	Written and graphical presentation and own assessment of the 'poverty line' Written report on recommendations by group and class
Concept: Social Class Simulation £100,000 share-out Booklet: *Rich and Poor in Britain* Statistics: Family expenditure survey, *Life on the Dole* booklet Booklet: *Housing and Homelessness* Case study: Carol Housing advice centre booklets Council housing application form Statistical tables from Black Report, *Inequalities in Health*	Class discussion, analysis and consideraion of case studies Group analysis of facts and figures: 'Finding somewhere to live in Northampton' Analysis, discussion and notes	'Diagrammatic' presentation of UK Written responses to questions to isolate factors determining social class Preparations of a weekly budget for a range of incomes Written presentation Presentations of a display using photographic tape-slide questionnaire techniques, in pairs or groups Written answers to determine class-influenced incidence of disease and mortality
Concept: Discrimination Video: *Discrimination at Work* Booklet: *Racism and Discrimination in Britain* Role-play: *Immigration* CRE Factsheet: *Immigration* Booklet: *Women in Britain*	Individual analysis, notes and class discussion Group discussion. Teacher input: the implications of the Nationality Act. Analysis of information on position of women at home and at work Boys and girls record their ambitions after school, linked to their performance at school Reading and class analysis in groups, then compared with responses of Liverpool sample	Written answers to questions and personal observations on video Pupil written responses to Campaign for Racial Equality sheet Devise own laws on immigration Written responses to questions Written analysis of results Written-up results.
Concept: North–South Exercise: Describing developing countries Draw a map of Africa with key facts CWDE North–South booklet Statistics on world debt World map to Arno Peter's Projection 'Samtisirch' exercise on ethnocentrism Simulation: Trading Game Worksheets: *Food First, World Food Supply* Video: *Politics of World Hunger* Case study: *Kenya* Booklet: *Kenya* Video: *Horizon Kenya*	Mental map of Africa Class discussion and notes Plotting figures and countries Discussion Reading and discussion Enactment and group discussion Notes Groupwork: notes, analysis and consideration of problem of health, education and welfare aid Contrast with Britain	Producing corrected map of Africa Written summary of main recommendations of *Brandt Report* Map display Written answers to questions Written reports Written answers and illustrative response to worksheets Written summary of recommendations to solve Kenya's problems Written, graphic, map and illustration work, designed to be produced as a display in pairs

Fig. 1.4 A planned example for a school's unit on equality/inequality (MEG).

❝ List of materials to be used to cover the topic ❞

❝ List of activities students may be involved in ❞

❝ List of tasks students may be required to complete – some of which may be assessed for the examination. ❞

SEG

The SEG syllabus also requires five topics to be studied during the course. A list of examples is provided, but schools are free to devise their own topics. The examples given are:

- Community and Environment
- Urbanisation
- Industrialisation
- Peace and Conflict
- Law and Order
- Education
- Environmental Management
- The Impact of Technology
- The Mass Media
- Race and Culture
- Gender Inequalities
- Unity and Division

- People and Work
- The Family and Child Development
- Recreation and Conservation
- Beliefs and Values
- Marriage
- Health and Welfare
- Political Movements
- Transport and Communications
- World Interdependence
- Prejudice
- Human Rights
- Wealth and Poverty

Each topic must be treated in such a way as to ensure that the four main Humanities *conceptual areas* are covered:

- Power and distribution – the political dimension;
- Ideas and ideologies – the moral dimension;
- Spatial interaction – the geographical dimension;
- Continuity and change – the historical dimension.

66 Areas and situations in which key ideas will be studied 99

66 Main concepts to be studied 99

SEG TOPIC GRID: URBANISATION					
CONCEPTS	INDIVIDUAL	COMMUNITY	NATIONAL	GLOBAL	% WEIGHTING
POWER		Pressure Groups and Community Associations	Government legislation on house types, New Towns, Green Belts, etc.	Government intervention in location, e.g. Brazilia	30
IDEAS		Community activities Recreation versus houses Rates-usage Government legislation	Planning policies Philanthropic movement Howard Corbusier		20
SPACE		Planning a local community	Size of New Towns and their characteristics The nature of cities	Population map of world and major cities	30
CHANGE	Viewpoints of Industrial Revolution Eye-witness acounts Life in a shanty town after a village		Push/pull factors during Industrial Revolution Movement of population to cities Rank/size rule		20
% WEIGHTING	10	30	40	20	100

Fig. 1.5 An example of an SEG topic grid.

These concepts must be studied at a range of levels, that is, at *contextual levels*. These are:
- the individual;
- the community and local environment;
- the whole country – the national scale;
- the whole world – the global, or international, scale.

Schools must ensure that each of the five topics studied involves a consideration of each concept and context.

NEA

The NEA syllabus outlines fifteen topic headings, or *modules*. From this list schools can either choose five to be studied or choose four and devise a fifth topic/module themselves. This must then be approved by the examination group.

The fifteen module headings, and the sorts of questions which could be explored are:

1	Belief	What are beliefs? What makes a belief moral, immoral or amoral? What are the main religious and political beliefs in societies? What is the significance of these beliefs?
2	The Community	What are communities? How have communities developed? How are communities organised? How do communities differ in attitudes, values and beliefs? How do central and local government policies affect the community and where do conflicts and disagreements arise? How do communities change and develop?
3	Conflict	What are the causes of conflict? What are the manifestations of conflict? What are the effects of conflict? How is war portrayed? What possibilities are there for the prevention and control of conflict?
4	Consumer Affairs	What are the main forms of buying and selling? How are products promoted and packaged? What are buyers' and sellers' rights and how does the law protect them?
5	Education	Is education the same as training? How far and for how long should education be made compulsory? What signs have there been of changing relationships in education? What is the relationship between social class, educational opportunities and life changes? How is the technological revolution affecting education?
6	The Family	What changes have taken place in the structure of the family? How have these developments affected relationships within the family and relationships of the family with society? What social changes have affected the extent to which the state accepts responsibility for some of the functions of the family?
7	Health	Does a particular environment dictate our physical and mental health? Is health a reflection of our diet? What is parental responsibility in relation to health? Why are some community health issues controversial? What aspects of safety help make our lives more healthy?
8	Inequality	What is inequality? What are the causes and effects of inequality? What are the possible solutions to inequality? How are solutions linked to causes? How is inequality relative? How is the world interdependent?
9	Law and Order	Why is it necessary to devise and enforce codes of regulation? How is law and order maintained? What personal and social factors determine the level of crime in society?
10	Leisure	How have leisure activities developed? What factors affect the leisure activities of individuals? To what extent are leisure and holiday patterns affected by media pressures? How may leisure patterns develop into the future?

11	The Mass Media	What are the main types of media? How have these media developed? What are the effects of the media? How far do the mass media reflect or determine the nature of their audiences? Who controls the media?
12	People and Work	Why work? How is work organised? What are the main types of work? What are the causes and effects of unemployment?
13	Persecution and Prejudice	How does prejudice become persecution? What examples of persecution and prejudice are there in the world today? What are the causes of persecution and prejudice? What are the effects of persecution and prejudice? What is the connection between prejudice, racism and sexism?
14	Politics and Government	How is power exercised? What are the main types of political systems? How are decisions made? How far does governmental responsibility extend?
15	Pollution and Conservation	What are the social, moral and political issues involved in the nature, distribution and use of the world's natural resources? What are the social, moral and political implications of pollution, conservation and ecological problems? What alternative technologies and lifestyles are available as potential responses to environmental problems?

7 ▷ TYPES OF ASSESSMENT TASK

❝ Make sure you understand which assessment objectives your tasks are aimed at ❞

The way in which the work on which you will be assessed is organised can vary between the three syllabuses, and even within one syllabus. This is because Integrated Humanities courses involve 100% coursework assessment, and it is up to individual teachers to decide exactly what you will study and how your skills and abilities will be assessed, though within the framework already outlined. In all the syllabuses, though, you will be expected to cover *five topics*, or *modules*, during the course, and you will be assessed in some way on *each* of them.

For all the syllabuses, you will be required to complete a wide range of tasks for assessment. 'Assignments', 'assessed pieces', 'studies', etc. could include tests which you complete under *examination conditions* – that is, a number of questions to be answered in a set length of time, without discussion with other candidates or reference to any other aid, such as your textbook, notes, etc. However, this would be an inappropriate way of assessing many of the objectives as it would not reflect the full range of skills and abilities referred to in the list of assessment objectives. So as well as the possibility of tests, your assessment could include:

■ written items – essays, descriptions, drama dialogues, summaries, diaries or logs, creative writing, transcripts from interviews, etc.;

■ visual items – display work, design, constructing models, producing a video, etc.;

■ oral items – group/class discussion, oral accounts, 'radio broadcasts', interviews, etc.

The examples below will give you some idea of the *range* of assessment tasks you may be asked to complete during your Integrated Humanities course. The examples will also show how particular tasks can be used to assess particular objectives.

EXAMPLES OF ASSESSMENT TASKS

Task A

A series of lessons on *inequality between nations* has included:

■ the North–South divide;

■ the history of the relationship between Europe and the developing world;

■ international trade and the role of the multi-nationals;

■ case studies of life in developing countries;

■ an analysis of suggested solutions to the problems of poverty in developing countries.

After these lessons you are asked in question 1 to describe, in one hour of class time, what is meant by the term 'developing countries'.

In your answer you should include reference to the problems experienced by developing countries, their causes and reasons for their continuance.

You are then asked in question 2 to design, outside lesson time, a leaflet or poster to make people more aware of the problems and extent of poverty in developing countries. Your leaflet/poster could invite them to a meeting, ask for donations, or just try to inform the public. The leaflet/poster must be entirely your own work.

Comment

Question 1 could be used to test an assessment objective focusing on *understanding* – that is, your ability to take in and use terminology, generalisations, concepts, different viewpoints and perspectives, etc. A successful response to this question would draw upon the work you have covered in your studies. It would probably include reference to a number of terms and ideas, with a view to demonstrating clearly that you have understood them:

- the terms development and developing;
- the measurement of development, with examples from case studies of developing countries;
- the key features of developing countries – for example, those relating to their economy, population structure, health, diet, working and living patterns;
- the unequal relationship between the developed (First) world and the developing (Third) world;
- the meaning of colonialism and its affect on the development of colonised countries;
- unequal trading relationships between developed world and developing world countries;
- an explanation of what multi-national companies are and their role in the international economy.

Question 2 could be used to test *communication* and *presentation*. A successful response would involve you in producing a strong, powerful and effective message which is clearly organised and presented, and which uses relevant material and appropriate techniques. It should show an understanding of who the message is aimed at and what is likely to be the most effective means of influencing that 'audience'.

Task B

After a study on the topic of *work*, and before the beginning of a week's work experience, the following task is set:

You are about to start your work experience placement. When you return to school after the week's work, you will be expected to give an account of your experiences. Below are some guidelines for you to use when preparing your account. Make sure you read these *before* you start in your placement, so that you can make relevant notes whilst at work.

Introduction

You must give an introduction, explaining what you are going to be doing. In this you should give details of:

- the firm – names, address, business (what it does/produces), size (small, national, multi-national), its competitors, etc.
- the workforce – number of employees, men/women, full-time/part-time, hours of work, any shiftwork, what skills/qualifications do they have? etc.

Your week at work

You need to give a description of your work – what you had to do, how much help you were given, what you felt about the work, whether you needed any special clothing, what you learned, what was the typical work day like? etc.

The organisation of the firm

You should find out about how the firm is run – who is in charge, of which departments/workers, is there a division of labour, what training is required/offered, are there any YTS employees there? Find out more about the workforce – what sorts of qualifications do they have, what are their normal hours, do they work overtime, what are their rates of pay, holidays, pension schemes, etc. Why do they work there, where do most of them live, how long have they been with the firm, are they in a union, how many trades unions are represented in the firm, have there been disputes recently, over what issues, does the firm offer any facilities – canteen, sports/leisure facilities, childcare? etc.

Conclusions

Describe your feelings during the week – were you made to feel at ease, did people answer your questions, how did you find the work in general, would you like to work in that firm, or have you had other ideas about your future? etc.

Comment

This task could be used to assess *investigation/enquiry*. You would be involved in collecting and recording information during the process of your work experience. This requires a familiarity with research methods, and with the use of a variety of them – for example, using any relevant *secondary* material (job adverts, promotional leaflets by the firm, etc.), or *primary* material in the form of your own observations, interviews with members of the workforce, and so on.

The information you collect must be directed towards a purpose – that is, towards the suggestions for enquiry set by the teacher. You must then make use of this, together with your wider understanding of issues such as technology, trades unions, and the changing economy. Your final account should not, therefore, be purely descriptive but should attempt to relate your experiences to wider issues. So, if you record your work experience in a work-experience diary, your account should not simply repeat the whole diary but rather be a selection of *extracts* which are relevant to the enquiry questions you started out with.

Task C

After a series of lessons on the topic of the *family and socialisation*, the task is set on the following extract:

This is the loneliest little boy in the world. He cannot hear. He cannot speak. His mind has been locked in silence for two years.

If he could break out of that silence, Robert would tell a story too extraordinary for the imagination to conceive.

He would tell us how he survived for three incredible years in the most treacherous area of East African jungle. He would tell how he was adopted by a family of monkeys after he lost his own parents in Uganda's bloody civil war.

He would tell how it was to *be* a monkey; how it was to be a Mowgli of The Jungle Book.

He would tell of the dangers he faced as a child among wild beasts. He would tell of their world – how they are, what they feel.

The animal kingdom was also his kingdom. But tragically – although perhaps mercifully, too – the trauma of his experience, and serious damage to his hearing, have plunged Robert into an isolated world where he can tell nothing of his life in the wild.

Robert, now eight, is being gently nursed back into the world where he belongs. At a Kampala orphanage he is learning how to discard the habits he learned from the animals, who adopted him as one of their own.

Doctors have pieced together fragments of his young life going back to the day when he was left for dead in the bush, near his village home. But medically they are completely baffled by him. To have survived at all, he has broken every previous record known to man. He has already lived longer and progressed further than any other of the strange, infrequent cases of feral children.

The hurt and bewilderment that show so vividly in his eyes are clues to the nameless adventures he lived through in the jungle.

It was 1982 when Obote's soldiers were raping and looting and murdering their way through the notorious Luwero triangle 50 miles from Kampala city.

Terrified families abandoned their homes and fled into the bush, to take their chances with the wild animals rather than face certain slaughter at the hands of the soldiers.

The looted villages were never to be rebuilt. Men and women were pursued and killed, children separated from their parents for ever. Many were kidnapped. Boys were turned into under-age soldiers, girls sold as servants.

Robert, just three years old, crawled into the undergrowth and cried himself to sleep. He wandered, filthy and lost, further into the jungle, a tiny orphan frightened and hungry.

It was three years before he was found in a clearing by soldiers on a route march through that same jungle area. A group of Vervet monkeys, jabbering with excitement, scattered as they approached.

Just one adult female remained, threatening to attack as they neared her. She was protecting a small ragged bundle – a human child.

That was 1985, and nurses at the orphanage were astonished by him as he was handed into their care. 'He was a wild-eyed emaciated little thing, all skin and bones and curled up like a small animal,' remembers Tereza Nansikombi, the nurse in charge of Naguru orphanage. She watched in horror as the boy ran around on all fours, his hands and feet turned under to adapt to life in the wild.

He weighed just 19½lbs. He was completely naked when he was found, his toenails and finger nails broken and overgrown, his teeth formed awkwardly in four separate rows. His diet of fruit and berries had failed to dislodge his milk teeth, and his secondary teeth had grown from underneath them.

Doctors and nurses had never seen anything like Robert. Tereza, who has nursed heartbreaking scores of war orphans, sometimes bringing them back to life after terrible mental and physical injuries, wept openly as she held him.

'I told the doctors I did not

known what to do with him,' she says.

'They put his age at six years, although he was nothing but an armful of filthy neglected half-animal, half-human. I just couldn't believe he would live.'

Tereza washed him carefull in an aluminium bath outside the simple orphanage buildings. An outer skin of roughened dirt peeled off in her hands.

The boy could not stand up straight, but could only squat, teeth chattering, like the monkeys who had taught him to be like them. He put his scrawny arms right round his neck and hid his face from her and from this strange new world.

He never smiled. He never spoke. And he turned to the mongrel dog wandering around the orphanage for friendship, rather than join the groups of other children, as curious about him as he was about them.

'I put his chances of survival at nil, says Tereza. 'He made a whining noise when he was distressed, and he grunted like an animal. He did not know how to sleep in a bed, and he ate grass and eath, even the clothes we gave him to wear.'

But Robert had survived on a jungle diet against all odds. He could only get better now that real nourishment was on hand.

He remained very sick for long months to come. For four weeks his life hung in the balance while he received hospital care for violent bouts of vomiting and diarrhoea.

Worst of all, at night he rocked back and forth on his haunches, holding on to the side of his cot. He whined piteously, and the nurses knew he was pining for his monkey family.

Doctors, battling against the impossible shortages of equipment and medicine in the aftermath of civil war, have only been able to ascertain that he has no brain damage, but suffers from lack of development of the muscles in his inner ear.

Now, thanks to the Mail on Sunday, Robert's case may be taken up by top British paediatricians who are currently studying video film of him I had taken and brought back with me from Kampala.

They hope to find a way by which he can communicate to others for the very first time.

The severe bruising to his upper arm where he had been roughly handled – perhaps carried along – by monkeys, has subsided. He teeth are strong and white, and he has learned painstakingly to walk with an ambling gait.

Toilet training has been successful, and Robert lies down to sleep at night among the 20 other children in one of the orphanage's sparse dormitories.

He has learned through human love from Tereza and her nurses, to respond to affection. But he still lives almost entirely in a world of his own, always eating and playing separately from the others. Always staring speechlessly into the distance, all the hurt still locked deep inside him.

'I love all these boys and girls, but my heart belongs to Robert,' Tereza says. 'Somewhere inside his mind is the key to his sadness. If we could only find it, we could unlock all his unhappy secrets and start to make him really better.'

She beams proudly at the little boy she brought back to life, and Robert will raise his arms to her, asking to be gathered up and cuddled.

Of all the 72 children at Naguru orphanage, he has found a link with only one. Eleven-year-old Julius Bogere, abandoned by a family split by poverty during the war years, is his special friend.

He sits hour by hour with Robert, wordlessly holding his hand or helping to wash him and feed him.

Poor little Robert! He cannot yet articulate, but his every expression echoes that final line from Mowgli's Song in Kipling's The Jungle Book:

'My heart is heavy with the things that I do not understand.'

Fig. 1.6 A newspaper extract to accompany an assessment task (Source: *Mail on Sunday*, 1987).

Questions

1   'Give me a child until he is seven and I will give you the man.'
    a)   In your own words explain what is meant by this phrase.
    b)   What evidence is there in the passage to support this view?
2   a)   How reliable do you think this evidence can be? (What are its strengths and weaknesses?)
    b)   In your opinion what are the major influences on the development of an individual?

Comment

This task could assess the objective of *interpretation* and *evaluation*.

In question 1 a) you are being asked to interpret the sentence, to explain in your own words what its author was saying about the effects of early influences and conditions on children, and the effects these can have on the rest of their lives. You are *not* being asked to agree or disagree but to *explain clearly* what was meant.

In question 1 b) you are being asked to search the newspaper passage to find *evidence* which might support your answer to 1 a).

Question 2 a) asks you to *evaluate* the evidence given in the newspaper passage. To do this you would need to consider whether there is anything about the passage which would lead you to doubt the accuracy of the evidence it offers. For example, is the information first-hand or second-hand? Would the newspaper have any reason for reporting the evidence in the way it does? (for example, might it wish to sensationalise the story by presenting it in an eye-catching and dramatic manner?) Also, is there anything in the article which would lead you to think that the evidence it offers is valid?

Question 2 b) goes beyond your interpretation and evaluation of the particular statement and the newspaper article, and asks you to *apply it* to your *own* understanding and knowledge of the influences on human development and behaviour. This is the basis for giving your opinion of the original statement.

Task D

As part of a study of the community, the following task is set:

Planning a community

You are going to take part in an exercise to plan a new community on the outskirts of the city of Wigginton, around the existing village of Riversham. You will discuss the development in small groups (three or four) and then produce a report to present your plans. Before the group discussions begin you will need to prepare for the task by considering the following information. Make sure you do this before the next lesson.

Homework: Introduction to the task

Riversham, a small village about eight miles from the centre of Wigginton, is surrounded by open countryside and has about 1,500 inhabitants. The housing is mixed – some privately owned and some council property. The village already has a post office/village store, a church with a church hall which is used several nights a week by local groups, (scouts, etc.), a small primary school and two public houses. There is also Cottage Crafts, an old posthouse now converted into a number of small workshops run by local people and employing about fifty. A variety of activities go on there, including weaving, pottery, leatherwork, carving and sculpture, and the centre attracts many visitors, who can watch people working, purchase goods and make use of the coffee shop.

Most of the villagers work in Wigginton. They travel there mostly by car as the bus service is poor (five buses a day during the week) and, although there is a railway line near the village, Riversham has no station. The main Colesley to Wigginton road, the A73, runs nearby and is linked to the village by two miles of minor road.

Wigginton itself does not have enough land to develop reasonably for housing newcomers and rehousing families living in the old area of the city, Allington, a twilight zone. The council has decided to develop a new community around Riversham, to cope with approximately 6,500 people who need to be rehoused. They also hope to attract industry to that area to provide work for the new community.

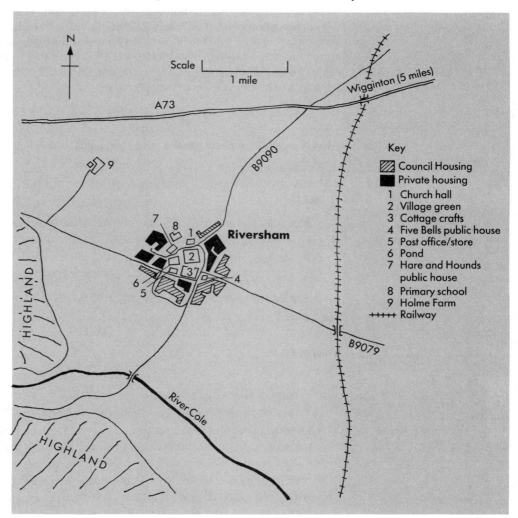

Fig. 1.7 A map of Riversham to accompany an assessment task.

Your group will have the task of discussing how the new community should be planned and developed. There are likely to be around 8,000 inhabitants altogether, who will need houses, shops, schools, youth centres, leisure facilities (sports and others), medical services, a library, etc. They will also need work, so there will have to be factories/offices, and the transport services and road communications will need consideration. You must also consider services such as a sewage farm, a refuse tip, etc. Services and facilities are not everything, however, and you should remember that if a community is to be successful people must feel that they belong and have a sense of identity. Riversham will work well as a new development if people who live there get on well together – if they co-operate. In your group discussion, try to work out how you could encourage people to feel part of the new community.

Further information is provided by the map of Riversham and surrounding area.

Classwork: Discussion and report

Using the information studied at home, your group should discuss the planning of the new community of Riversham. When you have reached agreement, the group must compile a report, justifying your proposals.

Comment

This task could be used to assess *interpretation* and *evaluation*. You are being asked to consider the information you have been presented with in the description of the community and the map, and you must identify details which will be of significance in the planning of a new community. You should also identify any limitations which will have an effect on the development. You will need to consider what features assist the formation of a successful community; not just the obvious amenities but also things such as community identity, a sense of belonging, etc. You should realise that any planning decision is likely to produce *conflict* as it will reflect the different opinions held by different people about such terms as *community* and those features of a community which are suitable for development. These conflicts should be reflected in your group discussion, in which you will discuss different recommendations and their likely consequences. In *evaluating* various suggestions you should be prepared to *relate them to the evidence*. Be ready to identify any lack of reasoned argument, inconsistency or failure to relate suggestions to available evidence. Your final report should clearly state *your* development plan and also deal with *alternative suggestions*, stating clearly *why* you do not support them.

Task E

After a series of lessons on the topic of conflict, the following task is set:

Nuclear arms

Produce a teaching pack for fourth-year students on nuclear weapons. Your pack should include:

- a clear statement as to what the aims of the pack are, how it should be used, a list of other useful material, addresses, publications, etc.;
- worksheets;
- a poster for classroom display;
- ideas for games, simulations, etc.;
- ideas for projects, surveys, etc.

Comment

This task could assess:

- enquiry – where you demonstrate your ability to discover (through reference and library work) lists of books, articles and relevant material;
- understanding – of key terms and concepts involved in a study of nuclear weapons – for example, multilateral/unilateral disarmament – and the issues underlying the subject;
- communication – where you demonstrate your ability to produce relevant material which is organised and accurate. You then show you can convey the ideas and information to your audience in a stimulating manner.

8 > EXAMINATION GROUP REQUIREMENTS

❝❝ What the examination groups ask you to produce ❞❞

As you can see, the sorts of tasks you may be required to do can involve you in a range of activities, and your results can be presented in different ways. Also, the number of pieces of work which are required for assessment can vary from group to group.

MEG

For the MEG syllabus, candidates present a 'portfolio' of their work at the end of the course. This will include eight 'assignments' – tasks of any kind – together with two 'special studies'. These must involve a 'sustained piece of enquiry or research' for which 'a significant amount of the materials used should have been collected independently by the candidate'. The special studies are clearly intended to provide evidence of your skills of enquiry, evaluation and interpretation, although these can also be assessed elsewhere in the 'assignments'.

The MEG scheme might appear to suggest that you will produce just *ten* pieces of work altogether during your course. However, you must remember that these are just the ten completed tasks presented for final assessment and moderation. You may be required by your teacher to produce more, from which a selection (the best!) will be put into your portfolio to be sent to the examiners for moderation as the basis of your final grade.

NEA

The NEA syllabus requires assignments to be presented for *each* of the *five* modules covered. Across the whole of the coursework, *all* the assessment objectives should be covered. The *sort* of task set can be decided upon by the teacher and the school, as can the *number* of tasks set for each module. To assess one module, for example, it may be appropriate to set a *number of tasks* – perhaps a test, an essay and the production of an information leaflet on the topic. For another module, on the other hand, you may be required to produce a continuous piece of work, such as a research study which involves several weeks' work.

SEG

The SEG syllabus sets out the most structured framework for assessed pieces of work of all three syllabuses. Tasks to be set are divided into *three types*. The *number* of each type of task which has to be completed is fixed, as follows:

a (Paper 1) *Five controlled assignments* (one per topic/module).
  'Controlled' indicates that all students will be set the same task, using the same materials, with the same amount of time available (which must not be more than the normal amount of time given to lessons in Integrated Humanities during a week).
b (Paper 2) *One personal research study* (based on any one of the five topics/modules).
  This will be an 'investigation' which 'should entail personal initiative and enquiry skills'.
c (Paper 3) *Four pieces of Coursework* (based on the four topics/modules for which the personal research study is *not* set).
  For four of the topics you study you must produce a piece of coursework, which might involve essays, interviews, surveys, creative writing, etc.
  The five controlled assignments will, together, carry 30% of the total final mark.
  The personal research study will carry 35% of the total final mark.
  The four pieces of coursework will, together, carry 35% of the total final mark.

So, the number and variety of tasks you must submit for assessment will vary between the three syllabuses. Indeed, they can vary between schools using the *same* syllabus. What you must always remember is that whenever you are preparing to tackle a particular assessment task, you have to be clear about *what is being asked of you*. Check with your teacher which of the assessment objectives are involved in the task. This will give you an idea of the standards the teacher will be using in judging your work.

Remember: you are not competing against other students; you are matching yourself against a number of assessment objectives.

❝❝ Make sure you know what is being asked of you in every assessment you undertake. ❞❞

9 ▷ MARKING YOUR WORK

Examples of assessment criteria (standards) from examination boards follow.

MEG

MEG produces marking criteria which consist of *seven levels of attainment* – one mark for each level – for each assessment objective. Each level is a 'statement' which describes the standard of work expected for that level (see Fig 1.8).

	UNDERSTANDING AND COMMUNICATION		
Mark	OBJECTIVE 1A	OBJECTIVE 1B	OBJECTIVE 1C
1	The assignment shows that the student has a tentative understanding of a few of the main ideas connected with the subject of study. These are described in simple concrete terms.	The assignment presents some of the main ideas relevant to the topic, described in straightforward concrete terms. The description is in outline, but accurate in essentials.	The understanding of another's situation is shown through brief references to the experiences of another.
2	The student shows understanding of a few of the ideas and can describe them fairly accurately using words and phrases which communicate some elements of the study.	The account is presented in outline, clearly communicating the main points or events, but with no development of detail or personal comment.	The understanding of another's situation is shown through brief references to obvious concrete aspects of that person's/group's surroundings and activities and the ways in which they deal with them.
3	The student shows understanding of several of the ideas connected with the study, and can describe them adequately using a few appropriate terms. Examples are used to illustrate the meanings of the terms.	The account is clearly presented, some thought has been given to its organisation especially its introduction. The main events or aspects are described on the whole coherently, but with little detail or comment.	The surroundings and activities of the person/people are described clearly and with some attention to detail. Simple descriptions of feelings, aims and intentions are included.
4	The student shows understanding of the main ideas and can describe them competently using some specialist terms. These are given brief definitions by examples from the study.	The account presents an organised coherent description with attention being given to details which help clarify the main aspects. It shows a sense of organisation, but may include irrelevances.	The student is able to show some understanding of how the context in which the people live affects their activities, beliefs and feelings.
5	The main ideas are described accurately using some specialist terms. Some ideas are understood as concepts which can be generalised, and are explained using a range of examples.	The outline of the account is presented logically and coherently. There is an obvious structure to the assignment. Events or points are detailed enough to help the reader, listener, or viewer form a clear picture of what is being recounted.	The student is able to show that the person/people described respond/ed in a distinctive manner to their situation – one determined by their understanding of the situation.
6	The student can explain concepts related to the study accurately and clearly, using appropriate terminology. Detailed examples are used to show the applicability of the concepts, and possible generalisations are mentioned.	A detailed account is presented which gives the reader, listener or viewer a clear picture of the subject. In outline it is well structured while individual sections are both related explicitly to the general direction of the account, and are internally coherent, with little irrelevant material.	Empathy at this level is demonstrated by the ability to show how the circumstances of the person/people affected their lives, and how their background influences the ways in which they responded to those circumstances. This is communicated through imaginative (i.e. 'in their place') or descriptive (i.e. a report) accounts.

UNDERSTANDING AND COMMUNICATION			
Mark	OBJECTIVE 1A	OBJECTIVE 1B	OBJECTIVE 1C
7	The student shows a detailed and sophisticated understanding of the subject of study through the use of a wide range of specialist terminology. Concepts are defined and discussed, showing how they might be applied to other material, and the possible limitations to their use.	A full detailed and well organised account is presented (as in level 6) with a wealth of detail at key points, personal comments where appropriate, and a sense of audience.	An extension of 6 with added imaginative or descriptive detail and flair, avoiding the confusion of empathy with sympathy.

Fig. 1.8 An example of marking criteria for MEG Integrated Humanities.

NEA

NEA does *not* give marking criteria. Instead it provides a list of *seven grade descriptions* for each of the assessment objectives (Fig. 1.9). These give an indication of the standards which will have to be achieved for a particular *grade* to be awarded for each assessment objective. Your teacher will use these descriptions to produce a mark scheme for each particular assessment task.

Fig. 1.9 NEA grade descriptions.

GRADE	a) Understanding and knowledge	b) Investigation		c) Interpretation and evaluation of argument	d) Transmission and presentation of argument
		I	II		
G	The candidate recognises and recalls a few specific examples connected with the study.	The candidate presents some material relevant to the investigations.	The candidate locates and selects some evidence from stimulus material.	The candidate attempts to interpret the information and attempts to formulate initial hypotheses, distinguish probable cause and effect and identify the subjective and objective nature of evidence at a very simple level.	The candidate describes issues in simple concrete terms with an attempt at linked arguments
F	The candidate recognises and recalls some specialist terminology and concepts and some conflicting perspectives by the use of a small number of specific examples.	The candidate investigates the subject of the research using two different sources of information in a simple way.	The candidate locates and selects material in a simple way.	The candidate interprets the information and attempts to formulate initial hypotheses, distinguish probable cause and effect and identify the subjective and objective nature of evidence at a simple level.	The candidate describes the main issues in simple concrete terms with linked arguments.
E	The candidate recognises and recalls some specialist concepts and some conflicting perspectives by the use of some specialist terminology.	The candidate investigates the subject of the research using at least two different sources of information in detail.	The candidate locates and selects a range of secondary evidence from stimulus material.	The candidate interprets the information, formulates initial hypotheses, distinguishes probable cause and effect and identifies the subjective and objective nature of evidence at a simple level.	The candidate's account shows an attempt at structure with linked arguments.

GRADE	a) Understanding and knowledge	b) Investigation		c) Interpretation and evaluation of argument	d) Transmission and presentation of argument
		I	II		
D	The candidate recognises and recalls specialist concepts and some conflicting perspectives by a range of examples using some specialist terminology.	The candidate investigates the subject of the research using a range of resources including primary sources.	The candidate locates and selects some primary evidence as well as secondary evidence from stimulus material.	The candidate interprets the information, formulates initial hypotheses, distinguishes probable cause and effect, and identifies the subjective and objective nature of evidence.	The candidate's account has a structure with relevant detail in linked arguments.
C	The candidate recognises and recalls concepts and conflicting perspectives by a range of examples, using specialist terminology.	The candidate investigates the subject of the research using a range of primary and secondary sources in detail and some of the appropriate techniques.	The candidate locates and selects a range of primary and secondary evidence from stimulus material.	The candidate interprets the information, formulates initial hypotheses, distinguishes probable cause and effect, identifies the subjective and objective nature of evidence and confirms, rejects or modifies the original hypotheses by an informed evaluation.	The candidate's account has a clear structure with relevant detail which forms a coherent picture.
B	The candidate recognises and recalls a range of specialist concepts and conflicting perspectives and explains these by the use of specialist terminology. Possible generalisations are mentioned.	The candidate investigates the subject of the research using a range of primary and secondary sources in considerable detail and a range of appropriate techniques.	The candidate locates and selects a range of primary and secondary evidence in detail from stimulus material.	The candidate interprets the information, formulates initial hypotheses, distinguishes probable cause and effect, identifies the subjective and objective nature of evidence, confirms rejects or modifies the original hypotheses and assesses the ethical implications of conclusions on her/his personal views.	The candidate's account is well-structured with a large degree of relevant and coherent detail.
A	The candidate recognises and recalls a wide range of specialist concepts and conflicting perspectives and explains these by the use of specialist terminology. The candidate is able to make clear generalisations.	The candidate investigates the subject of the research using a wide range of primary and secondary sources in depth and a wide range of appropriate techniques.	The candidate locates and selects a wide range of primry and secondary evidence in considerable detail from stimulus material.	The candidate interprets the information, formulates initial hypotheses, distinguishes probable cause and effect, identifies the subjective and objective nature of evidence, confirms, rejects or modifies the original hypotheses, assesses the ethical implications of conclusions on her/his personal views and formulates alternative views.	The candidate's account is presented in a logical, comprehensive and coherent manner.

SEG

SEG produces detailed mark schemes for each of the three types of task required by the examiners (controlled assignments, personal research study and coursework). Your teacher must use this when marking your work (Fig. 1.10).

Remember that the assessment of your work does not finish with the mark or grade awarded to you by your teacher. The examination groups each have their own methods to *compare* the marking procedures and standards of your teacher with other teachers of Integrated Humanities. Samples of work from every examination centre (usually the school) are compared, and the marks adjusted if necessary. Your final grade will be established only at the end of this process, which is designed to ensure that work of a similar standard is awarded the same grade throughout all the examination centres.

	MARK ALLOCATION
1 UNDERSTANDING	
The candidate	
a) has shown no understanding of any of the disciplines relevant to this Assignment	0
b) has shown some understanding of the disciplines relevant to this Assignment through the use of appropriate terminology	1–2
c) has shown basic understanding of some of the disciplines relevant to this Assignment through the application of appropriate terminology and concepts	3–4
d) has shown considerable understanding of the disciplines relevant to this Assignment through the application of appropriate terminology and concepts, at all the required contextual levels	5–6
e) has shown considerable understanding of many aspects of the disciplines relevant to this Assignment through the application of appropriate terminology at all the required contextual levels and in all the required conceptual areas	7–8
2 ENQUIRY	
The candidate	
a) has made no effort to identify or to discriminate between sources of information	0
b) has attempted to identify and to discriminate between sources of information	1–2
c) has successfully identified and discriminated between sources of information and used these critically and imaginatively	3–4
3 ANALYSIS AND EVALUATION	
The candidate	
a) had made no attempt to analyse or evaluate	0
b) has made some attempt to analyse the material presented/ collected, but at a very superficial level	1–2
c) has analysed the material presented/collected to the extent of being able to identify cause and effect	3–4
d) has thoroughly analysed the material presented/collected and drawn valid conclusions	5–6
e) has thoroughly analysed the material presented/collected and has drawn relevant and perceptive conclusions which are explored in depth	7–8
4 COMMUNICATION	
The candidate	
a) has not communicated effectively	0
b) has used effectively at least one means of communication	1–2
c) has used effectively a variety of means of communication	3–4
Total Marks Available per Assignment	24
Total Marks Available for Five Assignments	120

Fig. 1.10. SEG marking scheme for the five assignments (paper 1).

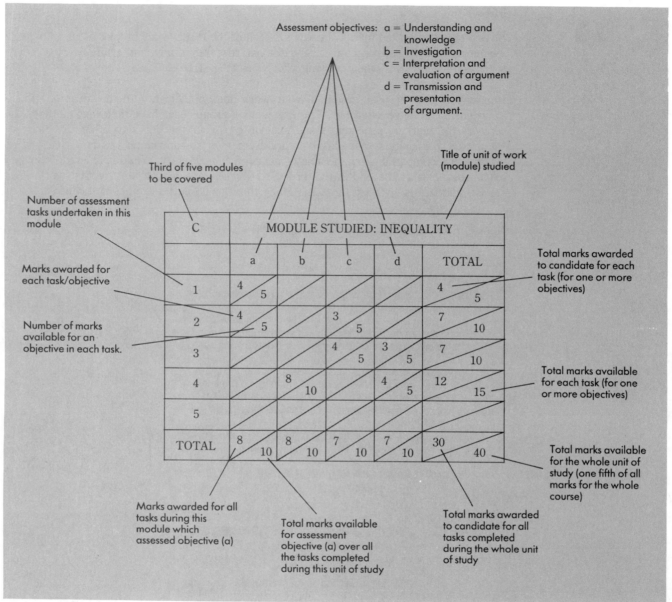

Fig. 1.11 An NEA record of marks for one module.

Integrated Humanities is an extremely flexible subject. It allows for a wide range of issues and topics to be selected and assessed through a variety of tasks. This means that it is not possible to present a list of key facts which must be learned or to describe every type of assessment task with which you may be presented. Instead, the following chapters concentrate on the main assessment objectives of GCSE Integrated Humanities. They suggest some of the ways in which you can develop your skills and abilities to meet each assessment objective and thereby improve your grade. Actual student work is presented on many occasions, with examiner comments to help you see the strengths and weaknesses of that work. The lessons you can learn from the experience of others should help you improve your own performance and grade.

UNDERSTANDING IDEAS

CONTINUITY AND CHANGE

CAUSE AND CONSEQUENCE

SIMILARITY AND DIFFERENCE

SPATIAL INTERACTION

EQUALITY, INEQUALITY AND THE DISTRIBUTION OF POWER

INTERDEPENDENCE

CONFLICT AND CO-OPERATION

VALUES AND BELIEFS

EMPATHY

GETTING STARTED

An explanation of Integrated Humanities, as the study of issues crucial to *people*, has been given in Chapter 1. What this chapter aims to do is give you an indication of some *key ideas* you may experience in your Integrated Humanities course. It is impossible to identify *every* idea as this will depend to some extent on your teachers. However, there is a variety of ideas and concepts which are common to many Integrated Humanities courses, and we are confident you will encounter most, if not all, of them. They are:

- Continuity and Change
- Cause and Consequence
- Similarity and Difference
- Spatial Interaction
- Equality and Inequality
- The Distribution of Power
- Interdependence
- Conflict and Co-operation
- Values and Beliefs

All Integrated Humanities courses also deal with Empathy. This chapter will offer an explanation of what this means, along with explanations of the other *key ideas* listed above.

ESSENTIAL PRINCIPLES

❝ What do the *key ideas* mean? ❞

The *key ideas* contained in this chapter will keep cropping up in your studies, so it will help to be aware of what they mean, and what the examiner is looking for in assessing your understanding of them. In addition, we have included possible coursework assignments and student responses to show how *you* might demonstrate your understanding of these ideas. Although we have explained each idea separately, it will soon become obvious how many of them overlap and are interlinked.

1 ▷ CONTINUITY AND CHANGE

❝ What has changed? Why have these changes taken place? How rapid have these changes been? ❞

Change is a constant feature of society. How and why things change is of great interest. Sometimes the changes are abrupt and clear-cut, such as the sudden change in policy which happens when a revolutionary government takes power. Changes in the lives of people also take place, but often slowly, over periods of many years. Change does not have a constant rate nor does it have a consistent direction. Developments in technology, warfare and culture, and political and moral attitudes have often been interrupted by great bursts of rapid change.

Points to consider when looking for change are:

1	The pace of change	When does change occur rapidly? When does change occur slowly? Which is more important, a period of slow or a period of rapid change?
2	The importance of change	Some changes are so important that they can be called '*turning points*'. After a turning point, things will be quite different in important ways.
3	'Dead-end' change	As a contrast to a turning point, some changes have no lasting effect; they in fact lead to 'dead ends'.

❝ Does change mean progress? ❞

4	Change and progress	People often talk about *progress*, meaning that they think things have improved or become more advanced. Do *all* changes make for progress? The development of the motor car has brought great changes to car-owning communites, but is this progress? What are the environmental effects of road travel? What is the cost in human lives? Think about the number of accidents on the road each year. Does driving increase stress-related illness?

❝ What remains the same? ❞

Despite changes, many things, such as peoples' attitudes, customs and traditions, often remain much the same. This is called *continuity*.

Change and continuity can both be identified when a *comparison* is made over time. For example, a comparison between weekly 'shopping lists' of 1989 and 1889 would illustrate many changes in the prices and types of item bought. It would also illustrate continuity in that certain items would appear on both lists.

QUESTIONS TO ASK WHEN LOOKING FOR CHANGE

❝ Ask questions ❞

- What is the nature of the change?
- Is it an important and significant change? Whom did it affect – everyone or only a few? In what ways did it affect them?
- Who has benefited and who has suffered from the change?
- Did the change occur suddenly or slowly?

In assessing your understanding of this idea the examiner will look for *evidence* that you have grasped some of the following points. Can you:

❝ What the examiner looks for ❞

- recognise that changes occur within the lifetime of particular people, in particular subject areas (for example, art, architecture, medicine) and in particular places;
- recognise that change is usually a *continuous process*, rather than a collection of isolated happenings;
- recognise *differences in the rate of change*;
- assess the *extent* of continuity and/or change between two points in time;
- recognise that change does *not* necessarily mean progress or development.

POSSIBLE COURSEWORK ASSIGNMENT

A possible area of study to show your understanding of *Continuity and Change* could be an examination of the changes in the life of women during the last century. In this you could try and identify changes in the following areas:

Has the role of women changed in the past one hundred years?

- the role of women in the house – Who performs the household chores? Who takes responsibility for bringing up the children? Has anything really changed?
- attitudes towards the role of women – Do people expect women to be the housewife and childminder?
- the occupational structure of women – Do women have the same jobs as men? Is there equality at the workplace?
- the education of girls – Is there equality of opportunity in education?
- legislation – Has a woman's life changed as a result of legislation?
- science and technology – Have there been any scientific or technological developments which have changed the lives of women during the last century?

Equality and inequality are linked with continuity and change.

During this investigation, remember to consider the points previously raised about *change*. Its pace, its extent and the progress and problems it leads to. Also, don't forget to highlight areas of *continuity* in the lives of women. If you present your results clearly, you should be able to show the examiner you have understood this idea of *Continuity and Change*.

2 ▷ CAUSE AND CONSEQUENCE

This *key idea* is also linked to the idea of *continuity and change*, because whenever we look at *how* things have changed, we also look at the causes for and consequences of making these changes. Actions and events in the wider world have different sorts of *causes*. Similarly, actions and decisions, whether ours, other peoples or those of governments and big business, have different sorts of *consequences*. These may include *intended* consequences (consequences expected to happen) and *unintended* (or unforeseen consequences, consequences *not* expected to happen).

Understanding cause and consequence can help you to understand events affecting your own life and those affecting others in the wider world. However, *identifying* cause and consequence is not always easy. Nevertheless, if you have been asked to identify change, the next stage is to ask:

Ask questions. What caused the change? What are the consequences?

- What *caused* the change?
- What are the *consequences* of the change?

In assessing your understanding of this idea the examiner will look for *evidence* that you have grasped some of the following points. Can you:

What the examiner looks for

- identify (and distinguish between) long-term and short-term causes;
- identify inter-related causes;
- identify intended and unintended consequences;
- assess the relative importance of different causes;
- support your analysis with precise evidence?

POSSIBLE COURSEWORK ASSIGNMENT

As part of a study of China in the twentieth century, this student was asked to complete the following assignment on the Communist take-over in 1949.

Mao Tse-tung: 'With our tactics . . . no enemy, however powerful, can cope with us.' How accurate is this as an assessment of why the Chinese Communist Party defeated the Kuomintang in October 1949?

In this piece of coursework you have to focus on the Communist victory in China in 1949. You have to decide why the Communists were successful.

You have been given a quotation from the Communist leader in 1949, Mao Tse-tung. Your task is to decide how far this statement explains the Communists success. Was this the major reason for victory? What other factors stated by Mao have anything to do with the Communist success?

To assist you in your decision you may wish to consider the following points:

- events usually have a number of causes.
- causes can be grouped into various areas – for example, political, social, religious, economic, racial, geographical, historical.
- some causes may be more important than others, acting as 'triggers' to others and making things happen.
- can you identify long-term and short-term causes?
- people make things happen.

Fig. 2.1 An assignment brief: China 1949.

Comments on the assignment brief

The way the set task is structured helps the student to complete the assignment. This type of assignment is likely to lead to good answers because it focuses the attention on causal factors. Without such a structure the student could easily get bogged down, presenting too much information in a long written answer that obscured the main point of the question. This would obviously be unsatisfactory as the main *purpose* of the work is to develop an understanding of *cause*. This is worth remembering. Before attempting questions related to the understanding of ideas, be clear about *which ideas* you have to show an understanding of. This will help to concentrate your mind on the task set.

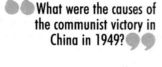 **What were the causes of the communist victory in China in 1949?**

EXTRACT FROM STUDENT'S WORK

What follows is a selection of extracts from a student's response to this assignment.

> Mao Tse-Tung, as leader of the Chinese Communist Party (CCP) lead the peasants through a revolution which resulted in the Kuomintang being defeated in October 1949 and the Peoples' Republic of China being proclaimed. As the quotation, suggests, Mao believed his guerilla war tactics were what allowed him to gain victory. But how accurate is this statement?
>
> There are several factors which induced Mao's victory over the KMT. There are short-term and long-term factors which helped Mao to win the war. One of these long-term factors is the mistreatment and inequality to the peasants.

Fig. 2.2 An extract from a student's response to a question about the success of the Chinese Communists in 1949: introduction.

❝ This is a sound introduction which outlines the terms of the answer and gets straight to the point of the question. A long-term *cause* is identified and the student goes on to explain about it, supporting the points made with *evidence.* ❞

> For several decades the peasants had been charged high taxes by their tyrannic landlords. The fields in which they grew crops was barely enough for each farmer to support his family, after almost as much as 70% of the produce was taken by the landlords as rent. When the haggard, illiterate peasants had paid their rent, their debt (when the previous harvest was a bad one), and their interest on the debt, there was hardly anything left. Mao wanted an end to this inequality and promised the peasants a better way of life and so they began to support Mao. The 'better way of life' meant, as one peasant commented, ' the poor will not have to pay taxes. The poor will not have to pay rent. Poor people's children shall go to school, and landlords will disappear'. Another peasant, talking about his conversion to communism said 'I especially liked the idea of the landowners being destroyed'. I believe none of the peasants were forced into supporting Mao, all of them were willing to, especially with the promise of a better life. Mao's aim was to persuade the peasants that his actions were good and well-intentioned ones, because 90% of the Chinese population were peasants, and once they were on Mao's side his battle to improve China was under-way. Mao had

great belief in the Peasant Revolution and in 1927 said, 'Without the poor peasants their would be no revolution. To deny their role is to deny the revolution. To attack them is to attack the revolution...' So Mao, in the meantime demanded that all the soldiers of the Red Army would not kill, pillage, or rape the women in the peasant villages, and that anything they damaged they would pay for. This, I assume, would build up the peasants confidence in Communism.

Fig 2.3 An extract from a student's response to a question about the success of the Chinese Communists in 1949: long-term cause.

❝❝ Here we have an *explanation* of how Mao's promises to the peasants and the behaviour of his soldiers helped the Communists to gain support. This support was a *long-term cause* of their success. ❞❞

The peasants hardship was a long-term political factor, although Mao's war tactics were a short-term cause which had great effect on the KMT (Kuomintang).
    Mao's war tactics were an advantage to him in Chinas' war against Japan between 1936—'45, because the KMT and CCP agreed to join forces in an effort to defeat the Japanese. By using guerilla tactics, the CCP won more battles against Japan than the KMT. This gave great credibility to the CCP and showed everyone of the CCP's capability at war tactics and fighting.

Fig. 2.4 An extract from a student's response to a question about the success of the Chinese Communists in 1949: short-term cause.

❝❝ The student now introduces a *short-term cause* for the success of the Communists, their victories against the Japanese. ❞❞

The setting up and organising of the Shensi Soviet also triggered the peasants into joining the CCP movement although this was not a major cause as to why the CCP defeated the KMT in 1949. The Shensi Soviet was an example to the peasants of the 'better life'. Cho Teh describes the Soviet of Hunan, 'An eight hour day was proclaimed, wages were raised and plans made for the relief of the unemployed. The property of landlords, militarists and officials were confiscated, and the landed estates proclaimed confiscated without compensation. Debts were cancelled'.

Fig. 2.5 An extract from a student's response to a question about the success of the Chinese Communists in 1949: Shensi Soviet.

❝❝ Another cause was the setting up of the Shensi Soviet. This was not a major cause, but it did give the Chinese peasants an idea of what life would be like under Mao. They liked what they experienced. ❞❞

To decide how accurate Mao's assessment of why the CCP defeated the KMT in October 1949, I have needed to discuss the many causes which may have helped him to gain victory. Each one of these causes overlaps with the other, but I found that the long-term mistreatment of the peasants and the effect it had on them to be of the most importance. If they had not been mistreated then Mao would not have a 'base' to work from, and would be unable to promise them a better life. As it happened, Mao was in a position where he could make promises to them, and in effect, all his work revolved around the peasants and not the industrialists. This is because of Chinas' population where 90% of the people were peasants.
    Mao had obviously studied hard the works of Karl Marx and agreed with the democracy, morals, and principles of Marxism. He projected his confidence among villagers and propagandists and persuaded those who were perhaps unsure, to join the CCP.

Fig. 2.6 An extract from a student's response to a question about the success of the Chinese Communists in 1949: conclusion.

❝ The conclusion is an assessment of *all* the causes which the student feels contributed to Mao's success, realising that there were many involved. There is an attempt to link the student's views of the causes to the original question set. ❞

Student assessment

Even by examining only part of this assignment, it is clear that the student shows an understanding of the main ideas. She can explain them competently, using appropriate terms. There is also a realisation that some causes are inter-linked. Short- and long-term causes have been identified, together with the effect these had on Mao's success. At the end of the assignment, the student attempts to tie in her findings with the question set. It is also good to see her support her points with evidence.

To improve, she could have included something about the influence of Mao himself in the success of the Communists. What part did his awareness, understanding of the situation and leadership qualities play in their success? Would the Communists have been successful without Mao?

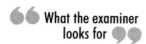

3 ▶ SIMILARITY AND DIFFERENCE

Similarity does not mean 'the same'. It means that things are alike in certain respects but not identical. This is an important difference, and one you need to be aware of. Two towns may look alike to an outsider but be very different places to the people who live there. It is often much easier to detect *differences* than it is to find similarities, as there are many different ways of doing things and not all human beings will do the same as you do. However, similarities do exist between people and events. It can be argued that people of all nationalities have a similar nature deep down, the same physical needs, wishes and hopes for, for example, friendship, love, happiness and enjoyment. Also, it is possible to identify *patterns* in events; a revolution in one country may be followed by similar revolutions in neighbouring countries. It is important to find out about, and to understand, both the differences between people and the things which people have in common.

In analysing your understanding of this *key idea* the examiner would want you to:

❝ Ask questions. What differences exist between people? What are the similarities? ❞

❝ What the examiner looks for ❞

- identify similarities within the context of the task you have been set;
- identify differences within the context of the task you have been set;
- *test* your conclusions once you have completed the identification process. How accurate are they? Are they based on reliable information?

POSSIBLE COURSEWORK ASSIGNMENT

A possible area of study to show your understanding of this idea could be a comparison of *your* lifestyle with that of someone in a different country. This could include an assessment of several aspects:

❝ People and the environment ❞

- needs and wants;
- homes;
- the family;

- education;
- employment;
- expectations;

- attitudes;
- leisure activities;
- choices available.

In all these you could seek to identify what is similar and what is different in the two lifestyles.

4 ▶ SPATIAL INTERACTION

The *key idea* here can be interpreted in various ways. For the purposes of this chapter we have defined it as an analysis of how the features of the earth's surface and its people are located and how they interact. Mainly, it relates to the relationship between people and the environment, and could include the following aspects:

- **Location**
  This is the position and distribution of people.

- **Interaction**
  This is relationship of people and their environment, which could include the response of people to the survival problems posed by the natural environment, or to a consideration of social issues and problems such as the problems of living in cities.

- **Distance**
  This includes investigating communication systems and the relationship between distance and time and how this affects the organisation of societies.

■ **Change**

Identifying spatial change; for example, why do people change their location? This aspect is obviously related to the *key idea* of *Continuity and Change* explained earlier.

An assessment of your understanding of *Spatial Interaction* by the examiner will depend on the particular investigation set up by your teacher. Your understanding will relate specifically to this. Therefore, it is impossible for us to give a definite list of what the examiner will look for in assessing your level of understanding. So, it is essential that you are clear about the main points of *your* investigation, and what it is you have to do to demonstrate your understanding of the main points. To achieve this *consult your teacher*.

POSSIBLE COURSEWORK ASSIGNMENTS

The explanation of *Spatial Interaction* just given has already suggested areas of study which could be used as coursework assignments. These include:

■ the response of people to the survival problems posed by the natural environment;

■ the problems created by living in cities;

■ an assessment of communication systems and how they affect the organisation of societies;

■ the reasons why people change their location.

To these could be added:

■ village or town studies;

■ the conservation of environmental resources, both renewable and non-renewable;

■ the problem of developing countries (this issue is examined in more detail in the explanation of the next key idea, Equality and Inequality).

5 ▷ **EQUALITY, INEQUALITY AND THE DISTRIBUTION OF POWER**

The *key idea* of *Equality and Inequality and the Distribution of Power* is strongly connected with other ideas included in this chapter. Indeed in many respects its understanding cannot be separated from them. As far as a definition goes, the *Chambers 20th Century Dictionary* defines 'equality' as the condition of being equal, and 'inequality' as a want of equality, difference, inadequacy, incompetency and unevenness.

There are many examples of inequality among people in the world, covering inequalities in:

■ freedom;

■ resources, including wealth;

■ opportunities, including the quality of life.

Most of these are bound up with the *Distribution of Power*, either in an individual country or in the world at large. People and groups with *power* are able to influence what happens in a country or in the world. In most situations, power is distributed unequally. This affects people's life chances, their freedom and their welfare. An awareness of this *inequality* raises important questions about fairness and justice.

In assessing your understanding of these *key ideas* the examiner will look for evidence that you can:

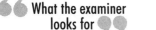 **What the examiner looks for**

■ identify inequality in the context of the task set;

■ suggest reasons for this inequality;

■ suggest possible consequences of this inequality;*

■ suggest ways, in the context of the task set, by which equality may be established.

POSSIBLE COURSEWORK ASSIGNMENT

Chapter 4 contains a possible coursework assignment on the so-called North–South divide in Britain. The resources included there could be adapted for an assignment which examines the possibility of inequalities between different parts of the United Kingdom. This work could be extended to include electoral voting patterns and constituency

*These points are linked to your understanding of the key idea of *Cause and Consequence*.

organisation, in an attempt to identify the distribution of *voting power* in the United Kingdom.

Another possible investigation for this *key idea* has been mentioned in the section on *Spatial Interaction*: namely, the problem of developing countries. What follows is an extract from a student's response to an assignment on global equality. The emphasis for the student here was on possible ways in which an underdeveloped country could improve its condition. This was part of a study which concentrated on the differences between developed and underdeveloped countries, identifying in particular the inequalities which exist between them.

Global equality and inequality is a good case study, and illustrates a point made earlier in the chapter, that *many* of the ideas you experience will be related to the *specific aspect* of your study.

❝How can underdeveloped countries develop?❞

EQUALITY AND INEQUALITY

Global inequality — A report to show how it is best for a third world country to develop

It is impossible for all of the countries in the world to be in identical situations in terms of their wealth. You always will get a scale with there more often than not being a large contrast between the top of the scale and the bottom of the scale, and the wealth of certain countries is no exception. The scale of countries wealth and situation is in three categories, first world countries, second world countries, and the THIRD WORLD COUNTRIES. The contrast between the first and third world countries is vast to say the least, with the third world countries grateful of any new enterprises that can aid their need for development. The struggling countries really are having great difficulties in giving their respective populations the opportunity to have the main needs in order to lead a reasonable and healthy life. The main needs that people need are 1) Food/Drink, in order to survive. 2) Health care, to also help the growing fight against death. 3) Employment, to earn vital money. 4) Making wealth. 5) Self respect, which may be the last of the needs but is an important part of most peoples character. To provide the basic needs there are two alternative approaches, the Capitalists approach, and the approach of the Socialists. These two respective views on development, are both very contrasting, using totally different methods. The Socialists approach involves the country reorganising itself. They feel that there should be a priority to feed the people, to care for the people and to introduce the use of intermediate technology. Socialists want the land to be shared and farmed more effectively without a lot of expensive machinery. The aim of the Socialists is to employ more people and therefore provide self-respect.

> ❝ A very good start. Definitions are given for the inequalities of countries and their division into First-, Second- or Third-World countries. Understanding is shown of several ideas, including basic needs and Socialist and Capitalist approaches to development. There is also an indication, from the manner in which this work is written, that the student understands the terms intermediate technology and multi-national technology. ❞

The Capitalists provide a contrasting alternative which is based on various ideas. There approach is based on multinational investment, to aid the food situation, to introduce the use of machinery and to concentrate mainly on only a few items of trade. The aim of the Capitalists is to create development similar to the western states.

The two alternative ways forward for a third world country do have their problems. The Capitalists approach involves low profits being made, inadequate food production, and a problem of providing employment. The Socialists steps to move a third world country forward has the danger of violence, unpopularity from aid, and a lack of profits for development.

> 66 The problems involved in implementing the two systems, Capitalism and Socialism, are adequately put, although specific evidence to support the points made would have helped. 99

Ghana, a third world country that needed to move forward quickly, introduced what was known as the 'Big Project'. They took a very big step in creating a dam, known as the Volta Dam. The whole project was devised by one man. NKruma, who along with the government, had the aim to produce cheap electricity for Ghana. The Volta Dam became the biggest industrial means of Ghana with 90% of the electricity being used for Ghana. The project was big, and that obviously meant that it was a very expensive project to set up, costing no-less than £50 million. The huge dam was built on the river Volta, producing a huge sheet of water covering over 3000 m. The new dam may well have produced a large expanse over water but at the same time it has deprived Ghana of 3000 miles of land. Which is a lot of farming land to lose in one big move. The project, which is a Capitalist project, was hoping to provide the population of Ghana with the main needs. I have already stated that this multinational investment has wiped out a large expanse of land and to go along with this fact around 80,000 people, who were living on this land, became homeless. Which is a huge step backwards before any benefits of this project materialised. To improve the situation for the people who became homeless the government did build many concrete bungalows for these people, but these were not really adequate for a family life. Along with the change of the landscape from earth to sea, the life styles of the people effectively changed too, from living on land, farming etc, to living on the sea.

> 66 Ghana as a case study is introduced. A clear explanation is given of the attempt by this country to move forward. Effects of the Volta Dam are clearly explained. The adverse effects are dealt with first. 99

Certain towns that were based alongside the dam became a lot better off for this project. They were able to form new lake side suburbs to gain from the sea industry, but despite this life was remaining rather tough, with there only being two busy days a week.

As well as providing Ghana with cheap electricity, which was the main reasoning behind the project, there were other minor industries that benefited from the 'Big Project'. One trade that boomed was the tomato trade. It was hopeful that the huge lake would materialise into a new waterway. A trade was formed because of the dam, providing people with their new transport boats. The boat trade took off providing jobs for a few.

The electrical power that was now being produced was sent to the Aluminium smelter. From all of the electrical power that was being received the Aluminium industry began to benefit more than any one or thing. While homes are being destroyed from the floods of the dam, the Aluminium smelter was benefiting greatly. Because of the 'boom' in this industry there was about 2500 jobs made available. Although this figure appears high, and it is a good benefit for Ghana, there would have been more jobs available if there were not so many machines which were doing manual jobs. People of Ghana were employed as control workers (black people) and through experience Ghanian technicians were created. These technicians shouldered a lot of responsibility for it was up to these type of workers to make it work for Ghana.

The aluminium smelter that was being produced did very little for Ghana itself, but it did benefit other first world countries, which was not really the whole point of the project. First world countries are able to take advantage of the less wealthy countries. One country that entered business with Ghana was America. They provided Ghana with a lot of financial backing for the project to enable Ghana to gain from cheap electricity, but this was not the only reason behind America entering business with Ghana. America made a good profit from the aluminium smelter.

> 66 Balanced argument, this page includes the successes of the project. A sound understanding is shown of how the First-World countries get involved with the Third-World countries. It is not for humanitarian but for financial reasons! 99

The main needs of the population of Ghana were aided in only a little amount by the 'Big Project'. The Ghana folk may well have benefited more from a variety of other projects that would have tackled the needs of Ghana with more success, for example ox-ploughing, looms, and windpumps. Although I said that there wasn't that much success from the project, there were some benefits that resulted. 2500 Ghanians were employed, there were developments of new markets, and it taught certain skills. There were trades such as boat building, the fishing trade benefited, but only on a small scale. The main aim of the project, to produce cheap electricity was fulfilled, but this along with the other benefit was rather little for the 50 million pounds that it cost. I get the feeling that the man who set up the 'Big project' was more concerned about himself, hopefully hearing his name to be remembered for many years to come, than the population of Ghana.

The 'Big project' based around the Volta Dam was a Capitalist's way forward, but development in Ghana was provided by the Socialists by at least as much and if not more. There were new developments of industries introducing textile factories, an airport and a motorway. The Government produced a lot of financial backing along with the ideas that were very doubtful as to whether the country would benefit from them.

> 66 A sound conclusion is given, based on a clear understanding of the situation. Both the positive and negative sides of the attempts at development are included, all of which illustrate a thorough understanding of this particular issue. 99

The Airport, obviously required vast financial backing and there must be doubts over whether the Ghanian government had their priorities right, for I feel that it was a waste of a lot of money which could have been used more wisely on new industries. The Government did obviously not feel this way, and probably thought that the pride and self-respect to have an airport like much wealthier countries was more important. The airport does not really have enough traffic to warrant it being open. It only has one day that is reasonably busy, a Saturday.

The textile factories included a lot of machinery and this really defeated the object of creating many jobs though the machines are capable of doing more work in these factories than man could. This fact rather dented the idea of textile factories.

Student assessment

The student shows a clear understanding of the different strategies recommended by Socialist and Capitalist perspectives. This is supported by the student's understanding of the specific effect of the Volta Dam on the lives of the people of Ghana, both negative and positive. To conclude, the student explains the main ideas accurately, using specialist terms where appropriate.

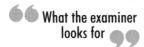

6 ⟩ **INTER-
DEPENDENCE**

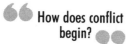
**People depend on each
other.**

**What the examiner
looks for**

People depend on each other in a variety of ways, from the giving of caring and emotional support to the exchange of goods and services. This *interdependence* is evident in every aspect of life, at individual, group and international level, and can have both positive and negative sides. It would seem that the most urgent problems facing humankind, the environment, peace and the satisfaction of basic needs, must be tackled on a world level and across national boundaries, as well as at the local level. When looking for solutions to human problems one often recommends working together.

An assessment of your understanding of this *key idea* is likely to involve your showing:

- an awareness of how people depend on each other in the context of the task set;
- recommendations for further interdependence in the context of the task set;
- an awareness of the circumstances necessary to allow interdependence to flourish;
- an awareness of the problems which could develop, in the context of the task set, as a result of increased interdependence.

POSSIBLE COURSEWORK ASSIGNMENT

This could involve an investigation into the economic and political organisation of countries. For example, in economic terms, if a country exports one major item to only one or two customers, what will happen to that country if the buyers stop purchasing the product?

7 ⟩ **CONFLICT AND
CO-OPERATION**

**How does conflict
begin?**

**What the examiner
looks for**

We live in a world of *conflict*. People continually disagree with each other. This happens in our own family, our own society, in other societies and between our society and others. Conflicts can be *resolved* in a variety of ways. Understanding how conflicts occur can make it easier to avoid them or resolve them constructively. One way to avoid conflict is through *co-operation*. Individuals, groups and countries often work together to tackle common problems. Co-operation often means that tasks which would not otherwise be performed, can be dealt with. Co-operation is essential if conflicts are to be resolved peacefully.

In assessing your understanding of this *key idea*, the examiner would look for evidence that you:

- could identify conflict or co-operation in the context of the task set;
- could identify the cause of this conflict or co-operation;*
- could identify the consequences of the conflict or co-operation;*
- could, if co-operation was not already evident, suggest ways in which it could be established, and so ease the conflict;
- understand the difficulties involved in maintaining co-operation between the parties involved.
- * These points are linked to your understanding of the key idea *Cause and Consequence*.

POSSIBLE COURSEWORK ASSIGNMENTS

Rather than suggest one particular coursework assignment we have included a line of study which gives a varied insight into conflict and co-operation.

- Introduction of possible *areas of conflict* between people in your immediate environment: conflict at school or in your family. How might co-operation reduce the conflict? How could this be achieved and what form would it take? Consider the notion of shared responsibility.

**How do people co-
operate?**

- Within the locality look at an *issue* causing conflict; for example, the need for a by-pass or a new leisure pool. How might co-operation ease the conflict? Consider the idea of community organisation, the establishing of pressure groups, marches, demonstrations, petitions and meetings.
- *National examples of conflict and co-operation*. This might be best achieved through case study material. The problems in Northern Ireland would be a good example. Identify the source of the conflict and then offer suggestions as to what sort of co-operation is necessary to solve the conflict.
- *International examples of conflict and co-operation*: the United Nations, the EEC, the Cold War, the Reagan–Gorbachev summits. What were the causes of the conflict? How has the co-operation been established? What has been its benefits? Illustrate the problems involved in maintaining co-operation on an international scale.

8 ▷ VALUES AND BELIEFS

People have different views about what is important. Ways of life, behaviour, and traditions vary. Our *values and beliefs*, our sex, our social and cultural backgrounds, affect the way we perceive people and events and the way other people see us. Finding out about the values and beliefs of other people can help us to understand them, and ourselves, better.

In assessing your understanding of this *key idea*, the examiner would want to see *evidence* that you could identify the values and beliefs of the people under study. The task you have been set may well ask you to make an assessment of how these values and beliefs affect the lifestyles of the people concerned, and how they interact together and with other societies. You may also be asked to identify similarities and differences between your own values and beliefs and the ones you have identified for the people you are studying. This last task is obviously linked to your understanding of the key idea of *Similarities and Differences*.

 **Ask questions.**

POSSIBLE COURSEWORK ASSIGNMENT

Is there a God?

This could include any investigation into the values and beliefs of individuals, groups, whole communities or countries. A fundamental study in this *key idea* could be: Is there a God? The following extract is from such an investigation, where the student looked at the beliefs of science, philosophy and the general public concerning this most vital of questions. The selected extract concerns the scientific interpretation of a God.

THE SCIENTIST
Looks at God
The scientist answers a question using facts. Therefore, to disprove God's existence, he needs evidence, as reliable evidence amounts to fact. The scientist has a number of points which are valid to oppose the Christian point of view.

These points are: opposing creation theories; evolution is responsible for all of todays living things and not immediate creation; everything must have an origin and an end therefore there can be no god as god is said to be eternal; and, a supreme being is not scientifically possible.

The largest controversy between religion and science is the evolution controversy, and the theory of how the universe came to be.

Scientists believe that the universe probably originated 10^{12} years ago due to the 'big bang' theory. That is to say that there was a massive explosion and the stars and planets were formed from the gases produced. Science also has evidence to support this theory that is, that:(a) the galaxies are continuing to move apart at high speed and, (b) post-explosion radiation has been detected throughout the universe. That is how science explains how the universe and earth came to be. The scientist says that the explosion was caused by gases from the sun, but the bible tells us different."

'In the beginning, when GOD created the universe,...'
Genesis:Ch1 v1

The bible says God not gases! The next part of the Science v's Religion controversy, also has something to do with creation, but this time it is the creation of life. It could be entitled:
CREATION 'v' EVOLUTION

In 1831 a naturalist by the name of Charles Darwin was invited to sail on board HMS Beagle as the ship's naturalist. During those five years, Darwin made many observations of living beings and fossils, these observations lead to an idea that plants and animals had changed with time, one species being developed into another. He returned to England in 1836 and from there on, he conducted numerous experiments of his own to develop his idea. In 1859, he published a book called 'The Origin of Species' which explained the theory of evolution. This means that ape forms as we know them today have been changed over millions of years. One species has been changed into another species. In his book, Darwin made it indirectly known that he considered the man had originated from ape. This caused a considerable uproar, but it did lead to further investigations into this theory by other scientists. Today it is scientific fact that man comes from ape and evidence such as skeletons and fossils have been provided to prove this. Scientists have also traced all life forms back to bacteria which first became evident 3500 million years ago, hominids did not become evident until about 10 million years ago. So what about the 6 day creation story as it is in the bible. Life in the form of plants was created on the third day and man only three days later. Scientists have proved that this is wrong, so god must therefore be a liar or non-existent. It says that man is made in Gods' image, it also says that man must not lie, therefore, God must not lie, so there cannot be a God.

The third point that the scientist makes is that God is supposed to be eternal and has infinite powers, ie. a being without beginning or end whose powers will never cease. This say the scientist is impossible. Everything has to come from somewhere and has to come to an end, it is impossible for something to have no end.

The final point is, that it is impossible for there to be a being so supreme as God is supposed to be. No being can possibly create something so vast as the universe, so small as the virus, and so complicated as the eye or the body, it is scientifically impossible.
CONCLUSION

There is no God, it has been proven that a God did not create the universe, or in fact life as it is said in the bible. It is impossible for any being to have eternal life and it is impossible that such a supreme being to exist. Therefore, there is no God.

---

9 > EMPATHY

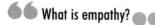 **What is empathy?**

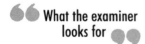 **Empathy is having an appreciation of others, based on evidence.**

What the examiner looks for

There is some debate among the examination boards as to whether *empathy* is an *idea* which you have to understand, a *skill* you have to perform or an *attitude of mind* which you have to develop. It is not our purpose to enter into this debate; instead, we will simply offer an explanation of what empathy means, consider what the examiner will look for when assessing your ability to empathise, and give examples of students' work.

WHAT DOES EMPATHY MEAN?

Empathy is being able to show some informed appreciation of the predicaments and points of view of other people, particularly people in cultures and situations different from your own. Empathising is not the same as identifying with or sympathising with people. It is a word used to describe *imagination, working on evidence*; it is an attempt to enter an unfamiliar experience.

In assessing empathy the examiner will want to see whether you can:

- reconstruct a situation with correct detail and show an understanding of the special and different patterns of thought of the people under study;
- show an understanding of another person's or group's situation and the ways in which this may affect them;
- show how the context in which people live or lived affected their experiences;
- show an appreciation of the way people respond or responded to their situation;
- show a clear understanding of the context in which people live or lived, of their responses to that situation, and of their feelings.

POSSIBLE COURSEWORK ASSIGNMENT

The type of assignments to *avoid* when submitting work for assessment in this area are those which ask 'Imagine you were'; all these tend to lead to are flights of indisciplined imagination! 'Imagine' is a word probably best avoided in setting assignments. This is because the key to empathy is showing an appreciation of people *based on evidence*; it is *not*

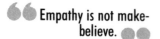 **Empathy is not make-believe.** 🙶🙷

make believe. The two student assignments which follow are very different, but both attempt to give informed appreciation of other people. The first concerns the past, the second the present.

EMPATHY EXERCISE ON HITLER AND THE JEWS

This piece of work was part of the introduction to the wider topic of Human Rights. As a stimulus the student had a selection of books, documentary material, and audio and visual material. The aim of the assignment was for the student to show an appreciation of what it might have been like to be a Jew living in Nazi Germany during the 1930's. To achieve this, the student adopted the position of a Jewish woman, Ruth Winterbaum. Three letters are written to her mother on different dates.

> 27th August 1935
>
> Hannah Braun
> 47 Seestraße
> Zurich 19
> Schweiz
>
> Dear Mother,
> I am writing this letter now, rather hurriedly as apparently laws are to be shortly passed restricting Jewish civil rights – if this is to include the sending of letters then I would feel better if you received a letter prior to the event explaining what is happening here.
> I can't believe what has happened in the two years since that ~~bastard~~ Hitler came to power. Does the rest of the world know what is going on here? Since 1933, he has requested by way of the media that 'true' Germans do not patronise Jewish businesses. This has meant a decline in our own grocery business.
> Mr Weiß, the lawyer has found himself unemployed since Jews were eliminated from the Civil Service, the legal profession and from education. We are portrayed as a lower species and contemptible, children are taught lessons in how to recognise Jews as bignosed, pennypurloining. We have malicious 'humour' directed at us.
> We can no longer easily become German citizens as citizenship has become heavily restricted. We also have virtually no rights to our inheritances.

🙶🙷 **Comments based on evidence: boycott of Jewish businesses began in April 1933; also, 1933, Jews forbidden to be part of the Civil Service.** 🙷🙷

🙶🙷 **Comments based on evidence: Nuremberg Laws, September 1935. No Jew can be a Reich citizen.** 🙷🙷

I desperately want to fight this crazed megalomaniac who is our leader. Jews should rise in force and crush his dictatorship. This, I feel, although the pessimists among us disagree, that this idea is plausible.

Hitler and his Germans hate us but we may not defend ourselves. He wants perhaps to crush and destroy every Jew on the planet, although he will never crush us completely - with the rest of the world watching his works he would not dare try. I am so angry inside, so too is Jacob

I leave you now to warn the rest of the world of our plight

your loving
daughter
Ruth.

> The letter illustrates a feeling of resistance. Here is a Jew who recognises that what is happening is wrong and is determined to do something about it. There is the expectation this can be achieved.

19th June 1937

Mother,

I trust you are keeping well. I was sorry to hear about the death of Herr Grünbaum, his wife must miss him dreadfully, as we all shall.

I send the children into your trusted care. Switzerland appears to be free from the damnable oppression of the Nazis. Hitler, our mighty leader, has encouraged Jews to emigrate. Jacob and I will spend time in our house. We do fear, however for Naomi and Golda's safety and wellbeing. We adults may resist taunting and abuse but I fear for the children and their innocence. They have had no school since 1933 so returning to school in Switzerland may do them good!

Please explain the situation to them and tell them that mummy and daddy still love them and we will see them

> There is still the desire to fight on, but tone is not so hopeful now. Particular concern is felt for the children.

> No school since 1933: a little early for this to occur. Is it out of context?

as soon as this foul business is finished.

The business is declining, due to the boycotts, but, unlike other shops, we have not been raided or smashed up. We continue by trading amongst the Jewish communities. Jacob feels we may not be able to continue this indefinitely he has heard that Hitler may close all Jewish business in this area. Whether this is true or not we have yet to find out. We shall fight anyone who tries to close our business. We want Jews everywhere to fight Hitler and be strong against his oppressive ruling. Dieter Brücker started an underground group. They were discovered and never heard of again.

Still, we keep cheerful and remain optimistic that we will one day be delivered, by the Allies or by our good Lord.

my love
Ruth

> A fear for the continued existence of their shop was well founded. All Jewish shops closed in December 1938.

> Mention of the Allies: what is meant by this? Is this out of context with the period?

Hannah Braun
47 See Straße
Zurich A
Schweiz

17 December 1938

Dearest Mother,

It is so long since we have spoken now, I can scarcely remember your voice. Each day I hope and pray that the ordeal we are enduring will end, so we may be reunited and all Jews may walk as free individuals, unmarked by the Star of David we must all carry, on our sleeves.

Ever since my last; which I hope the children gave to you, Jacob and I have been subjected arbitrary abuse, both physical and mental persecution. We no longer the strong and proud people you knew.

> Reference to the Star of David accurate: used as a means to identify Jews.

Our business has collapsed, partly because of boycotting and the restricting of our Jewish customs, but mainly due to the looting and pillaging, carried out by the Germans we once considered our friends, during the fearful night of the 9th of November known in Germany as 'Kristallnacht' because of the amount of glass broken from Jewish shops and houses.

Do you remember Kurt Weiß? He lived with us while we lived on der Hauptstraße. He was, regretably shot dead because he conre business deals as a non-Jew amongst the Jewish communities.

Our lives have become increasingly restricted we must follow those rules laid down for us by our German leaders who despise our race. A strict curfew must be followed, anyone found breaking it is shot on sight. Some houses are guarded and their residents may not make contact with the rest of the world - Rabbi Goldberg is in such a position. I must praise the Lord that I am able to communicate with you, mother and our children. I am only able because I find myself at the call to provide certain 'pleasures' for their Kommandant. In return for which, I may post the occasional letter and receive food not usually available in the shops. I am degraded by this, but if I am to remain alive, I must not refuse.

Perhaps death provides the answer to our troubles, cursed are we for what we are. I feel often like ending it all. Jacob, my dear husband and friend, gives me strength in moments of weakness; I would never desert him in such a cruel way. He says, 'Ruth we must be strong and fight, think of our children and the children of Israel.'

Time is ebbing away from us. I can sense a feeling of impending doom. If we are never to meet again, please remember we will always

Reference to Kristallnacht accurate: 9th November 1938

Tone of letter has changed from the first one. The student captures with sensitivity the degradation, hopelessness and despair of the race. Ruth has succumbed to the lowest levels in her quest for survival. Where is the fighting, optimistic Ruth?

remember your loving children, please do not shed a tear, but look after Naomi and Golda well for us and provide hope for others.

Your daughter,

Ruth

Student assessment

In this piece of work, the student shows a clear understanding of the context in which people lived, of their responses to that situation, and of their feelings. The letters accurately and sensitively make use of the events to provide a convincing impression of life for Jews in this period. The changes in the emotions of Ruth are illustrated extremely well and are supported by a clear description of the period. A super piece of work.

EMPATHY EXERCISE ON CRIMINALITY

This piece of work required the student to assess a variety of sociological and psychological theories of *criminality*. The student was also given information about a 'typical' criminal. From this stimulus the student had to create a 'typical' criminal, suggest possible circumstances which might have contributed to their turning to crime and offer explanations for their criminal behaviour.

Hearing at the London Court of Criminal Proceedings
on Tuesday, 7th March, 1988

Name: Barry Richard Mahrn
Age: 19 yrs
Address: 16a Barrow Flats'
        Central London
        Council Accommodation

Crime
Mr Mahrn assaulted Mr R James of 16 Park Close, London, on the night
of 16th December 1987. After beating Mr James about the head and
chest Mr Mahrn proceeded to steal his car and drive it approximately
twenty miles away to a bar. It is known that Mr Mahrn spent at least
two hours in the bar during which time he managed to get very drunk.
After the bar closed Mr Mahrn drove another five miles before
crashing the car into a hedge. No one was injured.
  Mr Barry Mahrn is charged with assault, theft of a car and drunken
driving.

Family Situation
Barry is the third of four children and the youngest boy. His parents
do not have a happy, stable relationship and rarely seem to talk to
each other and I believe that years of living around this situation
has affected the children's minds as far as relationships are
concerned. From what I can gather none of the boys seems able to hold
down a serious relationship or any major commitment to another
person. They always back off and it is my belief that this is a
result of their parents unsettling behaviour.

    **❝❞ Explanation offered regarding Barry's behaviour. He cannot form relationships
because of the experiences of his own family – lack of interaction between
mother and father. ❞❞**

Barry himself says that although his parents do not fight or argue
he still wishes that they would be friendlier or more sociable to

---

each other. In the past year, after leaving prison, Barry has not had a relationship with anybody. He says he prefers the company of friends who he can 'have fun with'. Barry doesn't feel any need to meet new people of any type and can be very antisocial when it comes to going anywhere without people he knows.

Barry appears to be very hostile towards his parents, especially his father. To his mother he can be very aggressive at times yet at other times he can be very sympathetic towards her. Basically I believe that this is because he doesn't want everybody to walk all over her like they do, he wants her to stand up for herself and fight back. This explains why he is sometimes aggressive and why he sometimes pities her. However, his mother does not see the situation like him at all so they are often at loggerheads.

It is hard to understand Barry's attitude towards his father. At first glance it would be easy to assume that Barry hates him, but deep down I do not believe that this is true. Barry has very strong aggressive feelings towards his father. To begin with Barry is angry with him for giving up with life and drinking. He dislikes the way his father treats his mother and the rest of the family. Yet underneath the anger Barry is very fond of his father, I think that perhaps when he was younger and his father was working and they were more secure financially, Barry was extremely proud and trusting of his father. But watching him throw his life away must have been heart-breaking for Barry and it is only now that all of his feelings for his father are beginning to show.

It seems to me that Barry has very little to do with any of his brothers and sister. He never speaks of his elder brother, who is currently in prison, and he will only say that his sister is nothing to do with him. It is as though he is disowning them both. At home he shares a room with elder brother Gary, who he likes and respects. I believe that he is slightly envious of Gary who has a steady job which he's been doing since he left school.

On the whole the family never eat together or do anything as a family. Although I am sure they do have feelings towards each other, they are never expressed and emotions are never shown.

Earlier History

Barry's family were first drawn to my attention five years ago when I was called to do a similar report on Barry's brother. At the time Barry was only 14 years old. Even at this time he was a very disruptive child who was developing the signs of somebody in emotional turmoil. He was loud and attention seeking, he was aggressive and no amount of discipline would restrain him. This was also reflected in his school reports, one of which said

'he has a total disregard for school rules and disrupts the rest of the class. He is generally very uncooperative in class situations and I find him very unsociable'.

> **Lack of togetherness of the family and lack of love and affection in the home means Barry cannot form relationships. He is ignored at home, which has caused him to become an attention-seeker. This is shown in his behaviour through aggression. Good reference to school report to illustrate this.**

After leaving school Barry managed to find himself a very good apprenticeship in a garage and looking back he says he was very happy there and foolish to have given it up. It lasted a mere six months and Barry was asked to leave as a result of his 'unsociable behaviour'.

In his own words he was loud and abusive and it was surely his own fault that he was asked to leave. I think that the job was okay as long as Barry was interested and people were interested in him, but

> **Psychological scars left on Barry as a result of the change in his father's lifestyle – drunkenness and cruelty to his mother.**

after six months the novelty wore off and he was no longer the centre of attention. After the garage job Barry had a job in the local packing factory but this was simply too boring for him and after a fortnight he gave up. I think that Barry's main problem is that he is too bright for the jobs he is academically capable of doing. His poor exam results do not do him justice and I think that he needs a far more demanding job than the two he has had so far. He needs a job with variety, something in which he will have to think about things. Unfortunately he does not have the academic qualifications needed for a job of this type and he has no hope of getting them as he refuses to attend night classes or similar courses.

External Influences

Barry has very few friends but lots of acquaintances. Many of them are known criminals or offenders. He has no particular friend but two or three characters who he hangs around with. I know that he never talks of his feelings or thoughts to anyone but keeps them bottled up to himself. He can often be seen in seedy parts of town at night with a couple of friends who he refuses to name. From what he tells me they never actually do much, he only says that they 'have a few drinks and have a bit of fun'.

It is hard to tell just what influence other people have on Barry's character as he clams up and will not tell anything of his movements during the nights. It is obvious that Barry is influenced by other people but I don't believe that there is one person alone who influences him. I think that he watches people in general and picks up many of his habits in this way.

Barry's Attitude

Barry has a bright and active mind and he realises exactly what is going on. However, he shows no remorse for his crime and seems to be wallowing in all of the attention he is receiving. This is one of the first times in his life that he has been the centre of attention and he is making the most of it. Whatever the outcome of the court proceedings this section of events will probably be followed by a period of depression as he becomes one of may people again and realises that he isn't important any more.

He will plead guilty yet although he isn't proud of what he has done he isn't ashamed either. At the time I do not think he set out intending to commit a crime I think that something must have clicked in his mind causing him to lose all sense. He believes that after this people will view him differently. They will think of him as extremely big and tough because he has been arrested/to prison. He believes that after this he will be able to say that he has had some excitement in his life and he will be able to boast about the whole episode. Unfortunately life is not always like this and I wonder what sort of life he will have ahead of him if he does serve another prison sentence. He seems to have no idea of the problems faced by people with a criminal record.

Assessment of Barry's Character

One of Barry's main problems is that he is not the type of person that he would like to be. Ideally he would like to hold down a nice respectable job and to be liked by people. However, he believes that this is impossible and has therefore given up hope altogether. Because he cannot be the type of person he would like, he seems to have made a conscious decision to be the type of person people expect him to be. He hangs around during the day and shouts abuse if anybody approaches him.

Generally he is a very mixed-up person. After years of having his feelings and emotions shaken up he doesn't know where to turn next or what to do with his life. His life at home is a total shambles and his

> " Turned to crime in the quest for attention, linked to the lack of attention received at home. "

social life is very secretive. He cannot hold down a proper relationship and is in many respects very much alone. He does nothing with his life and wanders aimlessly from day to day and in the life he leads crime is the only excitement he gets and the consequences do not matter to him because his life is going nowhere anyway.

One considerable problem is that he is far too bright to be leading the type of life-style he leads and he tends to suffer from excessive boredom. If Barry could only find himself a hobby or something which he could take a keen interest in then I believe his character would change as he has the potential to be an interesting person if only somebody could give him a little encouragement.

Recommendation
I have fully discussed this within the department and we all feel that it would be a grave mistake to send Barry to prison, as we think he will have severe psychological problems on returning to normal life.

We recommend that Barry should be put on probation for a year and during this time we request that he should come to regular counselling sessions once or twice a fortnight. I feel that Barry achieved a lot during the counselling sessions we had in order to write this report and I feel that with regular counselling Barry would discover a lot about himself and he would eventually learn how to handle his emotions instead of bottling them up as he does now. By the time he left the counselling sessions he would feel much more secure and assertive.

Student assessment

In this piece of work, the student shows a clear understanding of the context in which people live, and an appreciation of the way people could respond to this situation. The student is not saying *all* people who live in the same context as 'Barry' will turn to crime for attention. However, he has displayed a sound understanding of some of the reasons given to explain criminality. It is possible from this account to identify with 'Barry' and get a clear picture of why people might turn to crime. The account generates the feelings of a person trapped by the circumstances of their upbringing, unable to break free.

Here are some key points to remember:

- Make sure you are clear on what are the important ideas connected with *your* study.

- *Consult your teacher* to ensure you are aware of what you have to do to *show* your understanding of the ideas in question.

- remember, the ideas explained in detail in this chapter are *not the only* ideas you will come across in your Integrated Humanities course. They are, we think, the *key ideas* and so need highlighting.

- Empathy must be based on an appreciation of someone else's situation, based on evidence. *It is not a fairy story.*

GETTING STARTED

An important part of your Integrated Humanities course is the opportunity you will have to find things out, to handle and organise data, and to draw conclusions from information and evidence. Remember that your enquiry may provide *evidence* for the assessment of a number of objectives; for example, your *understanding* of the concepts and terms you use, your *interpretation* and *evaluation* of the material you gather, and the way you *communicate* your findings. This chapter concentrates on the skills you will need to **collect and record** evidence.

Your enquiries and investigations will take different forms. Some will be completed over a short period of time; others will be longer and more sustained pieces of work, taking as long as a term, or even more. Enquiries can also vary in the *degree of choice* you will have over the subject area of your research. For some, your *teacher* will focus your work into a particular area or topic; for others *you* will be given a greater degree of choice. There will also be great variety in the possible types and forms of materials which you will make use of. You may be involved in selecting and analysing information which has already been corrected *by others*, in books, documents or collections of statistics. Or you may be involved in collecting *your own* information, from your own observations or from questions you ask.

ESSENTIAL PRINCIPLES

Your enquiry will not earn marks merely for its length! Your work will be assessed according to your ability to:

- identify clearly an area or subject of research in such a way that you know exactly *what sorts of evidence* you will be looking for and you will be able to pose questions which you then answer through your research;
- collect and record information which is relevant to your study;
- use the material you have collected, to interpret it and to explain the things you have found out.

The keys to a successful enquiry are:

- being clear what it is that you are going to find out information about. Remember, you are not collecting material for the sake of producing a lengthy assignment. The information you obtain and use must be relevant and for a purpose.

> **Important points to remember for a successful enquiry** 〟

- deciding which are the most suitable methods to use to collect information. Preferably, you should use a variety of methods, which should be appropriate to the subject you have selected. The sorts of methods you use will depend on:
  - how much information you require, from a few people/places or from many;
  - where you need to go to find your information;
  - how you are able to record the information;
  - whether there are any particular problems associated with the methods you have selected, and how well you understand these difficulties and allow for them in your research.
- being able to order your material in a logical manner which addresses the research questions you identified.
- arriving at a conclusion which is derived from your findings and is related to, and attempts to answer, your research questions.
- being able to identify in your conclusion any weakness in your research, and how you could have improved it, for example, by using different methods, changing your research question, etc.
- managing the amount of time you have at your disposal. Your enquiry is your own work – you will be working on your own, or in a small group. Making sure that you make full use of the available time is essential. Your enquiry should be split into a number of *stages*. Set yourself clear goals as to the time by which each stage is to be completed and stick to them.

Proposed Subject Area:

Title:

What you intend to do/show in this assignment/study:

Resources to be used:

Timetable:	To be completed by (date):	(✓)
Planning and Organisation: (what you are going to find out, by what methods, using what sources, etc.)		

Timetable:	To be completed by (date):	(√)
Finding Information: (using research methods, primary and secondary)		
Using Information: (collating and analysing data, drawing conclusions)		
Presenting Information: (selecting appropriate forms of presentation, organising into Introduction, Chapters, Conclusion, etc.)		
Reviewing Information: (consider what you have done, is there anything missing, etc.)		
Date assignment due:		

Fig. 3.1 An organisation plan.

1 ▷ CHOOSING A SUBJECT/TOPIC

 **Points to consider when choosing the topic for your enquiry**

The research topic you choose must be one for which you will be able to discover and record usable and relevant information without too many difficulties. It is therefore important that *before* you begin your research you discuss with your teacher your choice of topic, what you intend to do, and how.

Before you start, consider the following points:

■ Is your choice of topic *relevant* to the course you have been following? Will you be able to *make use* of the skills, concepts and ideas you have already discussed and developed?

■ Is your choice of topic *narrow enough* for you to be able to research and produce usable information and explanations, but *broad enough* for you to be able to use a variety of methods and produce interesting results? Your topic must, above all, be *manageable* – too broad an area will bring the risk that you collect a considerable amount of unrelated, and so unusable, information.

■ Is your choice of topic realistic? Will it be possible for you to collect relevant information on the subject?

■ Is your choice of topic something you already know something about? The background information you possess on the subject will be important to you and will make planning the research easier.

■ Will you be able to have access to the subject area you have chosen, or might there be problems in contacting key people, organisations, etc.?

■ Is your choice something in which you are interested? Remember, your enquiry might last some time and you will have to motivate yourself. Having an interest in the area into which you are enquiring will be advantageous.

Start with a general area or theme. You must be able to examine the potential this has for research and then narrow it down into a manageable enquiry.

You should have few problems in thinking of a range of issues and questions for research. They could even be suggested by *one particular place*. Take for example, a *local factory*:

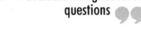

Developing a range of issues and questions about a particular place

- Why is it located where it is?
  - Historical factors?
  - Geographical factors?
- What does it produce? For which markets?
- What sorts of machinery are used? What resources are used?
- What is its management structure? Which trades unions are represented?
- How many people work there? How are they recruited? What is the catchment area for the factory?
- What skills do the workers possess? Are they trained at the factory? What qualifications are needed for the different jobs there?
- What effects does the factory have on the local environment and local community?

Similarly, for a broad theme such as 'education', a vast number of possible research questions can be 'brainstormed':

Brainstorming research questions

- Why are schools located where they are?
- What was education like in the past? How did schools begin?
- How are schools organised? Are they all the same?
- What is discipline like in schools? How does it vary from school to school? What was it like in the past? Are pupils becoming harder to 'control' than they were?
- What differences are there between state and private education? How many pupils are in private schools? How expensive is it?
- How many people work in schools? What are the different jobs? Who is responsible for appointing people to the jobs? What qualifications do people need for the different jobs?
- What sorts of teaching styles are there? Which do pupils prefer?
- What subjects do schools offer?
- What happens to pupils after the age of sixteen?
- Are all groups of pupils treated equally? Are male and female teachers treated equally?

These are just some of the questions which might be asked about schools; the wider topic of 'education' could suggest a vast number of issues to research.

Narrowing down your research area

The next step is to try to *narrow down* your research area. This might be done by selecting one of the questions you have already identified and thinking about what further questions it suggests. This process can then be repeated until you have identified an area which is manageable and suitable. Take, for example, one of the questions above: *'What subjects do schools offer?'*

Possible questions this suggests are:

- Do all schools offer the same subjects?
- Do schools in different countries offer different subjects?
- Which subjects are thought to be most useful?
- Which subjects are the most popular with pupils?
- Are some subjects offered only to certain groups of pupils?
- Are subjects taught in different ways?
- Has the choice of subjects changed?

We can then take *one* of these questions and, again, give it further consideration: *'Has the choice of subjects changed?'*

Possible questions from this are:

- How has the organisation of subject choice changed?
- Who decides which subjects are offered?
- Have any school subjects disappeared?
- Have subject choice patterns changed, for males/females?

In this way, the original theme of education has been considered and narrowed down into what might be a manageable and suitable subject.

2 > FORMING A HYPOTHESIS

66 **Turn your research area into a *question*. Suggest an answer to your question.** 99

A *hypothesis* is a statement of what you expect to find out. Your research will either prove or disprove your hypothesis. (It does not matter if you find that your hypothesis was wrong; what is important is that you have researched the topic well and that your conclusion is based firmly on the results of your research.) Your hypothesis should therefore be written in such a way that it is capable of being tested.

To form a hypothesis, first turn your research area into a *question*. For example, if you are interested in finding out whether boys and girls have the same opportunities at school, your question could be: *'Do boys and girls enjoy the same opportunities in education?'*

If your area of interest is the effects of soap operas, your question could be: *'Do soap operas affect the way we live?'*

Now suggest a possible *answer* to your question:

- 'Boys and girls do not enjoy the same opportunities in education.'
- 'Soap operas affect the way we live.'

These statements can, after research, be shown to be right or wrong. They are examples of hypotheses.

66 **Thinking ahead is an important part of planning your enquiry.** 99

Starting with a hypothesis can be useful, but is not always essential. Instead one can be produced when your research is already under way, or it can be changed or rejected. What is important is that *before* you start your enquiry you have a clear idea of what you are aiming to find out. A useful approach is to write a short paragraph, imagining that you have finished your enquiry and that you are describing your conclusions. Thinking forward in this way will encourage you to be clear about the aims of your research, and will help you to plan ahead and set yourself goals.

Arriving at a hypothesis, or research question, will give your enquiry a clear focus. The next stage is to plan it out in more detail outlining what your work is going to entail. Begin by breaking down your question into its component parts. For example, your hypothesis might be that, *'The local community does not adequately provide facilities for disabled people.'* To complete this enquiry it may be necessary to know something about:

- the range of disabilities in the community and their effects;
- the provision the community makes for the disabled;
- the problems likely to be experienced by disabled people in having access to community services and facilities;
- the work of voluntary organisations;
- the perceptions of the community in general to the problems experienced by the disabled.

66 **Identify your key words.** 99

If you start with a general area or a particular period or event, break down your research by producing a list of key words/ideas which are relevant to your work. This should help you to achieve your aims (Fig. 3.2).

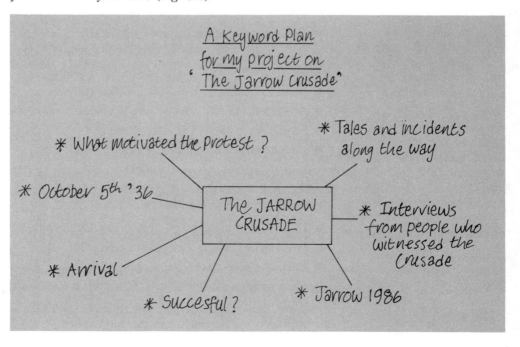

A Keyword Plan
for my project on
'The Jarrow Crusade'

* What motivated the protest?

* Tales and incidents along the way

* October 5th '36

The JARROW CRUSADE

* Interviews from people who witnessed the Crusade

* Arrival

* Successful?

* Jarrow 1986

Fig. 3.2 A key-word plan.

You can use your key words to keep a record of your research and the sources of information which you use (Fig. 3.3).

keywords	"The making of The welfare state" BOOK BY R.J.Cootes	"How we used to live." BOOK By Freda kelsall	"Observer Magazine" MAGAZINE 12th Oct.1986	"Official Jarrow 86 leaflet." LEAFLET Aut./Win.86	"The Times" NEWSPAPER October 6th 1936	"changing Horizons - Britain 1914-80." BOOK By W.O.Simpson.
Motivation	Page 53 Paragraph 1	Page 8 Paragraph 1	Page 26 Paragraph 1	Page 1	—	—
October 5th '36	Page 53 Paragraph 1	—	—	Page 1	Page 11	—
Tales along the way	—	Page 8 Paragraphs 2,3	Page 26 Paragraph 3	—	—	—
Arrival	Page 53 Paragraph 2	Page 8 Paragraph 4	—	—	—	Page 252 Paragraph 1
Success?	Page 54	Page 8 Paragraphs 5,6	Page 31 Paragraph 5	—	—	Page 252 Paragraph 1

Fig. 3.3 A key-word grid.

 Getting organised

When you have produced a satisfactory breakdown, you will need to consider what sources and methods you are going to use to obtain the information you need. You could then draw up a *timetable* for yourself, describing what you are going to do and when you intend to complete each stage (as shown in Fig. 3.1). You might also consider keeping a *diary* of your enquiry, in which you list everything you do, the letters sent, books read, interviews conducted, etc. (Fig. 3.4). Don't leave things until the last minute. You cannot guarantee that the books you need will be immediately available in the library, or that people and organisations you write to will respond quickly, and you may find you have to devise alternative strategies.

5 Jan 1988	Back to school
6 Jan 1988	1st Social Science lesson of the new year. Student guide to Personal Research Project handed out. Began thinking about project.
7 Jan 1988	Considered the area of women in the media.
11 Jan 1988	Finalised decision of women in the media.
15 Jan 1988	Drew spider diagram, organised a plan of action
22 Jan 1988	Article in Chronicle and Echo 'Prime-Time Asset' Read that page-3 girl Paula Ann-Bland to be at Northampton's Derngate theatre from 26 to 30 Jan. Think about possible interview. Prepare possible questions.
25 Jan 1988	Rang Derngate press officer who told me to ring S.T. Marketplan and speak to Caroline Morris. I rang S.T. Marketplan who said that they would try to organize an interview. I was told to ring back on Wednesday.
26 Jan 1988	Paula Ann-Bland in Northampton.
27 Jan 1988	Rang S.T. Marketplan, told to ring back tomorrow.

28 Jan 1988	Discovered interview not possible.
Feb 1988	In back issue of You - 'Mail on Sunday' - Magazine found article: 'Hot Rod Heroines'.
3 Feb 1988	Visit county library. Take out two books. 'Print and Prejudice' and 'The Manufacture of News. Deviance social problems and the mass media'. These books were found using the libraries catalogue system and so the Dewey Classification system. Using the Clover Newspaper Index found two articles concerning 'soft-porn' newspaper; 'The Star' In 'Independent' newspaper found article: 'Newspaper Posters Crude and Vulgar.' Accquired book; 'Ways of Seeing'.
11 Feb 1988	Read books, made notes.
13 Feb 1988	Made notes on newspaper articles.
14 Feb 1988	Wrote project's introduction.
15 Feb 1988	Accquired back issues of women's magazines. Went through magazines cutting out examples of stereotyped images and the like.
17 Feb 1988	Accquired two magazine articles: 'Sex and Gender' and 'Woman's Role'. Read these and made notes.
18 Feb 1988	Went into town to research into the addresses of possible people and organizations I could write to for resources. I wrote to the glamour modelling agency: Yvonne Paul Management Ltd., the pressure group: Women against Rape and the Advertising Standards Authority. I also wrote to Action For Women in Northampton asking about a possible interview. Sent letters (to leave next morning).
19 Feb 1988	Started first survey, 'Do you approve of Page 3 Modelling'. Local newspaper articles: Trafford Tanzi. HALF TERM...
20 Feb 1988	Continued with survey no. 1, began surveys no.s 2 and 3. Asking parents if they would approve of their daughter being a topless medel and asking if people considered the banned Daily Telegraph posters (see 10 Feb) to be sexist.
21 Feb 1988	Finished survey no. 1 and 2.
22 Feb 1988	Rang Equal Opportunities Commission to request information. Put together posters: SMASHING THE STEREOTYPE. Action Speaks Louder Than Words. Beauty and Brains Spells 'Bad'
23 Feb 1988	Put together poster SMASHING THE STEREOTYPE. Males Put Under Submission.
24 Feb 1988	Planned poster: 'What an alien would think about Earth from reading the popular press'.
4 March 1988	Made further notes (Page 3 as Humour)
8 March 1988	Covered all posters with protective plastic.
10 March 1988	Wrote 'Page 3' produced inlay card for Ruth Lewis interview.
13 April 1988	Wrote 'Women and Humour'.
14 April 1988	Began to write 'Women and Advertising'.
15 April 1988	Continued to write 'Women and Advertising'. Wrote bibliography
20 April 1988	Wrote conclusions.
28 April 1988	Acknowledge list and contents list.
29 April 1988	Received letter from 'Women against Rape'. Included letter to The Guardian from movement concerning pornography and the like. Too late to include in studies contents. Handed in project.

Fig. 3.4 An enquiry diary.

SOURCES OF SECONDARY INFORMATION

Your *sources of information* are all the places, people, organisations, books and documents, etc. which can provide you with the information you require for your enquiry. It is up to you to distinguish between them, to locate them, and to know how to go about approaching them and deriving information from them. The possible types and varieties of sources which you could make use of are enormous. The rest of this chapter looks at some of the main sources which are available to you, and how you can go about locating them and recording information.

It is customary to distinguish between *primary* information – that is, information you collect yourself from *your own* observations and questioning – and *secondary* information – that is, information which comes from *other sources*, usually already collected.

3 ⟩ USING PUBLISHED MATERIAL

The way you make use of published material will depend on the overall aim of your enquiry and the research questions you have set. You may wish to use published material to increase your background knowledge of the subject or topic you have identified, to help you to define and sharpen your hypothesis, and to help you to understand the terms and concepts you wish to make use of. They can increase your understanding of issues and problems you may encounter in the course of your enquiry, or you may use them to give you ideas and suggestions about the sorts of things you could study yourself, and the appropriate methods to use. Published materials, and the use you make of them, may form the entire content of a library-based research project.

The first place to begin is your *school textbooks*, the material with which you will be most familiar. Textbooks contain, in a condensed form, knowledge and views on particular

❝❝ **Using textbooks** ❞❞

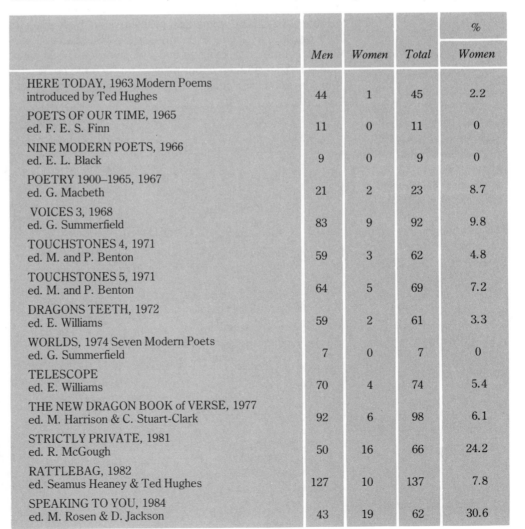

	Men	Women	Total	% Women
HERE TODAY, 1963 Modern Poems introduced by Ted Hughes	44	1	45	2.2
POETS OF OUR TIME, 1965 ed. F. E. S. Finn	11	0	11	0
NINE MODERN POETS, 1966 ed. E. L. Black	9	0	9	0
POETRY 1900–1965, 1967 ed. G. Macbeth	21	2	23	8.7
VOICES 3, 1968 ed. G. Summerfield	83	9	92	9.8
TOUCHSTONES 4, 1971 ed. M. and P. Benton	59	3	62	4.8
TOUCHSTONES 5, 1971 ed. M. and P. Benton	64	5	69	7.2
DRAGONS TEETH, 1972 ed. E. Williams	59	2	61	3.3
WORLDS, 1974 Seven Modern Poets ed. G. Summerfield	7	0	7	0
TELESCOPE ed. E. Williams	70	4	74	5.4
THE NEW DRAGON BOOK of VERSE, 1977 ed. M. Harrison & C. Stuart-Clark	92	6	98	6.1
STRICTLY PRIVATE, 1981 ed. R. McGough	50	16	66	24.2
RATTLEBAG, 1982 ed. Seamus Heaney & Ted Hughes	127	10	137	7.8
SPEAKING TO YOU, 1984 ed. M. Rosen & D. Jackson	43	19	62	30.6

Fig. 3.5 The representation of women poets in school anthologies (Source: *Gender Issues in English Coursework*, NATE Language and Gender Committee, NATE, Short Run Press Ltd, Exeter, 1988, p.10).

subjects and topic areas, extracts and reviews of original information and research. Textbooks can also be the object of study in themselves:

- Old history textbooks can illustrate how views of history and historical events have changed.
- They can be analysed for examples of racial stereotypes and attitudes.
- They can also be analysed for gender bias – for example, how many pictures are there of women/girls as compared to men/boys? What activities are the people in the illustrations engaged in? How many times are women/girls mentioned in the text? How many women poets are represented in school poetry anthologies (see Fig. 3.5)?

FINDING SOURCES

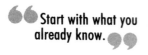
Start with what you already know.

You should first start with the material you already have: notes, textbooks and reading you have already done which is relevant to your research. Remember to consider work you may have done in school outside your Humanities lessons which may be useful to your enquiry. From the information you have, you should be able to identify where there are gaps, ideas for new areas to research, and lists of books and periodicals for further reading.

When you have identified books and articles that you know exist, you can consult the *library* author/title catalogue to find out where they are. Remember that your central or main public library will have a wider range of books than your smaller branch library, so is more likely to have the books that you are looking for. If a book or periodical is not in stock, it can be ordered for you (although this can take time). Locating a book in the library will probably involve you in using the *Dewey* Decimal Classification System, which is simply a means by which the subjects covered by books are classified by a system of numbers.

Using the library

Where you have identified gaps in your information but have not come across the title of a book or a relevant author to look up in the author/title catalogue, you can consult the library subject index. To do this you will first have to identify the key words in the topic you are looking for. If, for example, you are researching the importance of cocoa to the economy of Ghana, you would probably start by looking under 'Ghana', and then use the key words 'cocoa' and 'economy' to help you search. The subject index is an alphabetical list of hundreds of subjects and will give you the library classification number for each subject. You can then either browse through the books on the relevant shelves or consult the classified catalogue, which lists, in numerical order, all the books in the library

---

Dewey uses every number from 000 to 999, as well as the decimal point places in between them.

The main divisions are:	Each of these main divisions is then divided. For example, the last division is broken down as follows:	Again, each of these is broken down. For example, the 940 division (History of Modern Europe) covers the following:
000　General Topics (including encyclopedias)	900　General Works	940　General Works
	910　Geography	941　Scotland and Ireland
100　Philosophy and Psychology	920　Biography	942　England and Wales
	930　History of the Ancient World	943　Central Europe
200　Religion		944　France
300　Social Sciences	940　History of Modern Europe	945　Italy
400　Languages	950　History of Modern Asia	946　Iberian Peninsula
500　Pure Sciences		947　Eastern Europe
600　Technology	960　History of Modern Africa	948　Scandinavia
700　The Arts (this section includes Crafts and Sport)	970　History of North America	949　Other Parts of Europe
800　Literature (mainly books about literature, plus poetry/plays)	980　History of South America	Beyond this, Dewey uses decimal points to further classify subject areas, so that, for example, the section on France will then be broken down by period, region, etc.
	990　History of the Rest of the World	
900　Geography and History		

Fig. 3.6 The Dewey Decimal Classification System.

according to their classification number. In addition, most libraries will keep bibliographies, such as the British National Bibliography, which lists all books published in a particular year, arranged by author, title and subject.

PERIODICALS

A huge number of magazines or *periodicals*, covering a vast range of interests, research and areas of knowledge, is published every month. Periodicals have a number of advantages over books:

- They are more up to date (published every week, month or quarter etc.).
- They are relatively short.
- They can focus on a relatively well-defined subject area.

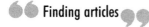

❝ Finding articles ❞

To help you find your way through the mass of periodicals you will find in libraries, you could refer to *Abstracts and Indexes*. There are a number of these covering a range of subjects and they are published several times a year. Indexes classify articles from a large number of magazines and will give you the author and title of an article, together with the name of the magazine it appeared in, the date of its publication and the page reference. Entries are arranged alphabetically under subject title, each title listing all the relevant articles which have appeared in the magazines and periodicals covered by the index. Be prepared to try alternative words for the subject area you are interested in. For example, for industrial disputes you may also need to look under labour disputes, industrial relations, strikes, etc. to find all the articles which might be of help to you.

Useful examples of indexes include the *Clover Information Index*, which covers a wide range of magazines on all subjects, and the *British Humanities Index*, covering Humanities publications.

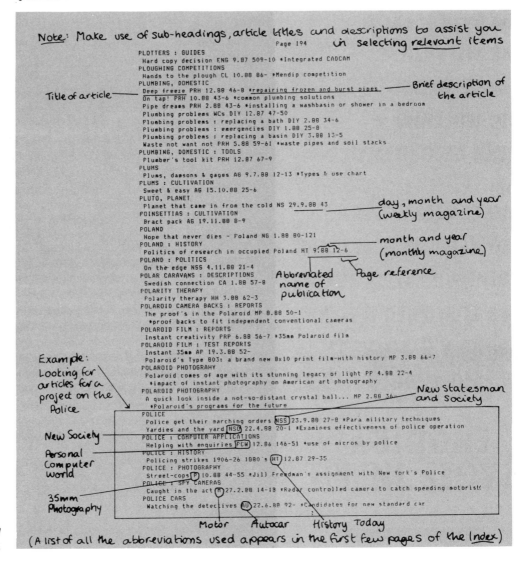

Fig. 3.7 *The Clover Information Index*, Clover Publications, 1988.

Abstracts are similar to indexes, but also contain a short description of what the articles listed are about. These can be invaluable in helping you to decide whether a particular article is going to be of use to you and whether you should try to locate it.

4 ❯ READING AND NOTE-TAKING

If you have been successful in locating a variety of published material, you are faced next with the formidable task of *extracting* and *using* relevant information from it. You must realise, as you approach the material, that you are reading for a purpose. This is the *aim* of your enquiry, and you should bear in mind, as you read, the headings and subdivisions under which you wish to collect information.

Not all your reading has to be intensive and word for word. Your initial task is to size up what you have found, and see if it has information relevant to you and your study and where that information is located. There are shortcuts to reading which will be useful to you.

❝❝ Reading for your research ❞❞

- **Skimming**
  This means flicking quickly through a book, chapter or article and reading headings and one or two sentences from each paragraph to gain a general impression of what it is about. This can be done to help you decide whether to reject the material or select it for future, more detailed reading.

- **Scanning**
  This involves looking quickly through certain sections of a book to search for specific information. To do this you should make use of the introduction, the contents list, chapter headings, paragraph headings and the index.

It is always important to make *notes*. Never rely on your memory to recall what you have read, or where you read it. Notes can be made in many different ways, but what is important is that they will be useful to you. In general you should bear in mind the following points:

- Make sure you record clearly *where your notes have come from*, giving the author, the name of the book or article, where it was published and the date of publication. You will need this if you want to find the information again, and, when you are writing up your enquiry, you should include a bibliography – a list of all the materials you have used.

❝❝ Make your notes brief, understandable and useful to you. ❞❞

- *Be brief*. Notes don't mean copying down what the author has said at great length. Try to use your own words and descriptions, summing up what you have read.

- Make sure that your notes are *orderly*: use *headings* and *subheadings*. Underline any sentences or phrases which you think are of key importance.

- Use *abbreviations*, but make sure that they are consistent and that you can remember what they stand for.

- Leave *wide margins* so that you can return to the points you have made and alter, or add to, the information.

- Look out for any *statistical information* or *short quotations* which you think will be of use, and make sure you copy down the information accurately, noting the page reference as well as other details of the book or article.

- Be prepared to be *critical* in your notes. You don't have to accept everything you read.

5 ❯ USING REFERENCE MATERIAL

Most towns will have a central reference library, which will usually be located in the same building as the central lending library. You will need the help of the librarians to find your way around the reference library. You will not be allowed to remove any material but there will be facilities for you to sit and make notes and, usually, photocopy. What materials exist in the reference library will vary from town to town, but they will all have the following types of information, which will be of use to you.

STATISTICAL INFORMATION

An extensive range of statistics should be available to you. Of particular importance will be:

- **Census information**
  This is collected every ten years from every household in Britain. Three main kinds of census information are produced:

- subject volumes, which give national and regional figures on particular subjects;
- county tables, for districts and counties;
- small area statistics, for areas smaller than local authority districts.

The main topics covered by the 1981 census were:

- sex composition
- age structure
- marital status
- fertility
- household structure
- population numbers
- country of birth
- population movement
- occupation
- employment statistics
- educational qualifications
- location of work
- method of travelling to work
- housing amenities and space
- housing tenure
- ownership of motor vehicles

Census information can be used:

- to provide general background information for your enquiry;
- to compare the results of your own questionnaires, interviews, etc. with the national picture;
- to answer your research questions – for example, to compare family size in different classes over different years.

For more details about the census, see Chapter 4.

■ The Central Statistical Office

This produces a constant stream of statistical data, on topics such as population, families, education, employment, income and wealth, health, housing, transport, leisure and law enforcement. These are available in the annually produced *Social Trends*, the *Annual Abstract of Statistics*, *Key Data* and *Regional Trends*, which produces statistics on various regions (see Fig. 3.8).

There is also *Economic Trends*, which provides economic statistics for and identifies trends in the UK economy. The *General Household Survey* produces information from a sample of 15,000 households on such topics as population, housing, employment, education and health. *British Social Attitudes*, although not an officially produced source, contains statistical information on people's attitudes to various issues of public concern. *World Statistics in Brief* summarises data from the *United Nations Statistical Yearbook*, and includes data about population, trade, education, tourism, health, etc. for every country.

■ Yearbooks

You will also find useful statistical information in various *yearbooks*, such as *The Statesman's Yearbook*, which contains international facts and figures, and in various commercial and business publications.

■ Central government departments

Additional statistical material is available from central government departments: for example, criminal statistics from the Home Office; monthly employment and unemployment statistics from the Department of Employment. Local council departments can also supply data, such as information about council-house waiting lists from the Housing Department. Individual institutions can offer particular data: for example, your school can provide you with examination pass rates for the school's pupils/ex-pupils. Statistical data can also exist in a number of different formats: for example, information on gender and inequality is available on micro software, published by Longmans.

Statistics give you access to a great amount of information on most areas which you would be interested in researching, but they need to be approached with care. They can be difficult to understand; they do not always exist in the form which might be of most use to you; you need to consider how they were produced and how reliable they are. For further advice on using statistics, see Chapter 4.

DIRECTORIES

Finding out about people and organisations

Directories are lists of organisations, businesses, etc. which can be used to find addresses or brief factual details, and can range from telephone directories to highly specialised directories. Some useful examples are:

- *Kelly's Directory* – published annually for larger towns up to 1976. They include lists of

Contents

Example: Project area – "Poverty". – Consult sections 2.3, 2.6, 2.9, 2.10, 3.4, 3.10, 3.11, 4.6, 4.9 [handwritten]

Fig. 3.8 The contents page, *Regional Trends 23*, Central Statistical Office, HMSO, 1988.

addresses of residents and commercial premises. Research uses could include comparing directories for different years as part of a study of housing turnover or migration; comparing uses of premises, such as town-centre shops, from previous years with the present, etc.

- *Sells Directory* of products and services – provides an alphabetical list of firms.

- *Who Owns Whom* – a two-volume directory of company ownership, which lists parent companies and their subsidiaries. Research uses could include finding out the names of the parent companies which own the shops you might have listed in a high-street survey; finding out which large companies own the subsidiaries producing branded goods you might find in a shopping survey of a supermarket.

- *Voluntary Agencies* – an annual directory, published by the National Council for Voluntary Agencies, together with *Charity Choice*, which has 2,000 entries, gives the aims and the addresses of voluntary agencies and charities. They can be useful for general research into such bodies, and for finding out how to contact particular organisations involved in the area you are planning to research.

- *Who's Who* – is a biographical dictionary, giving details, including addresses, of 'prominent people' (see Fig. 3.9). Research uses might include obtaining extra details about individuals you come across in your research, such as industrialists or those associated with particular pressure groups or charitable organisations. In studies involving personal details, the home addresses of a selected or sample number of prominent people could be located. The information given would also help in a study of the educational background of the rich and famous.

- *The Directory of Directors* – can be combined with *The Times 1,000: The World's Top Companies, Key British Enterprises: Britain's Top 25,000 Companies* and *Who's Who* to identify the top directors and leading industrialists.

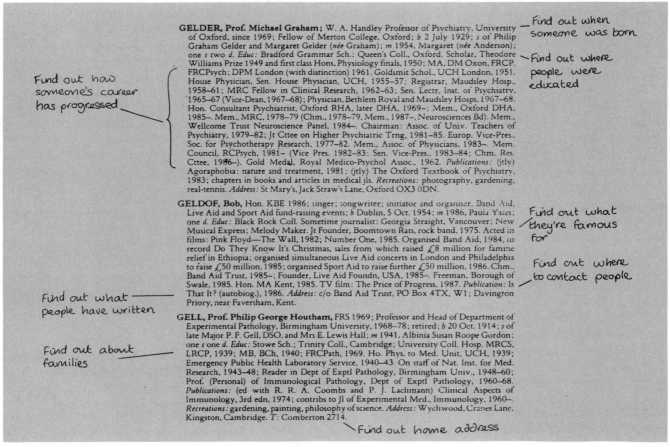

Fig. 3.9 The possible uses of *Who's Who* (Source: *Who's Who*, 1988).

BACK COPIES OF NEWSPAPERS

Although public libraries usually take a range of newspapers, few of these will be kept for very long. Reference libraries usually keep back copies of at least one local and one national newspaper – probably *The Times*. They will also be likely to have copies of *The Times*

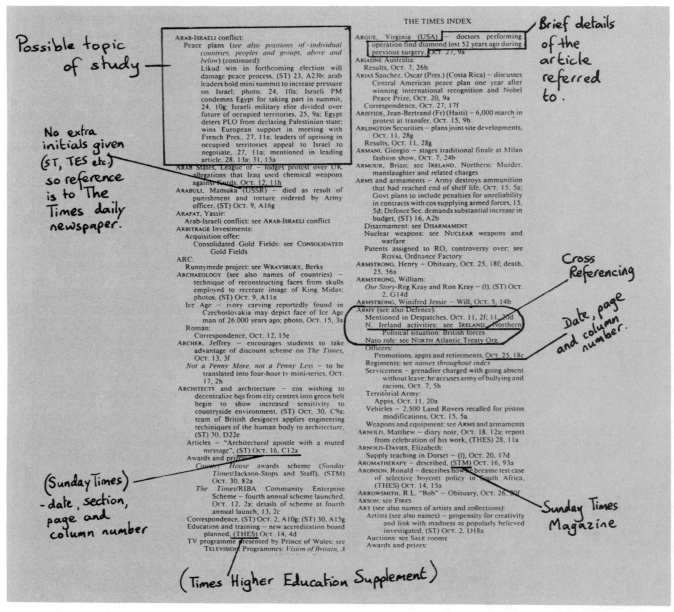

Fig. 3.10 *The Times Index*, October 1988, p. 4.

Index, updated regularly, which has lists of all the articles carried by any of the Times publications in the course of the year (Fig. 3.10). References are arranged alphabetically under subject headings, with a brief résumé of what the article was about, together with details of which publication it is in, the date, edition and page number. If you are studying, for example, the Arab–Israeli conflict, the *Index* will tell you where all the articles listed under that heading can be found.

A more recent index, started in 1986, is the *Clover Newspaper Index*. This is published weekly and lists articles, under subject headings, for all the country's main newspapers, not just *The Times*.

66 Finding out about events **99**

KEESING'S CONTEMPORARY ARCHIVES

This is a continually updated record of national and international current events. The information is taken from the press and from broadcasting, and is useful for researching the sequence of reported events in case studies from comparatively recent history.

The reference library will have more information than can be usefully classified and described here. On the shelves you will find *encyclopedias*, which can give general coverage of all knowledge or be subject-specific; atlases and gazetteers, to help you locate places, as well as historical atlases and those which provide visual information on a range of physical, socio-economic and political issues; and a range of general and specialist dictionaries, yearbooks and almanacs, and handbooks. There may also be a local history collection, which can be invaluable for historical studies and surveys of your locality.

COMPUTERISED SERVICES

Reference libraries will also have computer-searching services, with access to data bases which hold information on abstracts and indexes as well as some of the sort of factual information found in dictionaries and directories. Using these data bases has the great advantage of speed, thus increasing the scope and scale of the material you will be able to have access to. The problems associated with them, however, are cost and the care with which you must select the right key words to obtain the information you want. Because the system gives access to so much information, using broad titles will probably generate an unmanageable amount of data, most of which will be irrelevant. The best approach is to decide on a number of cross-referencing key words. The example used in our discussion of key words for public lending library subject indexes will illustrate the point. To find references to material on the importance of cocoa to the economy of Ghana, using just the key word 'Ghana' would generate far too much information. Adding the word 'cocoa', would help, but you would be given much irrelevant information concerning, for example, articles about how cocoa is produced in Ghana. Adding the key word 'economy' will narrow down the field, by giving more precise cross-referencing.

Viewdata are directories of current information which are similar to the Oracle and Ceefax systems you may have access to on your television set. Your reference library may have access to the Prestel system, which will provide you with continuously updated information. In addition, your reference library may have access to a local information service, giving pages of information on topics such as 'what's on' in your county, travel, transport, hobbies, etc.

6 > USING CONTEMPORARY MAPS

Maps are invaluable documents as aids in the collection of primary data and also as objects for study in themselves – to locate features of the environment, to study communications systems and to understand the location of, and relationships between, settlements. Contemporary maps can be compared with historical maps to study development, or with aerial photographs to identify and locate archaeological features. Places identified on maps could be checked in, for example, the *Oxford Dictionary of English Place Names*, or the English Place Names Society's county by county volumes, to discover their origins and find clues to land ownership, original physical features, trades, etc.

ORDNANCE SURVEY MAPS

These are the most detailed and accurate maps both for finding your way around and acting as a guide to land use and to road and settlement patterns. There are a number of scales of Ordnance Survey maps available, some of which are more suitable for the study of particular features than others. Remember that a map scale such as 1:50,000 means that, in reality, everything is 50,000 times bigger than it is on the map. Maps with scales of 1:1,250 are available for larger towns and conurbations, and 1:2,500 are available for most of Britain except larger towns. All are very detailed and will show buildings clearly. 1:10,000 and 1:25,000 maps are available for nearly all of Britain and will show clearly street patterns. The 1:50,000 range includes the whole of Britain and will give a good overview of an area.

GOAD MAPS

These are produced at a scale of 1:1,056, and show the shopping centres of towns and cities with a population over 50,000. They will name the shops and buildings and could, together with a copy of *Who Owns Whom*, enable you to map the commercial property-owning interests of shopping centres (Fig. 3.11 a) and b)). Goad maps will probably be available for you to look at in your reference library.

LAND-USE MAPS

These are available for particular areas, for particular years. They will include a detailed description of precise land use: individual crops, livestock, types of woodland, etc.

TOWN STREET PLANS

These are available for most towns and cities, and are useful for providing base maps for urban enquiries and for locating certain services and amenities.

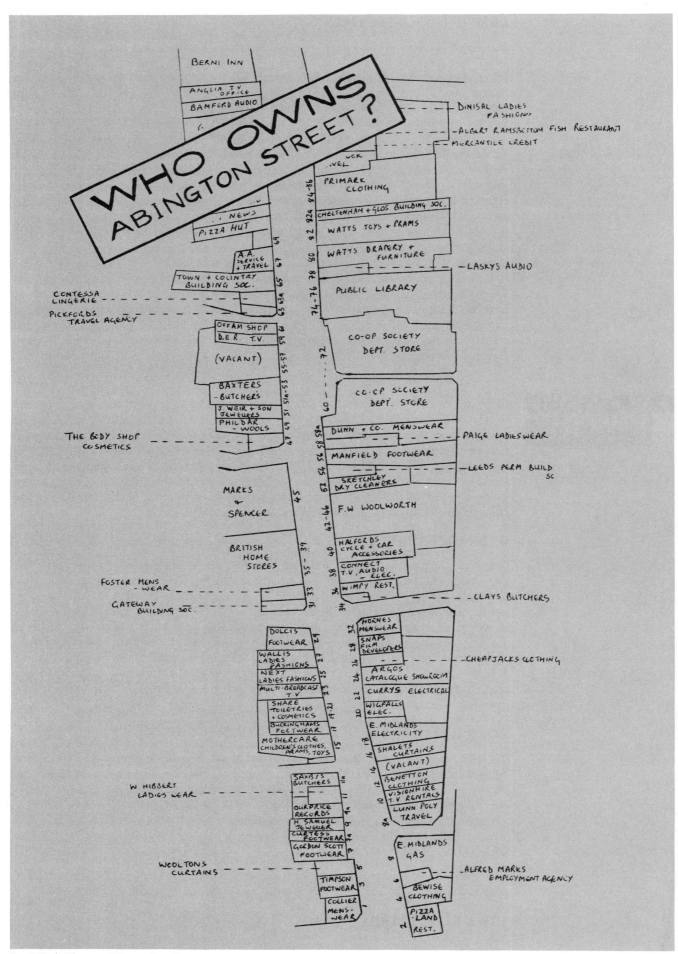

Fig. 3.11 a) Who owns Abington Street?

Shop/service outlet	Parent Company
Argos	BAT Industries plc
Baxters (Butchers) Ltd	Western United Investment Co. Ltd
Benetton U.K. Ltd	Benetton SpA Italy
British Home Stores	Storehouse plc
Cheap Jacks Ltd.	Church & Co. plc
Collier Menswear	The Burton Group plc
Connect Ltd	Granada Group plc
Curry's Ltd.	Dixons Group plc
Curtess Shoes	Sears plc
DER T.V. Rentals Ltd	Thorn EMI plc
Dolcis Ltd	Sears plc
Foster Menswear	Sears plc
Gateway Building Society	The Dee Corporation plc
Halfords Ltd	Ward White Group plc
Hornes Menswear - Retail Ltd	Sears plc
Lunn Poly	International Thomson plc
Manfield & Sons Ltd	Sears plc
Marks & Spencer	Marks & Spencer plc
Mothercare	Storehouse plc
Multibroadcast Ltd	Thorn EMI plc
Next	Next plc
Our Price Records Ltd	W.H. Smith Group plc
Pickfords Travel	National Freight Consortium plc
Pizza Hut Ltd	Pepsi Co Inc USA
Pizzaland	United Biscuits Holdings plc
Primark	Wittington Investments Ltd
H. Samuel Ltd	Ratners Group plc
Share	Woolworth Holdings plc
Sketchley Cleaners	Sketchley plc
Snaps Printing Ltd	The British Car Auction Group plc
Timpson Shoes Ltd	George Oliver Footwear plc
Visionhire Ltd	Granada Group plc
Wallis Fashions	Sears plc
J. Weir & Son	Next plc
Wigfalls Ltd	Dixons Group plc
F.W. Woolworth	Woolworth plc

Total outlets : 36'   Parent Companies : 25

Fig. 3.11 b) Information collected from *Who Owns Whom*, 1988.

LOCAL AUTHORITY MAPS

Local authorities produce their own maps, usually for planning purposes, which can be used to investigate planning decisions and to project future development.

7 > THE COUNTY RECORD OFFICE

Most counties will have a County Record Office. The Record Office keeps a vast amount of material on local history, and you will need help in both finding what you want and knowing how to use it. It may be advisable to contact your Record Office before your visit to find out if they will be able to help you at the time you were planning to go and if there are any rules about the use of documents which you need to know about in advance. Records Offices will contain documents from all over your county, ranging in age from medieval times to the present century. Most material, and certainly the material you will find easiest to use, will have been produced within the last 150 to 200 years. There are many different types of information you might make use of.

MAPS AND PLANS

- OS maps – the earliest are 1 inch and 2½ inch maps which date back to the early nineteenth century.
- Tithe maps – These were drawn up for most areas between 1838 and 1854, to a scale of 13 to 26 inches to the mile, when the tithe (the giving of one-tenth of the produce of the land to the Church) was converted into a rent. Tithe maps give a detailed picture of a village and can be used with lists of owners (called Glebe Terriers) to show land ownership, names of the occupiers of property, location of farms and houses, etc.

- Enclosure maps – These are maps which were drawn up at the same time as parliamentary enclosures of land in the eighteenth and nineteenth centuries.

In addition you may find maps produced by various individuals dating back to the seventeenth century, town plans from the seventeenth century, as well as plans connected with the building of railways, canals, tunnels, etc.

Research uses include looking at town development and growth, giving an historical dimension to a village or small-town study, locating and explaining the man-made features of the environment, tracing changes in land and building use, etc.

DOCUMENTS ABOUT PEOPLE

- Wills, often accompanied by inventories of personal possessions, can give you an insight into the lifestyles of individuals. Wills were accompanied by inventories until about 1740 and can provide details of household goods and equipment.
- Registers of baptisms, marriages and burials from parish registers.
- Census returns from over 100 years ago will give you details of individual households and their inhabitants. The first census was taken in 1801 and after that at ten-yearly intervals. Only returns after 1841 contain people's names. (For further information about using census documents, see Chapter 4.)
- Trade directories, produced on a county basis from 1850, give classified lists of the residents and traders of each parish, together with short descriptive accounts of the area.

Research uses can include reconstructing life in a village or street, a particular house or type of house, at a point in time as part of a study of migration or changes in occupational structure.

Record Offices will also hold many other documents which can be invaluable tools for the particular topics which you are studying. For example:

- **Poverty**

  Relevant documents include *workhouse accounts* and minutes from meetings of *Boards of Guardians*, which will give details of workhouse inmates, general conditions and diets, etc. Records of the *examinations of paupers* by the Justices, found in *quarter sessions* records, will give vivid accounts of the poor before 1834.

- **Education**

  Record Offices will hold copies of the *Victoria County Histories*, which are full of useful historic information, including histories of older schools which originated as endowed grammar schools. Some schools will have their own published histories. From the 1840s onwards you should also be able to find examples of *school logbooks*, which give details of the school curriculum (what was taught), attainments of children and references to assistant and pupil teachers, as well as registers, timetables and punishment books (Fig. 3.12).

  Research uses might include studies of the development of education, comparisons of particular aspects of education, such as discipline past and present, etc.

Record Offices will have many more documents which may be of use to you, such as local guide books, pamphlets and photographs, electoral registers, newspapers, and estate and family collections of documents. Tracing documents in the Record Office can be a highly specialised business, and you should not be over-optimistic about what you might be able to discover. You will require a knowledge of the period of the document and the particular laws or events to which it relates, and an understanding of the terms and language used. Documents do not necessarily speak for themselves and using them can require a lot of checking up; you need to consider not only when they were written, but also by whom, why and to whom. You should also realise that the Record Office is not the only source of historical documents.

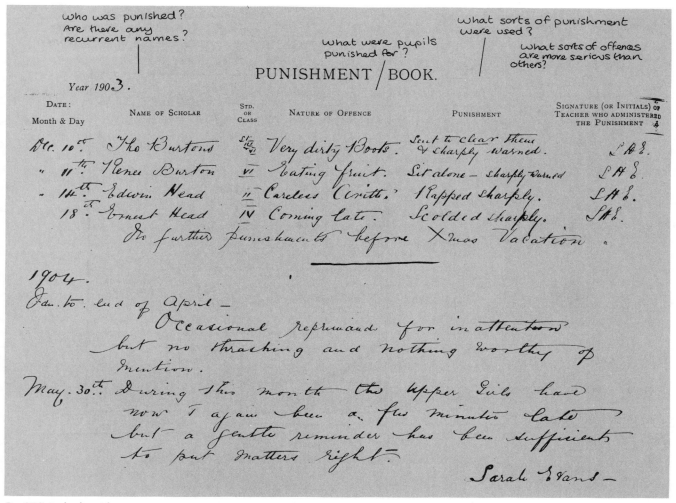

Fig. 3.12 A school punishment book (Source: Northants Record Office, doc. ref. 2B 122/96).

STUDENT'S WORK BASED ON THE USE OF DOCUMENTS

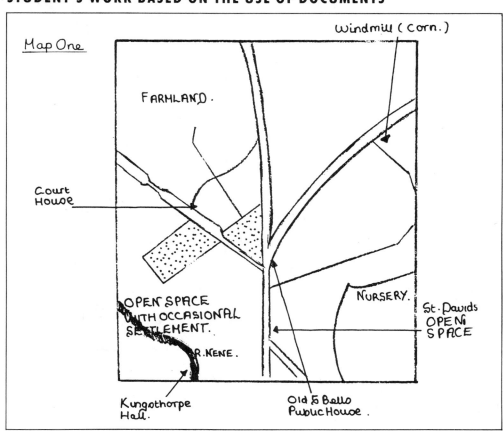

An Annotated Sketch Map of Kingsthorpe in Pre. 1900.

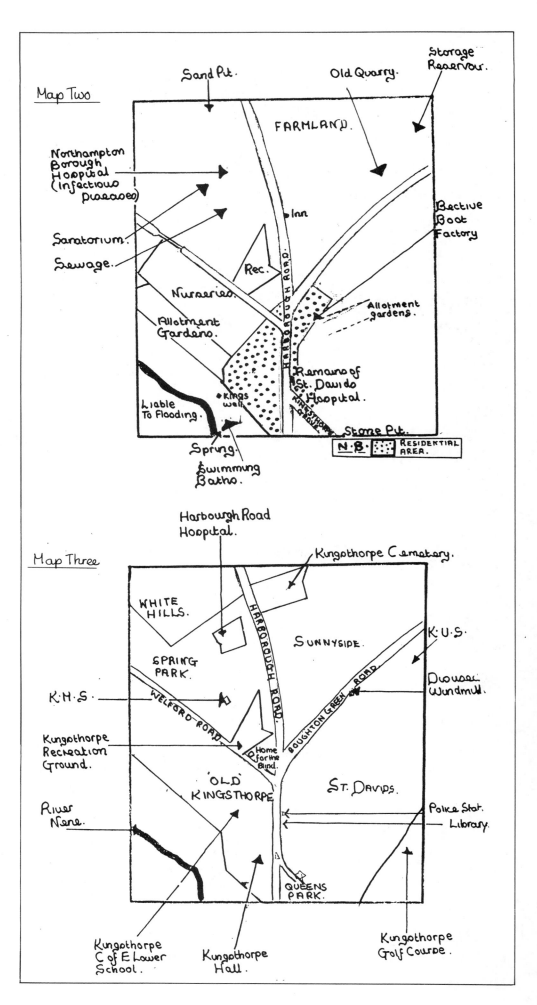

An Annotated Sketch
Map of Kingsthorpe in
1920.

An Annotated Sketch
Map of Kingsthorpe in
1977.

Our second section is called 'Important Buildings' and it takes a look at the growth of buildings, institutes and services in the three maps. The results from my analysis, I have tabulated below...

BUILDING, SERVICE ETC	PRESENT IN MAP	1..	2..	3:.
Cemetery			✓	✓
Windmill		✓	✓	✓*
Wardington C.*		✓	✓	✓
Bowling Green			✓	✓
Golf Course				✓
Police Station				✓
Post Office				✓
Recreation G.*			✓	✓
School(s)		✓	✓	✓
Hospital			✓	✓
Public House(s)		✓	✓	✓
Library				✓
Chapel		✓	✓	✓
Tennis Court			✓	✓
Kingsthorpe Hall		✓	✓	✓
Allotments			✓	✓
Nurseries		✓	✓	
Church		✓	✓	✓
Quarry			✓	
Lodge			✓	
Blacksmith			✓	
Boot factory			✓	
Kings Well		✓	✓	
Vicarage		✓	✓	✓

✳ Not Working.   C = Court.   G = Ground.

A TABLE SHOWING BUILDINGS, SERVICES IN THE THREE MAPS

As you can see from my findings 'map three' had the greater amount of buildings, institutes and services of a noteable nature. 'Map one' had the least number of important buildings and so therefore 'map two' fell in the middle. Well established buildings like churches, chapels, public houses and schools were found to be present in all areas under study. Two buildings have also stood the test of time in all three maps, these being the court house (Wardington Court) and Kingsthorpe Hall (within Thornton Park). My theory for the build up of buildings and services is this. As time progressed more residential areas sprung up; to meet the demand of important services and institutes for the residents on a local scale, buildings to serve the people had to be created. Long established Wardington Court and Kingsthorpe Hall can be seen on the pre. nineteen hundred sketch map shown earlier.

Our next section comes under the title of 'Patterns of Development', here I shall look at the kinds of residential property found in the three areas under study. In 'map three', a sketch map of which can be found on the previous page, one can see the popular residential areas such as Sunnyside, St. Davids, Spring Park, Whitehills and Kingsthorpe Village, but those areas haven't always been there. Residential property in 'map one' is basically here, there and everywhere. Ten percent of the land is residential and most of the dwellings are seen in private form in Kingsthorpe Village, the earliest property there built in the fifteen hundreds. The other buildings featured in 'map one' follow the left hand side of Harbourgh Road, near it's turn off with Welford Road. In 'map two' property has grown on the junction of Harbourgh Road and Boughton Green road, in the Bective area. These dwellings look very formal as they lie back to back in little blocks. Filling-in has also occured in the Queen's Park area along Kingsthorpe Grove, once again very formal. As we leave 'map two' and look at the final map we see the number of residential buildings has basically 'doubled' from twenty percent to ninety-four percent. In the fifty-seven years since map two was made builders had been very busy. The Northampton Borough Council had built the Sunnyside estate (in the fifties and sixties) and they had also built St. Davids(in the thirties). Private contractors had also been having a busy time building Whitehills, just before the second World War and Spring Park in the nineteen sixties.

Fig. 3.13 An example of a student's work based on the use of documents.

Comment

This is a good example of the use that can be made of historical maps and fieldwork observation to illustrate both urban development in the twentieth century and continuity and change in the community, by the comparison of maps of the same area from different periods. The sketch maps focus on the same area section, are drawn to the same scale and are used to isolate significant features. The extract of the candidate's study presented here relates to an enquiry of changing land use and the differences in the provision of buildings and services over the last 100 years, and the pattern of development of the area, focusing on the extent and nature of residential property in the area. An attempt is made to advance an explanation for the evidence collected and pattern of growth identified. This study could be developed further by using reference documents such as old trade directories covering the area, old photographs and the collection and use of oral histories from older residents.

8 › USING MUSEUMS

While Record Offices provide written historical sources for research, museums provide the opportunity to study historical artefacts. There are various types of museums and your access to them will, of course, depend on where you live.

LOCAL TOWN MUSEUMS

These will contain a wide variety of objects, most of which will be connected with the history of the town or area. There may be displays of particular trades and industries which have been associated with the town.

INDUSTRIAL MUSEUMS

Industrial museums have become increasingly popular in recent years and there are a growing number in existence. They concentrate on showing you industry and lifestyle, usually in the early part of the Industrial Revolution, and will contain working models, original machinery, everyday objects and documents and, sometimes, reconstructed houses, shops and streets. Examples include the Open Air Industrial Museum at Ironbridge, the Gladstone Museum at Longton in the Potteries and the Black Country Museum in Dudley.

RURAL LIFE MUSEUMS

These include reconstructed buildings and examples of traditional rural crafts. There are also farm museums, some of which are working museums where you can observe and study how farming methods have changed over the years.

SUBJECT MUSEUMS

These are found throughout the country, although many are concentrated in London: for example, the Natural History Museum and the Science Museum. For conflict studies, the Imperial War Museum in London has the best resources, including collections of oral histories, although local regimental museums can be of interest. For the mass media, the National Museum of Photography in Bradford has a wealth of information on photography, television and the cinema. For transport, the Railway Museum in York is very useful, and for buildings, the Avoncroft Museum of Buildings has over twenty re-erected buildings, covering six centuries, as well as displays of documents and domestic artefacts.

❝ Studying artefacts ❞

Museums vary in the extent to which you will be able to touch, closely examine and even operate the *artefacts* which are displayed. Being able to study objects in a first-hand manner gives you a sense of scale and weight, an understanding of an object's use and, therefore, a feel for the way of life in the period during which it was used. A museum object can raise many questions:

- What is it made from?
- How could it have been produced?
- What are the implications for the economy of the society which produced it? And for the lifestyle of the user?
- What was it used for?
- Do we know who used it, when and how?
- How did the object come to be conserved and acquired by the museum?

Reconstructed buildings can lead you to consider a number of questions about life during the relevant period, and the problems and difficulties of family life, while reconstructed or original machinery can give insights into industrial design, working conditions and practices.

Remember that museums increasingly pay considerable attention to how artefacts are going to be arranged and displayed, to ensure that collections are attractive, informative and help create a particular impression. Always be prepared to question the organisation of objects and consider if different arrangements would create a different impression. In the museum it would be an advantage if you have a clear idea of what you are looking for. Museums can present you with vast collections of material from many different periods and you might easily become sidetracked by things outside your research area.

You should have opportunities to make sketches and notes on the exhibits you see. Make sure you give an indication of size and use or function. Also, be prepared to give your responses and feelings about what you see: for example, your own response to a reconstructed building can be invaluable in providing you with a feel for, and understanding of, everyday life in other periods.

If you are in doubt about what sort of museums are available in your area, consult an edition of *Museums and Galleries in Great Britain and Ireland*, available in your reference library.

ARCHAEOLOGY UNIT

Your area may have a local archaeology unit. This will handle artefacts and have records of all historical sites, possibly with an extensive collection of aerial photographs of your area. You can find out about local archaeology units from your council. Remember, if you do have a unit, it is unlikely to be open to the public, so write to them or ask your teacher for advice.

9 ▷ THE MASS MEDIA

The *mass media* are all means of communicating with large audiences. These include television, radio, newspapers and magazines, advertisements and films. The mass media provide a vast amount of information about the world which will have relevance to your enquiry. They can provide you with information about events and stories to illustrate issues which you are researching, sometimes an analysis of these issues, different points of view and the background and sequence of events.

The media, especially local newspapers, can also tell you a lot about your community. For example, adverts for houses give a good indication of house prices in the community and the relative value and desirability of areas within a town, etc. The sphere of influence of a town can be researched by noting down the location of stories in the newspaper, as well as the location of advertisers. In this way a picture can be built up of the size and shape of the area for which the town is a centre for entertainment, shopping and work. Local newspapers can also give an idea of available leisure facilities, and situations vacant columns can tell you about employment opportunities and the wage/salary levels of various jobs. Advertisements can give an indication of the prices of goods, and if the sort of advert is related to the audience which a newspaper is aimed at (for example, 'quality' newspapers such as *The Times* are more likely to be bought by those in the higher social-class categories), they can give us an understanding of the marketing strategies behind the promotion of particular products. If you have access to newspapers from earlier periods you can gain an understanding of what everyday life was like and what were the concerns and worries of people at the time.

The mass media can also tell us a great deal about the sorts of things which our society thinks are important – or at least what the mass media believes we think are important – and the ways in which we should behave. The sequencing of items on the news, for example, will tell you which events are thought to be more important than others, and a study of soap operas may give you an indication of what family life and problems are thought to be like. The mass media both *reflects* public attitudes and also seeks to *influence* them. Forms of mass media such as advertisements are clearly aimed at influencing our behaviour. Certain newspapers may try to influence our political views and voting preferences, and there are other, subtler, ways in which the mass media may be seen as consciously or unconsciously having an effect on our views. Does the way news items are presented to us affect the way we think about events? How are certain groups of people in society presented to us? And what effects does this have on the way we think about them? Do soap operas affect the way we think about family problems, and do they affect our own behaviour?

Mass media organisations themselves could be an object for enquiry. Who owns television channels, national and local newspapers, and radio stations? What other companies do they own, and are there any implications in this? How are programmes, newspapers, etc. produced? Who are the audiences the producers think they are aiming at? What are the different types of programme and publication? Who decides, and how is it decided, what items should go where?

USING THE MASS MEDIA

You will not be rewarded for simply attaching extracts to your work, or for copying out large amounts from newspapers, etc. You must analyse and comment on the material you present. Analysing the content of the media can involve:

Analysing the mass media

- Measuring the amount of space (in newspapers) or time (in broadcasts) given to stories, or certain types of story. This can give an indication of the priorities of particular newspapers and radio/television news organisations, as can a consideration of where the items are located in the newspaper or broadcast.

- Analysing the words used in a news item. This can tell us a lot about what journalists and editors think, or want us to think, about the characters or groups presented in the story. Articles can be analysed to spot words which have negative images or which suggest violence, etc.

- The pictures or film which accompany news items are usually selected from a vast amount of material which could have been used. The ones which are finally selected can tell us something about the ways those who put the stories together want us to think about them. In newspapers, pictures are usually accompanied by a caption which not only tells us what the picture is but also how we should react to it. Sometimes the same picture will appear in a number of newspapers, but the message in the caption may be very different.

- The 'facts' reported in different newspapers can be compared. Who journalists choose to interview and quote, and even the way some facts are emphasised or exaggerated, can tell us something about the impression which those who have constructed the news item wish us to have. Headlines in newspapers, which attempt to condense stories and make them eye-catching, are also useful to compare, as an indication of how different newspapers wish to present the same story.

■ Cartoons, especially political cartoons, can give you information about the ways in which groups may be characterised and stereotyped.

■ Advertisements, especialy magazine advertisements, can be studied to identify selling techniques and the way, for example, women are presented – what are they doing and what products or types of product are they selling?

STUDENT'S WORK BASED ON THE USE OF THE MASS MEDIA

<u>News</u> .

1. <u>Break down of a Tabloid newspaper</u> . – <u>The Sun</u> .

All the information below was obtained from one copy of The Sun . printed on the 7th March 1988 .

The paper contained 28 pages in total which therefore means that the total printing area is 26551 cm², as each page has an area of 948.25 cm² .

From measuring the area of articles in the newspaper the following calculations were made :-

<u>National News</u> .
     Total Area = 2322.5 cm²
     No. of pages · 2.4 pages .

<u>International News</u> .
     Total Area · 28 cm²
     No. of pages 0.03 pages .

<u>Sport Features</u> .
     Total Area = 5084.5 cm²
     No. of pages · 5.3 pages .

<u>Photographs</u> .
     Total Area .= 3632.25 cm²
     No. of pages · 3.8 pages

<u>Classified Advertising</u>
     Total Area · 2071.5 cm²
     No. of pages : 2.2 pages .

<u>Display Advertising</u>.
     Total Area · 4779.5 cm²
     No. of pages · 5 pages .

<u>Letters</u> .
     Total Area · 1269.75 cm²
     No. of pages 1.3 pages .

<u>Cartoons</u>.
  Total Area . 859.75 cm²
  No. of pages . 0.9 pages .

<u>Special Features</u>
  Total Area : 2238.5 cm²
  No. of pages : 2.36 pages

<u>Competitions</u>
  Total Area : 484 cm²
  No. of pages . 0.5 pages

<u>Crosswords</u>
  Total Area . 199.75 cm²
  No. of pages : 0.2 pages

<u>Television and Radio Information</u>
  Total Area . 1509.75 cm²
  No. of pages . 1.6 pages

<u>Others (including scandal on personalities)</u>
  Total Area . 2285 cm²
  No. of pages . 2.41 pages .

$$\frac{360}{28} \cdot 12.857° \text{ per page}.$$

$$\underline{12.9°}$$

Type of News .	No. of pages	No. of degrees on pie chart .
National News .	2.4	31°
International News .	0.03	0.5°
Sport Features .	5.3	65.5°
Photographs .	3.8	49°
Classified Advertising	2.2	28.5°
Display Advertising	5.0	64.5°
Letters	1.3	17°
Cartoons	0.9	11.5°
Special Features	2.36	30.5°
Competitions	0.5	6.5°
Crosswords	0.2	2.5°
Television and Radio	1.6	20.5°
Others	2.41	31°
TOTAL .	28.0	361.5°

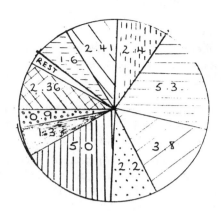

A Pie Chart showing the news included in a tabloid newspaper.

Key.

National News		Cartoons
International News		Special Features
Sport Features		Competitions
Photographs		Crosswords
Classified Advertising		Television / Radio
Display Advertising		Others
Letters		

NOTE :-

The statistics presented are only correct for one edition of the newspaper - 7th March 1988 - and are in no means true for all copies, as the amount will obviously change according to the time of year and news items!   good

" Good. "

Nevertheless, these figures do show many important truths about the tabloid press :-

1. The majority of the money needed for the paper to be profitable comes from advertising (The cover charge does not cover all costs) This can easily be seen as approximately 4.2 pages of the paper were advertising - one quarter of the total space.

2. The paper's readers are not very interested in business news or foreign affairs as there are only 0.03 pages on these subjects in total. Its following prefer sport coverage, photographs of, and special features on celebrities. In other words the readers want entertainment, which the papers set out shows and the reason behind the phrase, the 'popular' press.

Fig. 3.14 An example of a student's work based on content analysis of paper.

Comment

A good attempt at content analysis, carefully carried out. The well-presented data are clearly related to the analysis and conclusion. The working list of categories is useful, although the category of 'home news' could have been broken down into political news, crime, etc. The enquiry could be considerably developed if the tabloid paper was compared with a copy of the 'quality' press.

Analysing and evaluating the mass media is further discussed in Chapter 4.

10> **USING LITERATURE**

> Studying literature adds an important element to your enquiry.

What we normally refer to as 'literature' – novels, short stories, poetry, etc. – should be a significant element in an Integrated Humanities course and an important resource for enquiry and research.

Works of literature are not necessarily mainly concerned with providing a factual description of events. They may be interested in developing characters, ideas, views or hopes, or in telling an interesting story. Sometimes you may find it difficult to decide what is a work of fiction and what is a factual description. Even if you are reading an autobiography, there is no guarantee that the events described ever happened in the way the author claims they did. For your enquiry, literature should be treated in a different way from other sources of 'factual' information:

- Literature can help you to get an understanding of the atmosphere of a particular time, place or situation. This can, together with a study of historical documents, help to produce a deeper understanding of the past and the responses of people to conditions and events, or their thoughts about the future.

- Literature can give you an insight into the feelings and points of view of people and groups of people within our own and other societies, and can help you to understand and to illustrate concepts such as prejudice, inequality, etc.

- Literature can help you to express and reflect upon your own views, experiences and feelings towards places and events.

The list of possible novels, plays, books of poetry, etc. which you could use for your enquiry is almost endless. If you are going to draw up a list of possible sources from literature, your starting point should be the books you are already familiar with – those you have already read and the ones you are reading in your English lessons. Discuss relevant titles with your English teacher.

Your list of possible sources should involve a broad interpretation of the term 'literature'. Include not only novels and poems, but also scripts from plays and films, and songs. For example, what do the lyrics of 1960s pop music tell us about what it was like living at that time? Make sure that you know something about the book you are using – when it was written and something about the author. In your enquiry it is important that you study the book in its context. For example, there can be a great deal of difference between a novel written in the nineteenth century and a novel written recently but set in the nineteenth century.

Make a note of your response to a relevant book or poem you have read. Copy extracts of particular passages which strike you as being important, or which sum up particular attitudes, views, etc. Remember to record exactly where extracts and quotations have been taken from – you will need to give this information in your enquiry.

Draw up a summary of a relevant book, story or episode you have read. Remember, your enquiry is unlikely to be into a particular book itself; you will be using literature for what it can tell you about the subject you are enquiring into.

To give you an idea of the range of books, etc. which could be used in your research, the following are examples of some of the possibilities for a study of racism in America.

Novels

Dee Brown, *Wounded Knee*.
An adaptation of *Bury My Heart at Wounded Knee*. A study of the destruction of Native American Indians by white European settlers.

R. Ellison, *The Invisible Man*.
Southern States black boy comes to New York and meets black people representing different experiences of living in the ghetto.

J. Lester, *The Basketball Game*.
A story of a black family moving into a predominantly white area of Nashville in the 1950s, and the relationship between the son, Allen, and the white girl next door. An account of segregation in America.

M. D. Taylor, *Roll of Thunder Hear My Cry*.
A story of a black family's struggle to hold on to their land during the 1930s Depression in Mississippi; based on the experiences of the author's own family.

R. Wright, *Black Boy*.
Autobiographical account of black childhood in pre-war American South, and a growing awareness of racism and how it works.

Short stories and anthologies

L. Bennett Jnr, *The Convert*
Short story about the killing of a black preacher who entered a whites-only waiting room.

J. Lester, *Long Journey Home.*
Stories about slaves in Southern America.

J. Lester, *To Be a Slave.*
American slaves talking about their experiences, with comments by the author.

D. Parker, 'Arrangement in Black and White' in *The Best of Dorothy Parker.*
A woman from the Southern States asks to be introduced to a popular black singer, and reveals her prejudices in every word she speaks.

In addition

Howell Raines, *My Soul is Rested.*
This gives first-hand account of people involved in the Civil Rights movement.

Protest songs from the 1950s and 1960s.

American blues.
For example, Billie Holliday songs, such as 'Strange Fruit'; 'Young Gifted and Black', etc.

11 INFORMATION FROM ORGANISATIONS AND GROUPS

A vast amount of information on most of the subjects you will be researching into can be obtained by contacting the relevant organisations.

WHOM TO CONTACT

There are various types of organisation which may be of help to you.

- *Government departments* and bodies which are providing a particular state service: for example, the Department of Education and Science, the Department of Social Security, the Manpower Services Commission. National organisations which are financed by grants from local or central government: for example, the Commission for Racial Equality and the Equal Opportunities Commission.

- *Local authority departments.* Local authorities are a major source of information about the services they provide and also general statistical information concerning many aspects of the locality. General information available will include guides to council services, town guides, budgets and statements of accounts and annual reports, which will provide you with some idea of the scope of the work of the council and the finances involved. Planning departments will have information on development plans for proposed developments, structure plans, which will give a general outline of the authority's planning strategy, and local development plans. These documents will contain a range of statistical data and reports of relevant surveys, and also give you the opportunity to look at alternative strategies, to consider why they were rejected and to examine the assumptions that lie behind planning strategies. Transportation studies can provide useful information on subjects such as traffic flows and car ownership. Local housing statistics provide information on housing provision, supply, repairs and renovation, and homelessness. Most councils will provide some information about how rates are calculated and an idea of what services the money is spent on. You will also be able to inspect the rateable value of all property, which will give you an idea of property values in different areas. In addition, other individual council departments will be able to supply you with useful information on, for example, education, social services and environmental health.

- *Pressure groups,* which represent the interests of groups of people or put forward particular points of view, exist in great numbers. Because they are concerned to promote ideas or interests, they usually have available a useful amount of published information. Some pressure groups are paid for by the people whose interests they represent, such as trades unions, the Confederation of British Industry, etc. Others are funded by donations from the public to support certain causes or to put forward particular views on an issue: for example, the Royal Society for the Prevention of Cruelty to Animals, the Campaign for Nuclear Disarmament, Amnesty International, etc. Some pressure groups are permanent, because they are concerned with a range of issues connected to a particular cause: the RSPCA, for example, is concerned with the ongoing cause of animal welfare, and in pursuing this it will be involved in many issues concerning animals. Other pressure groups are concerned with a single issue only: for example, STOPP (School Teachers Opposed to Physical Punishment) campaigned against the use of corporal punishment in schools. When this had been abolished by the government, STOPP ceased to exist. Many pressure groups will be comparatively small, local organisations, concerned with a particular local matter for concern, such as whether or not a by-pass should be built, the siting of a new sewage works, keeping a local school open, the threatened closure of a hospital, etc. There are many other voluntary organisations which concern themselves with activities such as fund-raising for particular groups of people or which encourage self-help activities.

FINDING THE INFORMATION

Some information, especially from council departments and government departments such as the Department of Social Security, will be available from post offices and libraries, or from the local Citizens Advice Bureau or information office. To find the addresses of organisations you wish to contact for other information, consult the lists and directories you will find in the reference library. You will find *Whitakers Almanac* particularly useful, and you can always try the telephone directory for local organisations and departments.

Writing letters

Your letter must be clear and legible. Make sure that you say who you are, what you are doing and why you want the information. Make sure you say exactly what sorts of information you would find helpful for your research. Sending a joint letter, on behalf of a number of students, to an organisation may help if several of the members of your class are researching similar projects. Remember that many pressure groups and voluntary organisations exist on very small budgets and might have difficulty in dealing with a large number of requests. Keep a copy of any letter you send; this will be useful for keeping track of, and for demonstrating, what you have done during your research.

Fig. 3.15 An example of a letter.

```
Central Television,          Address you are
Central House,       ────    sending letter to         Make sure you include
Broad Street,                                           your own address
Birmingham
B1 2JP                                                    Students address
                                                          Date

        Dear Sir/Madam,
                        I am currently producing a study on Soap Operas    Explain what
        and how they affect our lives, for my GCSE Integrated Humanities. I   you want the
        would be very grateful if you could answer a few questions for me:    information for
        1. How do you decide how many Soap Operas to show at one time, and
        who decides on what time at which they are shown?
        2. Why choose one Soap Opera - How do you choose to show one Soap
        Opera and not another?
        3. In your opinion, what do you feel makes a good Soap Opera?
        4. Why do people decline to watch one Soap Opera, and concentrate
Clearly explain   on watching another?
what              5. Do you watch Soap Operas? If so, why?
information        6. Are there any restrictions on Soap Operas? Are any episodes cut
you would         from the series or edited in any way because they are too violent
like              or otherwise?
        7. Who decides how much physical violence or violent language there
        is to be shown in Soap Operas? How do they decide this (bearing in
        mind that most Soap Operas are screened before 9pm, when younger
        viewers are probably still watching television)?
                Also, any survey results or information on Soap Operas that you
        might have would be extremely useful to me - I would be very grateful
        if you could send me any.
                Thank you for your time.


                        Yours faithfully,


                        Signature
```

USING THE INFORMATION

> 66 Make sure you use any information you receive. 99

Simply attaching leaflets and information sheets to your work will not earn you any marks. A lot of the information you receive will have no relevance to your research. Marks will be awarded only for the use you make of the information: for example, to explain what the aims of a pressure group are, how it works, and what arguments it puts forward to support its views on a particular issue. You must *use* the information you receive, by writing about it, summarising relevant points yourself, or by extracting relevant pictures, tables etc. to include alongside your own writing, illustrating what you are describing.

Remember that many pressure groups exist to promote a particular view, so you cannot always expect the material they provide to be balanced and free from bias. It will be useful to find an organisation or pressure group which promotes an alternative or opposing view on a subject: for example, Life exists to oppose abortion, while the National Abortion Campaign exists to defend or extend abortion legislation.

Examples of Greenpeace's use of direct action

Aims of Greenpeace

GREENPEACE

Against all odds, Greenpeace has brought the plight of the natural world to the attention of caring people. Terrible abuses to the environment, often carried out in remote places or far out to sea have been headlined on television and in the press.

Greenpeace began with a protest voyage into a nuclear test zone. The test was disrupted. Today, the site at Amchitka in the Aleutian Islands is a bird sanctuary.

Then Greenpeace sent its tiny inflatable boats to protect the whales. They took up position between the harpoons and the fleeing whales. Today, commercial whaling is banned.

On the ice floes of Newfoundland, Greenpeace volunteers placed their bodies between the gaffs of the seal hunters and the helpless seal pups. The hunt was subsequently called off.

In the North Atlantic, Greenpeace drove its

inflatables underneath falling barrels of radioactive waste. Now nuclear waste dumping at sea has been stopped.
In the North Sea, Greenpeace swimmers

turned back dump ships carrying chemical wastes. New laws to protect the North Sea have been promised.

Peaceful direct action by Greenpeace has invoked the power of public opinion which in turn has forced changes in the law to protect wildlife and to stop the pollution of the natural world.

GREENPEACE STANDS FOR A SAFE AND NUCLEAR-FREE WORLD · FRESH AIR · CLEAN WATER · THE PROTECTION OF WILDLIFE AND THEIR HABITATS

Greenpeace has: Stopped French testing of nuclear weapons in the atmosphere.   Helped bring an end to legalised commercial whaling.   Prevented baby seals being killed in Newfoundland and the Orkney Isles. Fought a long campaign against radioactive discharges

into the Irish Sea.   Won agreements to end the dumping of chemical sludges into the North Sea.   Forced an end to the burning of hazardous waste in the North Sea. US coastal waters and the Mediterranean.   Stopped the dumping of radioactive wastes at sea.   Worked to protect threatened seals and dolphins round the UK coastline.   Helped persuade the government to spend £200m cleaning Britain's beaches and £600m cleaning aerial discharges from coal-fired power stations.   Reported on the scandal of imports of endangered species products into the EEC.

Greenpeace is an international environmental pressure group which maintains complete independence from all political parties anywhere in the world.

Methods used by Greenpeace – direct action to influence public opinion

Examples of Greepeace's achievements

As a pressure group, Greepeace is independent from political parties

Fig. 3.16 A Greenpeace leaflet.

COLLECTING YOUR OWN INFORMATION

> 66 Information *you collect* is *primary information.* 99

Information for your enquiry does not only exist as prerecorded and collected data and documents. You can collect *your own* through your own questioning and observations. Information which you collect in this manner is usually referred to as *primary information.* Going out into 'the field' to collect your own information presents you with a number of problems. Even if you are clear about the sorts of places and people you want to get information from, you will probably still be left with a vast number of possible places and people you could observe or question. How do you decide who, or what, to select?

12 > SAMPLING

Your research may concentrate on the study of one place, or one small group of people: for example, a particular factory, a community centre, the growth and location of a particular village, etc. You may, however, be interested in finding out more general information from a larger number of people or places. Whether you are interested in a particular case study or more general information, it is important to explain why you chose to obtain information from, or about, the places or people you *did* select, and not from others. In many cases your decision will be made for you by what is available, relevant or convenient for you to study. Where there is a large number of possible sources of information which you could use, so that you have to select, it becomes more important to explain your selection. Unless you can say that the sources you have selected are *representative* of all the possible sources you could have chosen, you will not be able to claim that your findings and conclusions portray a real and accurate picture of what you are studying.

Sampling is the means by which you identify a part of all the places and people you are interested in studying which will be representative of the whole.

SAMPLING PLACES

The first thing to start with is a list of all the places or a map of the whole area you are interested in studying. Then, select systematically a small number of locations. For example, in an urban transect, select a number of houses from a map which you have covered with a grid, a number of grid intersections or grid squares. This collection of all the possible areas of study is called the sample frame. The key to sampling is the way in which you go about the selection. It should be random: that is, the selection should not be consciously decided on by you. If it was, it may reflect your own views and biases. To make sure the selection is random, use a predetermined formula: for example, select every tenth house, grid square, etc., or make use of a random number table.

Stratified random sampling

You may sometimes want to be sure you sample certain categories of, for example, land use, types of building, etc. which random sampling may miss out. To make sure that no category which you consider important is missed out, first divide your sample frame into the categories you want to include and then sample the required number from each category.

SAMPLING PEOPLE

The same principles of sampling apply equally to the selection of people you may wish to question. For example, if you wish to give questionnaires to pupils in your year in school, first find a list of all pupils – your sample frame – and then randomly sample the number you want: for example, list every tenth name. If you wish to ensure that your sample contains an equal number of boys and girls, then you can apply stratified random sampling techniques: for example, divide your sample frame into boys and girls and take a sample from each.

Quota sampling

If you intend to question passers-by in the street, the methods of sampling mentioned so far are obviously inappropriate. Quota sampling involves deciding first on the number and the sorts of people you want to talk to: for example, five women over thirty, five men over thirty, etc. The sorts of people you list are your quota. You then have to identify people in these categories until your quota is filled. In this way you can be sure that you talk to a cross-section of people, and, if your quota is made up of the same proportion of categories of people as appear in the population as a whole, you can be sure that your sample is representative.

13 > OBSERVING AND RECORDING PLACES

The most straightforward method of gathering information would seem to be using the evidence of your own eyes. Observation as a method of information collection in the Humanities involves:

- understanding precisely what sorts of information you are looking for and how you will recognise them;
- devising a method for adequately recording the information you are looking for.

There are four main methods of field observation and recording which will be of use to you:

- photographs;
- field sketching;
- sketch maps;
- recording surveys and transects.

MAKING A PHOTOGRAPHIC RECORD

This would seem to be the easiest way of making a record of what you can see. All you need is access to a camera; a sophisticated knowledge of photographic technique is not necessary. The basic rules are:

- Use black and white or colour print film, not slides.
- Remember that the photograph you take will capture only a small part of what you can see in front of you.
- Make sure that the object you want to photograph fills the viewfinder.
- Include if possible something in your photograph to give you a sense of scale: for example, a person, a car, etc.
- Make sure that you understand enough about your camera to avoid under- or over-exposure, so that the photographs you take will be reasonably clear and usable.

Photographs can be used to:

- draw attention to a particular object of detail;
- give a general view of a place, building(s) or landscape;
- capture contrasts between, for example, urban and rural, etc.

Remember that photographs are selections from reality; they do not simply copy it. How a photograph is taken (the angle, etc.) can produce different impressions of the scene being photographed. Don't think that pointing your camera in the general direction of the scene you are observing will capture all that is necessary; give some thought to what you want your photograph to show and to constructing and selecting the view you wish to capture. Make sure you make a note of what you photograph, and from where.

Using your photographs

Your photographs may be generally illustrative of the topic you are researching. Alternatively, you may wish to use them in a more specific way, making them central to your work. However you intend to use them, ensure that they are relevant, that if they are to be included alongside your text they are located at the appropriate place, and that they are accompanied by your own explanations of what they show and where they were taken from.

Fig. 3.17 a) Using photographs to draw attention to details and making a comment on urban decay and housing conditions.

Fig. 3.17 b) (above) Using
photographs to capture contrasts:
how does human activity affect the
rural landscape?

Fig. 3.17 c) (below) Using
photographs to provide a record of
observations and features to be
explained.

FIELD SKETCHING

Sketching the *object* of your observation provides you with a record and, unlike a photograph, gives you the opportunity to emphasise the features you are particularly interested in for your study. Sketches also give you the opportunity to label and add relevant notes while you are out observing. Your sketch does not have to be of great artistic value. It will be adequate if it is a relatively accurate record of what you can see. Sketching has the great advantage over photograhs that it forces you to think carefully about what you see as you go about building up your sketch and adding details.
General advice:

- Make sure you have a firm base for your paper and use a pencil.
- Make sure that you clearly understand the purpose of your sketch, so that you know what features you wish to draw attention to.
- Draw a framework to give you a guide (see Fig. 3.18).

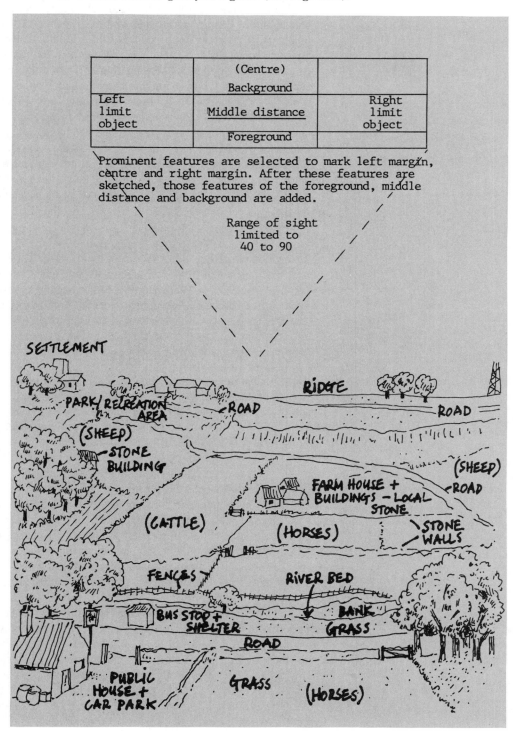

Fig. 3.18 Making a field sketch.

- Draw the main features according to the purpose of your research.
- Label the main features.
- Jot down any relevant notes you want to make on the side of your sketch.
- Make sure you make a note of where the sketch was made, if necessary giving grid references and compass points, showing the direction the drawing was done.
- Don't worry about the quality of your field sketch; as long as what it records is accurate, you can improve on it later.

Examples of field sketching

The key to successful field sketching is knowing what you are going to include in your sketch and what you are going to leave out.

- **Landscapes**

  If you are interested in mainly physical details, then information about, say, electricity grid cables is not necessary. If you are sketching a view of a farmstead, your drawing should show general relief and features such as rivers, roads, houses and farm buildings. If your view is broad and from a long distance, then particular features will be very small scale, so that you will need to identify particular features, types of building, etc. by clearly labelling them. If your study is concerned with particular types of farming, you will need to label the fields you sketch according to the types of crop, livestock, etc. In a study which involves researching the impact of human beings on the local landscape, be prepared to spot and highlight those features of the landscape which have been made or altered by people: for example, houses, villages, factories, roads, ditches, quarries, forest clearances, etc. You could also include features which have been altered by nature: for example, the effects of wind and water. You could also attempt an imaginative fieldsketch about what the landscape may have looked like before the influence of human beings.

- **Buildings**

  A study of a particular building or group of buildings can involve you looking for information about the function, present or past, of the building, its present condition, its location relative to other features, its age, etc. The focus of your study will dictate what particular features of a building are important and which you will emphasise. If you are interested in recording the age of buildings, you should first be aware of the styles of architecture, building materials, etc. associated with particular historical periods, so that you will know what to look for.

RECORDING WITH SKETCH MAPS

Recording with *maps* enables you to make a record of the location of the features you observe: their relationship to each other, types of land use, distribution of particular services, etc. Sketch maps are rough documents produced 'in the field'. You should feel free to make notes on them to remind you of anything which you think might be useful in making a more permanent record later. You will need to give some indication of the scale you are using and you should attempt to be as consistent as possible in your use of scale.

You will find it useful if, before your field work, you produce a *base map*. To make a base map, find an appropriate scale OS map or street plan and trace out the relevant area, ensuring that you include grid lines and any detail which will be necessary for you to place what you observe on the map with accuracy. Be prepared to enlarge the map to give you enough space to record the information you need. To enlarge your base map you can either use the enlarging facility on a photocopier or make the enlargement yourself, by tracing a copy of the original, drawing measured grid lines on it, then redrawing the map but increasing the distance between the grid lines so that all the information on the map is drawn to a larger scale.

In recording information, you will need to make use of a key. The greater the variety of information you wish to record, the more complex the key which you devise will need to be. If, for example, you are interested simply in the distribution of one particular type of service, then a simple dot map will be sufficient. If you wish to locate types of industry, shops, services, etc., then your key must reflect all the possible types which you might find. Make sure that you think out your key in advance of your fieldwork. For land-use surveys, you can make up your own key or use the detailed and extensive classification schemes that already exist for these sorts of surveys.

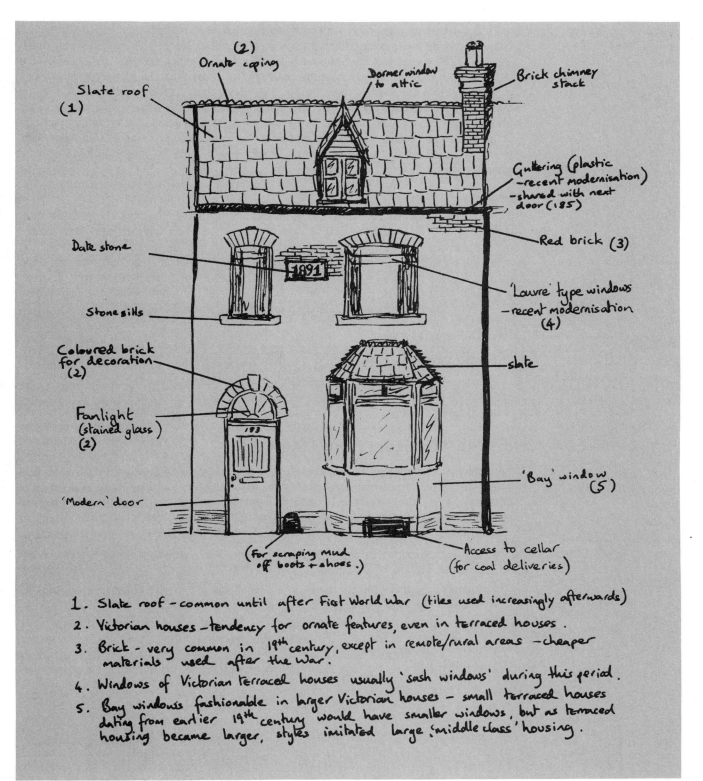

Labels on diagram:

(2)
Ornate coping

Dormer window to attic

Brick chimney stack

Slate roof (1)

Guttering (plastic – recent modernisation) – shared with next door (185)

Red brick (3)

Date stone

1891

'Louvre' type windows – recent modernisation (4)

Stone sills

slate

Coloured brick for decoration (2)

Fanlight (stained glass) (2)

183

'Bay' window (5)

'Modern' door

(For scraping mud off boots + shoes.)

Access to cellar (for coal deliveries)

1. Slate roof – common until after First World War (tiles used increasingly afterwards)

2. Victorian houses – tendency for ornate features, even in terraced houses.

3. Brick – very common in 19th century, except in remote/rural areas – cheaper materials used after the war.

4. Windows of Victorian terraced houses usually 'sash windows' during this period.

5. Bay windows fashionable in larger Victorian houses – small terraced houses dating from earlier 19th century would have smaller windows, but as terraced housing became larger, styles imitated large 'middle class' housing.

Fig. 3.19 A Victorian terraced house – 183 Rothwell Street.

If you are making up a key, you might choose to represent derelict land by heavy pencil dots; open space by the letters OS; animals by the letters indicated in capitals – HOrses, DOnkeys, Sheep, Dairy Cattle; arable land cereals – Wheat, Barley, Oats, Rye; and ley legumes: CLover, TRefoil, VEtch, LUcerne, etc.

Mental maps

An interesting method of obtaining information is to ask people to draw their own map without reference to an existing map or plan. The result is a *mental map*, which will tell you a lot about the individual's recall and experience of an area: which parts they are most familiar with, which have importance for them, which landmarks stand out, etc. Mental maps can be compared with existing maps to demonstrate which areas of the community, country, etc. individuals feel most strongly about.

Mental maps by a number of people can be compared to find out which parts of the community are most accurately portrayed or mentioned, and this will indicate which aspects of the community have the most significance for which groups of people. Maps of the neighbourhood produced by a range of people will also reveal that there are differences in the geographical extent of the area which people identify as their neighbourhood, while differences in scale might indicate individual experiences in travelling certain routes. Mental maps can provide information on people's attitudes to the environment and might help you to understand the basis on which people make decisions: where is the best place to buy a house, which areas of the community are thought to be more desirable than others, etc.

Choropleth maps

These are shading maps which you can use with a prearranged key of shading or colours to represent different values of different parts of an area. For example, to investigate the distance/time from a particular transport point, start at the bus station and shade in all the buildings within three minutes' walking distance; this could be repeated, starting from other transport points, such as car parks. The completed map will show you the most accessible areas: that is, those that lie within all, or most, of the shaded areas. You can use this sort of map to record the existence of different zones of a town or region.

Isoline maps

These are similar to choropleth maps but use lines to connect points of equal value, such as the contour lines you will find on a relief map. For example, in a study of noise pollution, using a noise meter, take readings on the meter at predecided intervals; plot these readings on to your map. The isolines can then be drawn in, connecting the points at which similar readings were taken.

RECORDING SURVEYS AND TRANSECTS

Your observations can focus on a number of areas and aspects of the environment which will be convenient to record in a format other than maps or sketches. As with all forms of observation, the first concern is to be clear about what you are looking for and how you will record it. This will mean you have to know how to classify places and land use.

Take classifying industry as an example. There are three main classes of industry:

- primary/extractive industry – for example, mining, quarrying, forestry work, power stations, etc.;
- secondary/manufacturing industry – for example, textiles, vehicle assembly, confectionery and baking, etc.;
- tertiary/service industry – for example, nursing, shopkeeping, transport, etc.

For a detailed study of types of local industry, it will be necessary to produce a list of possible industries. The *Standard Industrial Classification* (HMSO, 1979), available in your reference library, classifies all industry into ten broad divisions; these are broken down into different classes (sixty in total), each of which is made up of a number of groups (222 in total) which, in turn, are made up of a number of activity headings (334 in total).

STANDARD INDUSTRIAL CLASSIFICATION REVISED 1980

Division
0   Agriculture, forestry and fishing
1   Energy and water supply industries
2   Extraction of minerals and ores other than fuels; manufacture of metals, mineral products and chemicals
3   Metal goods, engineering and vehicles industries
4   Other manufacturing industries
5   Construction
6   Distribution, hotels and catering; repairs
7   Transport and communication
8   Banking, finance, insurance, business services and leasing
9   Other services

Fig. 3.20 *Standard Industrial Classification*, HMSO, 1979–80.

Shopping surveys

You can produce extensive lists of different types of shops with the help of the *Thomson Directory* or the *Yellow Pages*. For the purpose of a survey you will need to create broader categories: for example, food shops, household shops (furniture, television, hardware, etc.), clothes shops, service shops (estate agents, cafés, laundrettes, etc.), sports and hobbies shops, etc. When you are constructing your key, make sure that you have a 'miscellaneous' category – shops for which you had not already planned a category. For the purposes of your survey, your categories could be even broader. For example:

- convenience goods shops – that is, shops to which people are generally not prepared to travel far, such as grocers, greengrocers, general stores, newsagents, chemists, butchers, bakers, off-licences, etc.;

- comparison goods shops – that is, shops which tend to stock more expensive goods, to which people are prepared to travel further and visit less frequently, such as clothes and shoe shops, jewellers, record shops, furniture shops, electrical goods shops, etc.

Your survey may also concentrate not just on the type of goods or service which the shop provides but also on the type of premises: for example, hypermarket, supermarket, department store, etc.

Urban transects

A *transect* is a line or route which is preplanned, or sampled, and involves you in simply walking along the route and recording the features of all the buildings and land you pass, or a sample of them – for example, every fifth building. A transect will enable you to record a large amount of information and help you to compare different parts of the location you are studying.

Building size can be recorded by measuring the frontage of buildings, pacing it out and drawing it to scale. Building height can be recorded by plotting on graph paper one graph square for each storey. The measurement of building frontages can be used as an indication of housing density in different areas or zones of a town. Housing size can be compared in different zones or related to other observable features, such as pedestrian density, etc. Transects can also be used to record building use, using appropriate categories and symbols. For example, with an industrial and commercial category:

Shops	S
Banks and offices	O
Doctors, dentists, etc.	D
Cafés	C
Public buildings	P
Places of entertainment	E
Transport facilities	F
Industrial premises	I
Residential	R
can be subdivided into house or flat type:	
terraced houses	t
semi-detached houses	s/d
detached houses	d
bungalows	b
flats	f
multi-storey flats	m/s

Remember that individual buildings can have more than one use. You can either record only the ground floor use or ensure that you are equipped to record the use of more than one storey.

You could also record building age, style, and building and roofing materials on a transect.

The range of information which can be collected with an urban transect makes this method well suited for the testing of a wide range of hypotheses and concepts concerning urban development and spatial organisation: for example, suburban housing is built to a lower density than in inner-town or city areas; buildings will be higher the nearer they are to the central business district; towns develop through a series of concentric zones, etc. Transects can also be combined with a variety of other techniques to produce more detailed knowledge of towns: for example, with pedestrian counts, questionnaires, shopping surveys, etc. These will help in answering questions about the identification of the focal point of a town or investigating the relationship between two features, such as building height and pedestrian density.

STUDENT'S WORK BASED ON KETTERING TOWN CENTRE

'Kettering town centre is a focal point for the town and the surrounding area, and it is expanding'

INTRODUCTION
   The above title is the hypothesis that I will be testing in this assignment. It says that the town centre of Kettering is a FOCAL POINT, a place where people go, or focus in on. It states that it is a focal point for both Kettering itself and the surrounding area and also that the town centre is expanding, ie getting larger.
   To begin with, we must establish where the town centre is, Fig 1, shows my idea of Kettering Town Centre.

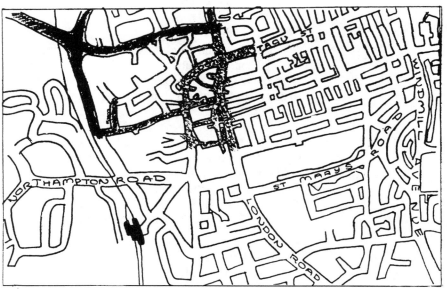

Fig 1

   The shaded area shows the town centre, but it is outside the town centre where I think it is expanding.

DATA COLLECTION
   To establish the accuracy of my view of the town centre, we spent a morning doing fieldwork in Kettering.
   Groups were dropped off at various points around Kettering, this was so that we could do transects from around Kettering, into the town centre. Along our given route we had sample points which we had to stop at and mark down the building use. These sample points were about every 100 yards.
   When we got back to the town centre, we were given a pedestrian count to do. We had to count the number of people that passed us along a given route, marking down our starting and finishing times.
   When this was completed we did an economic survey and a shopping survey. Our economic survey was about superstores and we had to investigate the site of B + Q/Comet. Most of the groups did more than one economic survey, but we only did one because we did a shopping survey (questionaire) instead.

Once we had finished our shopping survey, we repeated our pedestrian count and then came back to the school.

Other data that I thought would be useful was a bus timetable, as it gives a picture of what the surrounding area of Kettering is. I also traced an ordanance survey map of Ketterings surrounding area to see how many towns have a frequent bus service to Kettering indicating that Kettering may be an important focal point to those towns. I also found out where most of the major superstores were in Kettering as I thought that most of them were built away from the town centre, which may suggest expansion.

> 66 A good, coherent introduction and explanation of methods 99

RESULTS OF DATA COLLECTION

In the next few lessons after we got back from Kettering we swapped our data with other groups, for data that we required. Then when we had all the data, we started to put it into some sort of order.

The first thing I tackled was the transects. There were 8 in all. I plotted them onto graph paper (Fig 3) and then used a key to show the building use, (for example, see Fig. 2).

A four storey building with a basement. The ground floor is a shop. The first floor is offices and the second and third floors are residential, probably flats.

Fig 2

> 66 Examples of some of the transects; originally drawn on graph paper by the student 99

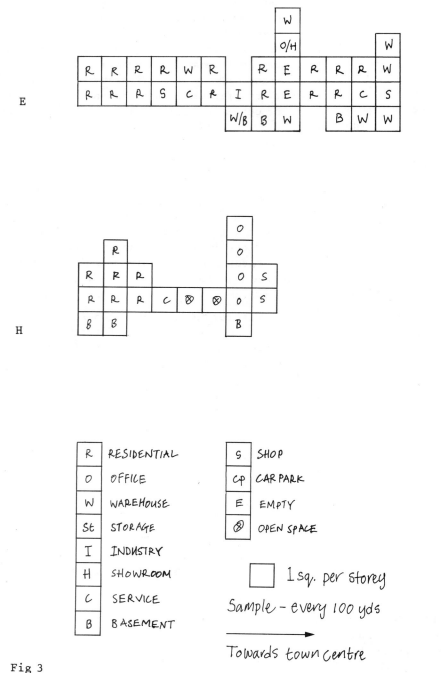

Fig 3

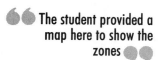

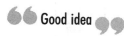
Once I had done that, I was able to draw up a zone map from the
transects. I made three zones, Residential, Mixed Use and
Shops/Services. Around the outside we have the residential area,
where the people live, inside that we have an area of mixed use, ie
shops, services, industrial and residential. Then in the centre, we
have the shops and services, the CBD (Central Business District),
this covers the area which I pinpointed to be the town centre, which
therefore backs up my theory.

After this I decided to take this line even further, down to which
streets made up the town centre, to do this, I required the
pedestrian counts. I drew them up using a scale of 1mm = 1 person.

Here the student provided evidence of her pedestrian counts

These showed that the streets with the most people in were Gold street and the High Street, this depicts a focal point, a lot of people going there. The next thing I did was look at the shopping surveys and the bus timetables to see who the people were who went to Kettering town centre.

Below are part of the results of two shopping surveys which show where people in Kettering town centre on a late Thursday afternoon come from.

WHERE DO YOU COME FROM?

Rothwell	Des	Thunderwood	Kettering
⌢⌢⌢ |||	⌢⌢⌢ /	||	⌢⌢⌢

This could have been presented in a clearer manner

Sample could have been larger

WHERE HAVE YOU COME FROM?
Kettering   ⌢⌢⌢ ⌢⌢⌢ ⌢⌢⌢ ||
Rothwell |||
Corby ||
Rushton   /
Loddington |
Scotland   \
Draughton   \
Wellingborough |

Most people came from Kettering, this shows that Kettering Town Centre is a focal point for the town, there were also people there from other places, mostly from Rothwell and Desborough.

I then looked at the bus timetables, and onto my traced map of the surrounding area I marked on the places which had a bus route to Kettering, and saw how frequent the buses were and whether they ran at weekends or Sundays. Most of the bus routes came from the north and north-east of Kettering, expecially the very frequent ones. I have put this down to the fact that Wellingborough is south of Kettering, and most people would go there instead. Most of the bus companies gave more services on a Saturday and the bus services were all much less frequent or non-existent on a Sunday. This shows that Kettering Town Centre is more of a focal point on a Saturday and is not a focal point on a Sunday.

Good idea

The next important thing was to find out why so many people went to the town centre, my theories were that there were a lot of large shops there, ie. giving varieties and also the prices in the shops would be lower as there would be competition between shops.

Firstly, I looked at my shopping surveys.

WHY DO YOU COME TO KETTERING?

Shopping	Entertainment	Other
⌢⌢⌢ ⌢⌢⌢	||||	
⌢⌢⌢			

```
WHY HAVE YOU COME TO KETTERING?
Work                      HHT III
Shopping                  HHT HHT
Services (eg. Bank)       HHT
College                   I
Visiting Relatives        I
```

The most common answer, by far, was shopping, followed by work. This
backed up my first part of my theory. Next I had to find out whether
there were a lot of large shops in Kettering Town Centre, ie. Chain
Stores. To do this I used economic survey 1, which shows where most
of the chain stores in Kettering are (fig. 4).

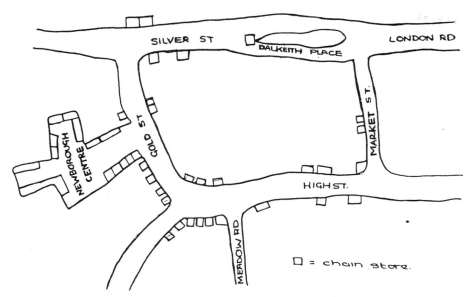

Could have named the stores

Fig 4

Why?

    As you can see, most of the chain stores are around Gold street and
the Newborough centre, which backs up my theory of where the town
centre is. So this shows that Kettering Town Centre has shops which
offer variety, but do they also offer competitive prices? To answer
this question, I looked at Economic survey 2, this dealt with
evidence of competition between shops.
    The people who conducted this survey found competition in shops,
Building societies and Chemist shops (see fig. 5 for details).

```
SHOP                      EVIDENCE OF COMPETITION
Curry's                   Hitachi TV  £449.99
Dixons                                £459.99
Timms                                 £479.99



BUILDING SOCIETY          Different interest rates
Lloyds
TSB

CHEMIST SHOPS
Superdrug                 Varying medicine prices
Boots
```

Fig 5

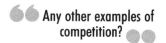

Any other examples of competition?

```
    Different prices for the same thing depict competition between
shops, and therefore lower and better prices.
    The final part of this investigation is whether or not Kettering
Town Centre is expanding, I looked to see if shops were being built
outside of the area, identified to be the town centre. I found a
number of shops that were.
    Do It All, B + Q/Comet and the CO-OP superstore have already
recently been built outside of the town centre. The new Sainsbury
superstore is nearing completion and an M.F.I. is being built up
near the hospital on the Rothwell Road.
    All of these are outside the town centre.
```

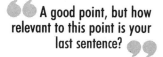

Student provided a map of the town centre showing the location of the superstores: DO IT ALL
MFI
B&Q/COMET
CO-OP
SAINSBURY'S

```
    As you can see from the map, the superstores are being built on
the North/North-east side of town, but whether or not this means
that the town centre is expanding is debatable. Another theory is
that because the superstores are big and well known, they do not have
to be sited in the town centre as people will travel to them anyway.
    This means that there rates will be lower as the further away from
the town centre you are, the lower your rates will be.
```

A good point, but how relevant to this point is your last sentence?

Fig. 3.21 An example of a student's work based on Kettering town centre.

Comment

This study begins with a hypothesis on the importance of the town centre and its expansion. It illustrates the importance of bringing together a range of research methods to produce the necessary evidence to prove or disprove the hypothesis, and also the importance of students working together in order to gather the necessary volume of information. In order to carry out this study the candidate has:

1   Considered what she thinks the town centre to be and where it may be expanding, using a base map.
2   Attempted to assess the accuracy of these ideas by:
    a) transects to identify building uses, enabling zone maps of land use to be drawn (residential, shops/services, etc.);
    b) pedestrian counts to identify the busiest points;
    c) economic surveys to locate chain stores, etc. and help define the town centre and possible area of expansion;
    d) surveys of shoppers to identify where people came from and so the area of influence of the town. (This was supported by a study of bus timetables, with the relevant OS maps, to identify the accessibility of the town centre by public transport.)
3   To consider the second half of the hypothesis the candidate again used economic surveys to look at competition between stores, and plotted on a base map the sites of new large stores and of those being built.

The first part of the hypothesis is well researched and convincingly established. The candidate's approach to an examination of whether the town centre is expanding is not as well covered. Additional surveys of shoppers' habits could have been made and consideration could have been given to whether the town centre was expanding or whether alternative and competing shopping centres were developing.

Rural transects

Rural transects can be used to record:

- **Crops**
  Make sure that you can identify the main legumes, root crops and cereals. Try to distinguish between different types of grassland – rough grazing, permanent pasture, ley, etc.

- **Soil**
  Sample soil from your transect could be described in terms of its colour, texture, whether it is fine, coarse, smooth, etc. and its water content, etc. Soil profiles could be examined and soil samples could be removed for acidity tests. From your findings the quality of the soil could be related to, for example, slope and altitude, or they could be used in a study of the ways in which people alter and affect topsoil.

- **Relief**
  The relief of each field – that is, is it flat, a steep slope or a gentle slope, etc. This can be described generally or more accurately in degrees with the aid of a clinometer. You should also give the direction of the slope – for example, slopes away from the road, towards road, etc.

- **Buildings and field walls, etc.**
  This might involve noting the age, building materials, etc. of the various buildings and field walls.

Rural transects can be used to examine the extent to which land use can be related to features such as soil and slope, or to suggest the presence of other factors: examples of the way farming activities can modify the rural environment; change in land-use patterns, when transects are compared to older land use maps, etc. Transects of valleys can be used to test the relationship between height of land, aspect, vegetation and temperature, or to consider the implications of any of these for housing, etc.

Vegetation sampling can be used to examine the effects of trampling alongside a path as a transect of, for example, a woodland reserve. This could be used as part of a study which examines the management of rural reserves and the dilemmas surrounding the relationship between access and conservation.

Hedgerows along a field transect could also be dated, by identifying the number of shrub species, using the formula one shrub to every 100 years. This could lead to the identification of features of the historical landscape.

Fig. 3.22 A rural transect.

KEY:	Buildings etc.	Relief	Soil	Crop	Length of field (Paces) ▼ ▼		Crop	Soil	Relief	Buildings etc.
Relief – F: flat G: gentle slope St: steep slope		St NE SW	C g	Cl	16 wire fence	16 wire fence	P	C g		
Soil – C: clay S: sandy g: grey y: yellow b: brown bl: black/dark brown		G NE to SW	F	K	25 CANAL	25	O	C g	F	Old Barn? – stone walls (no roof) derelict
Crop – W: Wheat R: Rye B: Barley Cl: Clover K: Kale O: Oilseed Rape P: Permanent Grass M: Miscellaneous	Public footpath along side of hedge.	F	S b	C/ S b	33 Hedge	17 Hedge	O	C/ S b	F	
	Farmhouse brick; slate roof. 2 large outbuildings.	O	S b	P	11 Hedge	24 Hedge	K	C/ S b	G NE to SW	Footpath running alongside of hedge.

Start:...

Grid Ref:...

In studying the environment you may wish to ask questions about its quality: what people feel about places and what features and amenities they value highly. When recording your observations on the quality of the environment, you are not recording something which is immediately visible. You must first list the sorts of things the presence or absence of which you feel are indications of the quality of the environment you are studying: for example, litter, broken and cracked windows, noise, parked cars, missing roof tiles/slates, peeling paint, graffiti, etc. You can investigate the presence of these using a scale of points along an urban or a rural transect. An example for an urban transect might be:

	Severe 1	Marked 2	Some 3	Little 4	None 5
Litter					
Broken/cracked windows					
Noise					
Parked cars					
Missing roof tiles/slates					
Peeling paint					
Graffiti					

The score along your transect will give you some indication of the quality of the environment in different parts of the town.

14 OBSERVING AND RECORDING PEOPLE

Observing people, looking at how they behave, listening to what they say and making careful records can be used to gain a wide range of information. By observing people in their 'natural setting', at work, shopping, going about their leisure activities, etc., you are seeing them as they really are and not just relying on what they say they do. People take a lot of their day-to-day activities for granted and may not think something important enough to mention. Observation can help us to focus on these activities and highlight them, providing data that the straightforward questioning of people about what they do might not fully capture.

Observation, as a method of information-gathering in the Humanities, involves:

- understanding clearly what you are looking for;
- devising a method for adequately recording the information you are looking for.

To prepare for your observation, try going through the following stages:

1 What is the purpose of your research? How will observation help you?

2 What sort of behaviour is going to be observed? How are you going to recognise it?

3 How is the behaviour going to be classified? What system are you going to use to record it?

4 Where are you going to observe? Do you require a map or diagram? Is it going to be important to show where people are, as well as what they are doing?

5 Over what period of time is the observation going to take place? Remember that if you are going to compare a number of periods of observation, they should last for the same duration.

Fig. 3.23 The observation process.

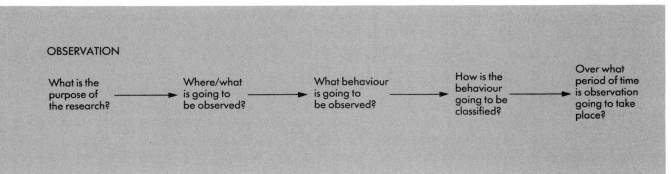

OBSERVATION SCHEDULE

If you follow these steps you will end up with an *observation schedule* – a list of things you are going to look for and a system for recording what you see. Your observation schedule will vary according to the behaviour you want to observe. Where you are looking for straightforward behaviour, such as the number of pedestrians passing at different points in order to establish where the busiest part of town is, then your observation schedule will be simple – a space to tick every pedestrian that passes you within a predetermined period of time.

Pedestrian Count – Abington Street, Outside Our Price Records.						
Date + Time / Direction	Tuesday 9.30–9.40	Tuesday 11.00–11.10	Tuesday 12.30–12.40	Saturday 9.30–9.40	Saturday 11.00–11.10	Saturday 12.30–12.40
Walking towards the market sq.	⊞⊞ ⊞⊞ I 11	⊞⊞ ⊞⊞ ⊞⊞ ⊞⊞ ⊞⊞ 11 27	⊞⊞ ⊞⊞ ⊞⊞ ⊞⊞ ⊞⊞ ⊞⊞ I 31	⊞⊞ ⊞⊞ ⊞⊞ 11 17	⊞⊞ ⊞⊞ ⊞⊞ ⊞⊞ ⊞⊞ ⊞⊞ ⊞⊞ I 36	⊞⊞ ⊞⊞ ⊞⊞ ⊞⊞ ⊞⊞ ⊞⊞ ⊞⊞ ⊞⊞ III 43
Walking towards the monument	⊞⊞ ⊞⊞ ⊞⊞ ⊞⊞ III 23	⊞⊞ ⊞⊞ ⊞⊞ IIII 19	⊞⊞ ⊞⊞ ⊞⊞ ⊞⊞ IIII 24	⊞⊞ ⊞⊞ ⊞⊞ IIII 19	⊞⊞ ⊞⊞ ⊞⊞ ⊞⊞ ⊞⊞ ⊞⊞ 30	⊞⊞ ⊞⊞ ⊞⊞ ⊞⊞ ⊞⊞ ⊞⊞ ⊞⊞ I 36
Totals walking in both directions	34	46	55	36	66	79

Fig. 3.24 An example of a pedestrian count.

The greater the variety of behaviour you wish to observe, the more sophisticated your observation schedule. For example, in an observation of leisure activities in a park, your questions could be:

- What are the range of leisure activities which take place in the park?
- Are there age differences in the types of activities which take place?

Key: Active – formal activities/sports: football, cricket, ball games, etc.
       Active – informal activities, involving movement, etc. but no visible rules to game.
       Non-active – sitting, sunbathing, picnicking, reading, etc.

ACTIVITY	under 10	11–20	21–60	over 60
Active formal Active informal Non active				

Sometimes it may be more relevant and convenient to record your observations in diagrammatic forms: for example, in research into gender differences in pupil play recreation.

TITLE OF STUDY: Gender difference in pupil play/recreation.

WHERE OBSERVATION CARRIED OUT: playground in secondary school (lower school).

WHAT IS BEING OBSERVED: Types of activity/interaction amongst pupils.

HOW OBSERVATIONS RECORDED: Plan of pupil distribution. key O = girl   □ = boy. N = non-active. T = active team games. Gt = active small group games.

TIME OBSERVED: 15 minutes (general impression)

Fig. 3.25 a) The notes for a playground observation.

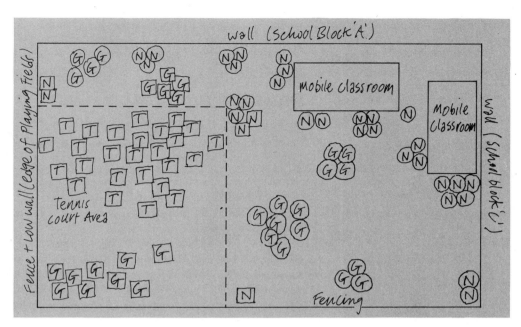

Fig. 3.25 b) The playground observation plan.

When you are constructing an observation schedule it is important that you have a category for all the different types of behaviour you are interested in. Sometimes this can lead you into producing quite long and complicated lists: for example, in research into teacher discipline in a fourth-year Humanities lesson, where your aim is to see if girls and boys are treated by teachers in the same way.

Classification for observation of classroom discipline

1. Teacher asks pupil not to talk, move, chew, etc. _____
2. Teacher tells pupil, quietly not to talk, etc. _____
3. Teacher raises voice to tell pupil off. _____
4. Teacher shouts loudly at pupil. _____
5. Teacher moves pupil to another seat. _____
6. Teacher makes pupil stand. _____
7. Teacher sends pupil out of room to corridor. _____
8. Teacher sends pupil to year tutor. _____
9. Teacher sends pupil to Head of Lower School. _____

10. Teacher gives pupil extra work. _____
11. Teacher gives pupil lines. _____
12. Teacher puts pupil on report. _____
13. Teacher keeps pupil behind after lesson. _____
14. Teacher gives pupil detention. _____
15. Other. _____

Key:

M = individual male   MG = male group
F = individual female   FG = female group
W = whole class   X = mixed group

Fig. 3.26 A classification for classroom-discipline observation.

VISITS

Where your observation is to take place during a *visit* to, for example, a workplace, a community centre, a council meeting, etc., your observation schedule should consist of a list of general areas that you are interested in and a series of points or questions to remind you of the sorts of things you are looking for, plus space to make your general observations and impressions.

Example: visit to a day centre

Where your observation is going to take place over a period of time in which you are going to be involved in a place or job (for example, a community placement work experience or pupil exchange with another school), it will be more convenient to begin with a list of what you want to find out and what you are going to look for, and then record your observations and experiences, as well as your feelings and responses to the environment of your work experience, etc., in the form of a diary, which you can consult and analyse later.

Visit to a day centre for the handicapped — Observation Schedule

1. **physical surroundings:** — Is the building big enough for its purposes? — condition of the building — e.g. well-decorated, comfortable, etc. — are there gardens?

2. **Facilities/Equipment:** — What evidence can you find of alterations, specially designed equipment, etc.? — are there sports facilities? refreshments?

3. **Staffing etc.:** — how many staff are there? Male/Female? — are there any other able-bodied people helping? how many? Male/Female? — Can you see any evidence that the centre offers advice to the handicapped? about what issues?

4. **Activity:** — What activities are people involved in? — are they working/playing in groups? — is there any evidence of organised social activities? what sorts? When?

5. **Other issues:** — What evidence can you find of transport arrangements? etc.

Fig. 3.27 An observation schedule from a visit to a day centre for the handicapped.

Styles of observation

Observation is usually seen as belonging to one of two types:

- direct observation, where you look at a situation as a visitor or outsider who is not part of the event, scene, etc. which is being observed;
- participant observation, where you join in with or are part of the situation you are observing.

Participant observation has the advantage that, being part of the group, you will have a clearer insight into what is going on. You may, however, find it difficult to be objective in your observations if you are too involved with a group.

The type of situation you can use for an observational study is almost endless. Apart from the more obvious, you could consider your own and your class's reactions to a role-play or simulation which is relevant to your study, or an observational study of people's reactions to everyday situations such as queuing or being in a job centre or the reactions of different groups of people to street buskers, etc.

STUDENT'S WORK BASED ON OBSERVING PEOPLE

Survey of public reaction to Street Busker

Subject: pavement artist (chalk picture)
Location: High Street (market place end)
Time: Saturday morning, between 11 a.m. and 11.20 a.m.

Pedestrians walking past	Pedestrians pausing to look:	Age Range	Giving money	Any other reaction or comment
⊥⊥⊥	f	t	–	
⊤⊤⊤	f + f	m+c	✓	mother talked to child about the picture
⊥⊥⊥	m + f	t	–	
⊤⊤⊤⊤	f + f + m	m + 2c	–	little girl wanted to give money but mum said no
⊤⊤⊤	m	P	✓	talked to artist + said it was very good.

‖‖‖	f + f	2p	✓	stood & talked — one gave money.
‖‖‖	f	m	✓	
‖‖‖	f + m	m	—	man put his hand in pocket but wife said "come on".
‖‖‖	f + f + f	2t + c	—	one said something then they laughed & went.
‖‖‖	f + m	m	✓	girlfriend (wife?) gave money.
‖‖‖	m + m	2m	—	pulled face.
‖‖‖ ‖	f + m	m + c	✓	mother gave coin to child to give to artist.
	f	m	—	stood watching — artist looked at her & she walked off (embarrassed).
64 walked past without stopping	f + m + f + m	4t	—	said how good it was.
	f + m	2p	—	talked to each other & old man told artist to "carry on the good work".
	m	t	—	
	m + m	m + c	✓	man lifted little boy up to see it better.

m = male	c = child	✓ = yes
f = female	t = teenager	— = no
	m = 20-60	
	p = over 60	

Conclusions

Out of the seventeen people or groups of people who stopped to look at the street artist only seven gave any money to him. As the tables show, five of those giving money were female. None of the teenagers who stopped gave any money, and a group of three girls laughed. This could show that teenagers aren't as generous as older people, but it might be because they have less money to give away. Five of the groups that stopped included young children, and in four cases it seemed that the adults stopped to let the children watch the artist. Three of these groups gave the street artist money. Only five people over sixty stopped, and all of them looked very interested. The first elderly person to stop gave money and talked to the man. Following him, two elderly women stopped, one of which gave some money. The last two, a couple, didn't give money, but the gentleman talked to the artist.

From this observation I found that women over twenty were the most likely to stop and give money, and that teenagers were the least likely to give money. I also found that older people were most likely to be friendly and talk to the artist. I had expected some people to complain about the artist being in the way, especially as his picture was quite large and there were people stopping and standing watching, but I didn't hear any complaints at all, even though there were a lot of people walking in that area. I was also surprised at the number of people who walked by without stopping, but perhaps this was because the street artist had been there before.

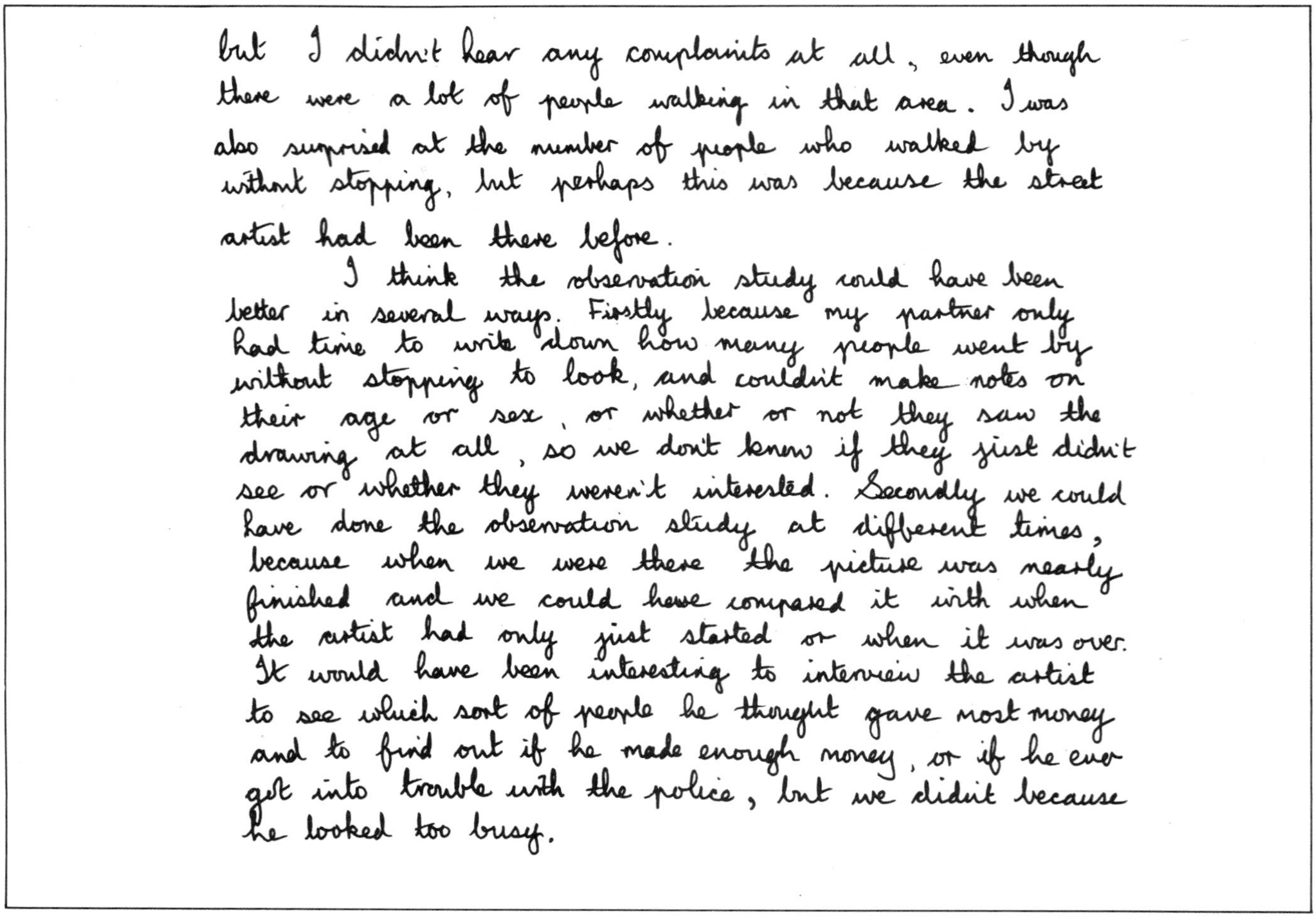

I think the observation study could have been better in several ways. Firstly because my partner only had time to write down how many people went by without stopping to look, and couldn't make notes on their age or sex, or whether or not they saw the drawing at all, so we don't know if they just didn't see or whether they weren't interested. Secondly we could have done the observation study at different times, because when we were there the picture was nearly finished and we could have compared it with when the artist had only just started or when it was over. It would have been interesting to interview the artist to see which sort of people he thought gave most money and to find out if he made enough money, or if he ever got into trouble with the police, but we didn't because he looked too busy.

Fig. 3.28 An example of a student's work: A survey of public reaction to a street busker.

Comment

An imaginative idea for a piece of research, it demonstrates a systematic approach to the collection and recording of information and illustrates one of the many uses of observation. As a piece of research, its major weakness is the lack of other observations with which it could have been compared, such as observations at different times or at different locations. Using other research methods – for example, interviews with the artist, street questionnaires with passers-by – would provide for a more detailed enquiry.

Analysing your results

How you go about analysing your results will depend, of course, on what you have observed and how you have gone about recording it. Where your observations have been about noting particular, easily identifiable aspects of behaviour, your analysis will involve adding up your results under their various headings, making comparisons and reaching conclusions. Where your observations have produced some sometimes lengthy notes describing what you have seen, your task will be more difficult. Try to organise your notes under a number of headings and summarise your notes, giving particular examples where you can.

ASKING QUESTIONS: QUESTIONNAIRES

A *questionnaire* is a list of questions. They can be sent through the post or given to people for them to fill in, and then returned or collected, or they can be completed by you if you read the questions to people and note their answers. Questionnaires are a convenient method for collecting a relatively large amount of information from people. If the information is to be of any use for your enquiry, you must be careful to make sure that:

■ you give some thought as to whom you want to collect information from – that is, the categories of people you want to include in your sample – and how you intend to contact them;

- the questions are really asking for the information you want;
- the questions are clear and will be easily understood;
- the answers you record will be in a form which you can use easily.

Types of question

There are two types of question:

- **Closed questions**

  This is where answers are given for the respondent to select from by ticking a box, etc. Closed questions make it easy for you to collect your information and so are particularly useful for collecting information through quota sampling and street interviews. Closed questions have the advantage of being straightforward to analyse, as the results can be easily added together. Care must be taken to ensure that if you are using closed questions, you provide enough possible answers to enable all your respondents to reply as they wish. Closed questionnaires are useful if you wish to produce statistics and graphs from your questionnaire.

- **Open questions**

  This is where you do not provide answers to be chosen from but simply provide a few lines for the respondent to write down their own answer.

      Example: Do you think Britain should continue to build nuclear reactors? Why/why not? Please give reasons for your answer.

  Open questions are useful if you want your respondents to give more detail in their answers and to express opinions. They have the great advantage of enabling people to reply in their own words, but the disadvantage is that replies are more difficult to compare and to analyse.

Problems with questionnaires

'Don't you agree that people should not be allowed to kill foxes for fun?'

This is a leading question: the wording encourages respondents to give a particular answer.

'Where did you go on holiday last year?'

This is a presuming question: the question presumes that the respondents had a holiday last year.

'Do you think that smoking is bad for your health and should be banned in public places?'

This is a double question: the respondent may agree with the first part but not with the second.

'Do you support unilateral disarmament?'

The question assumes that all respondents will understand unilateral.

'How old are you? Under 21, 21–30, 30–40, over 40.'

There is an unclear choice of answers here: which box should thirty-year-olds tick.?

'How often do you go to the cinema? Regularly, occasionally, hardly ever?'

These answers are unclear: the words regularly and occasionally could mean different things to different people.

Questionnaire checklist

- Are you sure that the respondents you are going to approach will be a representative sample?
- Does your questionnaire allow for any factual information you will need: for example, sex of respondent, etc.?
- Are your questions clear and easily understood?
- Are your answers clear and will your respondents be able to select one of them?
- When you are writing your questions think about how easy it will be to analyse and present the results you obtain.
- Before you start using your questionnaire it may be advisable to try it out on a few people first to check for any problems.

STUDENT'S WORK BASED ON USE OF QUESTIONNAIRE

66 A well thought out sample. 99

66 A good example of a testable hypothesis 99

THE VIEWS OF THE GENERAL PUBLIC

A survey was conducted to get a cross section of the communites opinions of nuclear power. Out of a sample of twenty, I decided that there would be six categories in which the sample of twenty people could be placed. They were, 1) male, 2) female, 3) adults, 4) students, 5) people who live in Shepshed, and 6) people who live in other towns or villages.

The questions I asked were:-

Question 1: Could you name any types of nuclear reactors?

Question 2: Could you name any ways in which nuclear waste is stored?

Question 3: Do you think that the Chernobyl disaster could have been prevented?

Question 4: Do you think that there is still radiation from Chernobyl around? Do you think we should have nuclear power stations in Britain?

Question 5: Do you think we should have nuclear power stations in Britain?

I asked the questions 1 and 2 as I wanted to find out whether the public knew anything about the nuclear power stations in this country or elsewhere in the world and also whether they remembered any of the publicity of Nirex's case to obtain land which was in the news recently. I also wanted to know whether British Nuclear Fuels statement which said that there was a failure in communications with the public over this matter was true. I asked questions 3 and 4 as I wanted to find out what the publics opinion was after a major disaster and whether they took any notice of newspaper reports, television and radio broadcasts. Lastly I asked question 5 to find out (after the Chernobyl disaster) whether the public thought it was still a good idea to have a nuclear power station in this country.

The following tables show the answers that I received for the five questions used in my survey.

SOCIAL SURVEY ON _Nuclear Power_ BY _____ DATE _30/6/89_ SAMPLE SIZE _20_ SHEET NO. [ ]

NUMBER IN SAMPLE	1	2	3	4	5	6	7	8	9	10	11	12	13	14	15	16	17	18	19	20	TOTAL
INITIALS	SR	BH	SR	H.T	K.Y	M.S	P.B	M.H	I.B	P.B	M.G	D.H	V.R	J.G	M.Y	CS	CH	CR	VR	CR	
AGE	M.A	M.A	MA	M.A	M.A	15	15	15	14	15	MA	MA	MA	MA	MA	15	15	14	15	15	
SEX	M	M	M	M	M	M	M	M	M	M	f	f	f	f	f	f	f	F	F	F	
TOWN OR VILLAGE LIVED IN	C	CD	S	S	S	CD	S	K	S	K	S	CD	S	R	S	CD	S	C.D	CD	S	
SOCIAL CLASS: MIDDLE OR WORKING CLASS																					
QUESTION 1 Could you name any types of nuclear reactors?	N	Y	Y	N	N	Y	N	Y	Y	Y	N	N	Y	N	N	Y	N	N	Y	Y	Yes=10 No=10
2 Could you name any ways in which nuclear waste is stored?	Y	Y	Y	Y	Y	Y	N	Y	Y	Y	Y	Y	Y	N	N	Y	Y	Y	Y	Y	Yes=17 No=3
3 Do you think that the Chernobyl disaster could have been prevented?	D.K	Y	Y	Y	Y	D.K	Y	Y	Y	Y	Y	Y	Y	Y	Y	Y	D.k	D.k	Y	D.K Y	Yes=15 D.K=5
4 Do you think that there is still radiation from chernobyl around?	D.K	Y	Y	Y	Y	Y	Y	Y	Y	Y	Y	Y	Y	Y	N	Y	Y	Y	Y	Y	Yes= No= D.k=
5 Do you think that we should have nuclear power stations in Britain?	N	Y	Y	Y	Y	Y	Y	N	Y	N	Y	Y	Y	U	Y	Y	N	N	N	Y	Yes=13 No=6 U=1

Key Y= Yes   N= No   M.A = Middle Aged
D.K/U = Don't know/Undecided

Question 1: Could you name any types of nuclear reactors?

	Total	Total %	Male	Female	Adults	Students	Shepshed	Other towns & villages
Yes	10	50	6 / 60%	4 / 40%	3 / 30%	7 / 70%	4 / 40%	6 / 60%
No	10	50	4 / 40%	6 / 60%	7 / 70%	3 / 30%	6 / 60%	4 / 40%
Don't know	0	0	0 / 0%	0 / 0%	0 / 0%	0 / 0%	0 / 0%	0 / 0%
Totals	20	100	10 / 100%	10 / 100%	10 / 100%	10 / 100%	10 / 100%	10 / 100%

Question 2: Could you name any ways in which nuclear waste is stored?

	Total	Total %	Male	Female	Adults	Students	Shepshed	Other towns & villages
Yes	17	85	9 / 90%	8 / 80%	8 / 80%	9 / 90%	9 / 90%	8 / 80%
No	3	15	1 / 10%	2 / 20%	2 / 20%	1 / 10%	1 / 10%	2 / 20%
Don't know	0	0	0 / 0%	0 / 0%	0 / 0%	0 / 0%	0 / 0%	0 / 0%
Totals	20	100	10 / 100%	10 / 100%	10 / 100%	10 / 100%	10 / 100%	10 / 100%

66 Results clearly presented for comparison 99

Question 3: Do you think that the Chernobyl disaster could have been prevented?

	Total	Total %	Male	Female	Adults	Students	Shepshed	Other towns & villages
Yes	15	75	8 / 80%	7 / 70%	9 / 90%	6 / 60%	9 / 90%	6 / 60%
No	0	0	0 / 0%	0 / 0%	0 / 0%	0 / 0%	0 / 0%	0 / 0%
Don't know	5	25	2 / 20%	3 / 30%	1 / 10%	4 / 40%	1 / 10%	4 / 40%
Totals	20	100	10 / 100%	10 / 100%	10 / 100%	10 / 100%	10 / 100%	10 / 100%

Question 4: Do you think that there is still radiation from Chernobyl around? Do you think we should have nuclear power stations in Britain?

	Total	Total %	Male	Female	Adults	Students	Shepshed	Other towns & villages
Yes	18	90	9 / 90%	9 / 90%	8 / 80%	10 / 100%	10 / 100%	8 / 80%
No	1	5	0 / 0%	1 / 10%	1 / 10%	0 / 0%	0 / 0%	1 / 10%
Don't know	1	5	1 / 10%	0 / 0%	1 / 10%	0 / 0%	0 / 0%	1 / 10%
Totals	20	100	10 / 100%	10 / 100%	10 / 100%	10 / 100%	10 / 100%	10 / 100%

Question 5: Do you think we should have nuclear power stations in Britain?

	Total	Total %	Male	Female	Adults	Students	Shepshed	Other towns & villages
Yes	13	65	7 / 70%	6 / 60%	8 / 80%	5 / 50%	6 / 60%	7 / 70%
No	6	30	3 / 30%	3 / 30%	1 / 10%	5 / 50%	3 / 30%	3 / 30%
Don't know	1	5	0 / 0%	1 / 10%	1 / 10%	0 / 0%	1 / 10%	0 / 0%
Totals	20	100	10 / 100%	10 / 100%	10 / 100%	10 / 100%	10 / 100%	10 / 100%

CONCLUSION
RE SURVEY RESULTS.
Question 1: Could you name any types of nuclear reactors?

The percentages for the above question were the same for both answers (yes and no 50%). This proves that half of the sample in the survey had either read about it in the newspapers or had watched the television when this topic had been in the news. More males (60%) knew about the nuclear reactors than females. This might have been because women are not as interested in the nuclear reactors as men. A greater number of students (70%) knew about the reactors than adults. This may have been as the younger generation have been brought up with nuclear power. People who lived in towns and villages (60%) other than Shepshed knew more about the reactors than Shepshed people. This is probably because the majority of the village people live near to a coal-fired power station.

Question 2: Could you name any ways in which nuclear waste is stored?

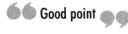

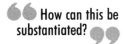

The percentage for this question differed, 85% answered that they knew how Nirex buried nuclear waste. This contrary to the British Nuclear Fuels statement "BNF have failed to communicate with the general public in order to make them aware of waste disposal". On the other hand, the public are probably now more aware of waste disposal due to the publicity given to Fulbeck in Lincolnshire where Nirex tried to commence work on a disposal site but was prevented from reaching the site by protesting residents. The survey also showed that more males (90%) knew about the ways in which the waste is stored than females. This again is probably because men are more interested in this topic than females. A greater number of students (90%) knew about the ways in which waste is stored than adults. This may have been because the younger generation is more aware of the disposal sites as they will have to live with it for a longer time. A larger percentage of people who live in Shepshed (90%) knew more about the waste than other people who live in towns or villages.

Question 3: Do you think that the Chernobyl disaster could have been prevented?

Most of the people that were interviewed thought that the Chernobyl disaster could have been prevented (75%) but 25% of the sample were not sure. I think that the 25% of the sample were undecided as the Chernobyl disaster was of a very large scale. A greater proportion of males thought that the disaster could have been prevented (80%) but 70% of the women also thought that the disaster should not have happened. I think that the people who answered 'yes' to the above question realised that the operators who were conducting the experiments were at fault. Most of the adults (90%) thought that the disaster could have been prevented. This may have been because the older generation were more worried about the contamination released and took more notice of reports given by the media than did the younger people. A larger percentage of Shepshed residents interviewed thought that the disaster could have been prevented (90%) than others interviewed outside Shepshed. The Shepshed residents interviewed seemed to be more interested/concerned in the effects of Chernobyl.

Question 4: Do you think that there is still radiation around from Chernobyl?

90% of the people who took part in the survey thought that there was still radiation in the environment. I think this is because they have heard about the radiation from television debates and have also read about it in the newspapers. The percentage of males and females who thought that there was still radiation around was the same (90%). All students interviewed thought that there was still radiation about (100%). 80% of the adult group surveyed also thought that there was radiation in the environment, but there was also 10% that were not sure. 100% of the people who lived in Shepshed thought there was still radiation around whereas only 80% of the people who live in villages thought that there was still radiation. This may have been because Shepshed residents might have been more worried about the cloud which formed after the Chernobyl incident and this is probably the reason why 100% thought there was still radiation around.

Question 5: Do you think that we should have nuclear power stations in Britain?

65% of the people interviewed thought that it was still a good idea to have nuclear power stations in Britain. 30% of the people interviewed did not wish to have nuclear power stations and 5% was undecided. I think that the 65% group probably thought that since fossil fuels will not last for many more decades nuclear power, which is efficient and cheap, should replace it. The 30% group interviewed probably thought that since large scale accidents can happen in nuclear power stations there should be an alternative, such as hydro-electric power or solar generated electricity. The 5% group probably thought that nuclear energy was of a good idea but the safety standards should be greatly improved and waste disposal sites would have to be better planned.

7% of males thought that we should have nuclear power whereas only 60% of women thought nuclear power was acceptable. I think this is because women worry about the dangers of radiation more than men. A larger percentage of adults (80%) thought that we should have nuclear power whereas the students were undecided, as 50% answered 'yes' to the question and 50% answered 'no'. I think the students were split in this question due to the fact that they will most probably have to live with nuclear power longer than the older generation. 70% of the people in villages other than Shepshed thought that we should have nuclear power whereas 60% of the people who live in Shepshed thought that we should have nuclear power.

❝ Good. ❞

❝ What reasons can be put forward for this? ❞

❝ The suggestions given for the results go beyond the available evidence. Further questions could have been designed to test these ❞

Fig. 3.29 An example of a student's work: The views of the general public on nuclear power.

Comment

This is an excellent piece of work. There is a clear statement about the categories included in the sample and the aims of the questions. The questions are clearly stated and the findings are presented in a comprehensive and easy-to-understand manner. There is a good attempt to analyse the results in terms of the sample, to discuss the relationships between the findings and to suggest explanations and reasons.

INTERVIEWING

Interviews are conversation with a purpose, ways in which information about a person or subject can be gained through face-to-face questioning and answering. There are a number of reasons why you may want to collect information through interviews:

- To obtain more detailed information on a subject than you can get through a questionnaire.
- To obtain information from an 'expert' – someone whose position or job means that their views and knowledge can be particularly important to your research: for example, an interview with a headteacher in research about the organisation and running of schools; a police officer in a study of local crime; a member of the local council or planning department in a study of the issues involved in a local development project, etc.
- To obtain oral histories. If you wish to obtain information about the history of an area, an institution or a particular period, if may be important to allow respondents to speak in their own words, to allow them to give sufficient details and to talk about events which you may have known nothing about when you begin your research.

Contacting respondents

Make sure you contact your respondents before the interview and give them an idea about what you are doing, the sorts of questions you want to ask and the length of time it will probably take. Ensure that you have their agreement to take part and that you have a time and a place for the interview. The people you contact will depend on what the purpose of your research is. Make sure that your respondents are suitable and that they are able to provide you with the information you want. Remember that if you wish to interview 'experts' or anyone whose time is valuable, you will have to give them a good deal of notice in order to allow them to find a suitable time. If you are collecting oral histories, then a useful starting point could be the social services day centres and homes for the elderly, or your own school's parent-teachers association.

Asking questions

Interviews vary from formal interviews, in which most of the questions are written down and simply read to the interviewee, to more informal interviews, in which the interviewer starts with a list of general points to be covered, allows time for respondents to develop their answers, and is more flexible than in a formal interview. Whichever type of interview you think is most suitable, to make the most effective use of the time you have available it is essential that you are well prepared for it and have studied any background material and prepared the sorts of questions you want to ask. Your list of questions, or interview schedule, is best arranged first by making a list of all the factual questions you think will be

```
      Purpose: To find out why males/females opt for different subjects

      Closed questions: Age: ................... Sex: .......................
                        Which subjects did you opt for? ...................
                        .................................................
      Main areas:

      1. What sorts of advice were you given about subject choice?

         Related questions: What advice was given by parents?
                                                       teachers?
                                                       careers teachers?

      2. What did/didn't you like about the subjects you did/didn't take?

         Related questions: What was the teachers' attitudes  to you?
                            What sorts of skills did the subject concentrate
                            on?
                            What sorts of activities went on in the classroom?
                            What did your parents feel about the subject?
                            How do you think your friends felt about the
                            subject?
                            What sorts of problems did you have with the
                            work?

      3. What sorts of future careers do you think the subjects are suitable
         for?

      - Complete related questions
```

Fig. 3.30 a) Interview with 4th Year students

```
          Closed questions: Age ...........
          Sex: ........... Town/Village: ....................................

          Main areas:

          1. School life

              Related questions - what subjects did you do?
                                  did you take any examinations?
                                  what sort of punishments were used in your
                                  school? etc.

          2. Home life

              Related questions - did your parents work?
                                  how many brothers/sisters did you have?
                                  what sort of jobs did you have to do around the
                                  house?
                                  how did you pass your time in the evenings, etc.

          3. Leisure/entertainment

              Related questions - how often did you go out? where to?
                                  what sorts of entertainments did you prefer?
                                  how much did they cost? etc.
```

Fig 3.30 b) Oral History interview –
What was life like for a young
person sixty years ago?

of use to you: for example, age, sex, occupation, position, etc. Secondly, make a list of the general areas which you wish to cover in your interview and think of a question you can use to introduce each area. Finally, under the heading for each general area, make a list of questions related to each one. Make sure that none of your questions, apart from those designed to obtain factual information, can be answered by one word answers such as 'yes' or 'no', so that they are invitations to your respondents to explain and describe. Figs. 3.30 a) and b) show examples of interview schedules.

During the interview

- Be prepared for the interviewee to move from topic to topic; don't be constrained by the order in which you have listed the questions.

- Use your list as a checklist to ensure that all the areas you want the interviewee to talk about have been covered.

- Take care about the way in which you ask questions; avoid giving your own opinions and views. Interviewers can, by their choice of words and even expressions, influence what the interviewee says.

- Make sure that you are prepared to ask people to clarify questions and statements you are not sure of, and to steer them away from areas you feel are not relevant to your research. The following list gives some examples of phrases which you will be able to use in controlling the course of the interview:

  - Is it really?   Checking for exaggeration,
  - Why?   contradictions and inconsistencies.
  - Yes, but didn't you just say. . .?

  - What do you mean by. . .?   Clarification.
  - Could you give some examples?

  - Do you believe. . . ?   Searching for opinions.
  - What do you think of. . . ?

  - Do you mean. . . ?   Putting things another way.
  - In other words. . . ?

  - Someone else might say. . .   Playing devil's advocate.

Recording your interview

Making notes and writing down answers is effective only in a fairly formal interview. You will find it difficult to record responses fast enough in a more flexible and wide-ranging, informal setting and keep track of the conversation at the same time, unless you can take someone with you to help with note-taking. Making a tape recording of your interview will be a more convenient method of retaining the information. Make sure first that you know how to operate the tape recorder and that the recording will be audible. Remember that background noise or an inappropriately placed microphone will result in an unusable recording. It is advisable to make a short test recording first and play it back to check that the recording level is suitable. Always make sure that you have first asked the interviewee's permission to make a recording.

Using the interview

Collecting the interview material is only your first step. What you have recorded needs to be related to the area you are researching. The next move is to find out what sorts of information you have. It is unlikely that you will have the time to transcribe the whole tape. Make up a list of headings, listen to the tape a few times, and make notes and quotes from the interview. What you do with the information depends on the sort of interview you have conducted and its purpose. If your interview was aimed at collecting an oral history, you should try to transcribe longer extracts under broad headings. If you have conducted a number of interviews, then your extracts can be briefer, illustrating some of their comments, and your notes and quotations from each interview can be compared, looking for similarities and differences. In your final write-up of your interviews they should include the questions you asked, how and why you contacted the respondents, and any observations you made during the course of the interview which you think are relevant.

Fig. 3.31 The interview process.

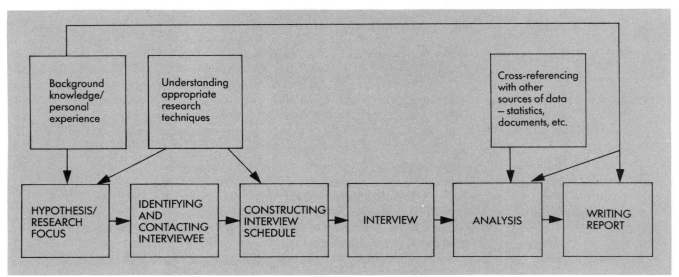

<table>
<tr><td>Background knowledge/ personal experience</td><td>Understanding appropriate research techniques</td><td></td><td>Cross-referencing with other sources of data – statistics, documents, etc.</td></tr>
</table>

HYPOTHESIS/ RESEARCH FOCUS → IDENTIFYING AND CONTACTING INTERVIEWEE → CONSTRUCTING INTERVIEW SCHEDULE → INTERVIEW → ANALYSIS → WRITING REPORT

15 ▷ WHICH METHODS SHOULD YOU USE?

Whatever your research question is you should be able to produce a lengthy list of possible sources of information. For example, if your research area is Conservation and the Environment, and your research question is *'Is There Conflict Between the Conservation of the Environment and the Use of the Environment for Leisure Activities?'*, possible sources of information would be:

- libraries, for relevant books and periodicals for background information;
- organisations – contact national groups such as the Friends of the Earth, the Council for the Protection of Rural England, the Town and Country Planning Association, the Council for Environmental Conservation, the National Trust, the Forestry Commission, the National Parks Commission; local organisations and bodies such as the local planning department; local voluntary organisations such as trusts for nature conservation, wild life trusts, etc.;
- historical information – old maps, local documents, etc.;
- contemporary maps, for a study of access to conservation areas from urban areas;
- observational study of visitors to country park, nature reserve, etc.;
- visitor count at the above, and questionnaires to discover where people come from, frequency of visits, etc.;
- vegetation sampling to discover damage along pathways in conservation areas, litter counts, etc.;
- interviews with wardens of country parks, representatives of wild life trusts, planning departments, etc.;
- literature – stories, poems, etc. on the importance of the environment and the dangers facing it.

The sources you select will depend on the topic you wish to research and the sort of research questions you set. Different sources will obviously require different approaches and it is important that you understand clearly the techniques and limitations associated with the different ones. Remember that different approaches will produce different types of information, which can be used for different purposes. Some will provide you with relatively large amounts of straightforward information: for example, secondary statistical information, questionnaires distributed to a large sample, a traffic or pedestrian survey, etc. Others will produce more detailed information from a smaller number of people, a case study of one place or organisation, etc.

It is important that your enquiry should contain more than one method of enquiry. Using a variety of methods will enable you to:

- examine the relationships between more than one source of information where each type requires a different method – for example, the influence of stereotypes portrayed by the mass media would require a content analysis of the media to discover the extent of, say, the stereotyped portrayal of women, and questionnaires/ interviews to discover public reactions and attitudes; to examine the relationship between pedestrian density and the type of shop or service available would require information from pedestrian-flow and density surveys, and mapping the shops and services within a given area;

- look at a case from different points of view – for example, your observations of a workplace could be completed with interviews with personnel;

- add different dimensions to your research – for example, observations of a village, small town, etc. will be complemented by a document study to provide information about its history and growth, etc.

Using a variety of methods will provide you with a variety of data, help you to demonstrate your ability to use methods of enquiry and provide you with a more balanced and detailed study.

16 > WRITING YOUR CONCLUSION

What you do with the information you have gathered will depend on the sorts of tasks and questions you set yourself at the start of your enquiry. If you began with a clearly defined hypothesis, or a series of research questions, then you must reconsider them and, using the evidence you have obtained, either provide answers or confirm or reject the hypothesis. Where your enquiry has been of a more general nature – for example, to trace the growth of a town, village, etc., or to describe an organisation or the lifestyle of a particular group – you will have been discussing and commenting upon the results of your enquiry as you uncovered the information and built up your study. In this case at the end of your work you will need to focus on the main features of your study and highlight any important findings. Make sure that:

- any conclusions you draw from your work are clearly related to the results of your research;

- you are prepared to compare your results with other studies you have access to in a similar area. Are they the same as yours or different?

- you attempt to explain your results. The information you have gathered will help you to answer the questions you set yourself at the start of your work. Now you need to give some thought to why you think your information has given you these answers. This will involve thought and imagination and will draw on your background knowledge of your topic;

- you don't claim too much from the results of your research. It is unlikely that you will be able to collect information on a large number of places or people from a large sample, so you should be cautious about claiming that what you have found out about one case or group of people would hold for others. Be cautious about making claims that one thing you have been studying causes another. You can be sure about making such a claim only if you are certain that there are no other possible factors which could also have had an influence. This is particularly true when studying the behaviour of people. It is almost impossible to itemise and separate all the possible influences on people and so to be sure that one has a greater effect than others;

- you describe honestly what went wrong with your research. It is inevitable that you will make mistakes, and being able to identify them will demonstrate your

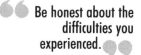
Be honest about the difficulties you experienced.

understanding of the process of enquiry. Were the methods you used successful? Should you have tried a different approach? Did you allow enough time for the different stages of your work? Were the questions you started with adequate? etc.

```
'Women in the Media'
CONCLUSION... (TO THE SUBJECT UNDER STUDY)
  When reading the newspaper, watching the television or glancing
through a magazine one just doesn't realise to what degree we are
being bombarded by sexism.
  We see hen-pecked housewives struggling to keep their whites
'whiter than white' and young ladies passively posing to please.
Although women's portrayal in the media IS improving still a great
amount of work has to be done before sexism is finally tamed. It will
be a hard job to beat the likes of 'The Sun' and 'Benny Hill' after
all why change a successfully proven formula?
  Personally I am against sexist images of women in the media. I feel
that society as a whole would benefit from seeing them abolished.
Many attitudes and predjuices connected with sexism in the media,
such as women being thought of as sex-objects and not capable of
leading a professional life in a 'mans world', could hopefully meet
their doom. I feel that the media is so impressionable some steps
must be taken to beat sexism before society is damged beyond
repair... many say it is already; I tend to agree with them.
  Until sexism is beaten society will continue to endure sexuality
and domesticity as a substitute for the REAL portrayal of women in the
media.

'Women in the Media'
CONCLUSION ... (TO THE PROJECT'S PRODUCTION PROGRESS).

  I am most satisfied with this my G.C.S.E. Personal Research Project in
'Women in the Media'. I found it both interesting and very enjoyable to
put together.
  I feel I have covered all of those points that I intended to cover in my
aims. Particularly difficult to find resources on I found was the
topic of the treatment of women by newspapers. I found no statistics
or written record on the subject. To overcome this problem I studied
a selection of newspapers and drew my own conclusions. The result
was the poster: 'What an alien would think about planet Earth if
reading a copy of the popular press.' I missed out any record of the
quality press and their handling of women but did draw this
conclusion; they too project images of women as sex and domestic
objects but their messages aren't so 'crude' and obvious as the
popular press.
  I found that many of the resources I used were biased. The most
biased, I found, were text books. They reinforced views as well as
facts. I tried to make my views as non-apparent as possible when
writing the project. My interview with Ruth Lewis was, I felt,
fairly biased. As my questions provoked opinion this was only to be
expected but one should realise that the interview only covered one
side of argements for women in the media.
  I used many types of research when putting the project together. I
used text books and magazine articles to draw statistics and to use
leads I could possibly follow using other means. Using examples from
the media I highlighted points as demonstrated by ads and the like. I
pulled examples from television, newspapers, general magazines,
women's magazines and even comics. Using interviews and surveys,
even at one stage a small observation study I researched opinion to
see if views supported the points laid down by my study. I wrote to
many organizations to see if they could pass on resources. This
proved to be both successful and unsuccessful.
```

> ```
>     I tried to put every aspect of the study in its own self contained
> unit but each aspect linked onto other. The imagery of women and the
> ideas behind this was the same for many areas. For example the sex-
> object implications of 'Page 3' link onto those of advertising. As
> women in the media have these as their two main images it was
> inevitable that this would happen.
>     All in all I can honestly say that I feel this study has been a
> success. I also feel that I have accomplished my overall aim which
> was to investigate all aspects of sex inequality associated with the
> portrayl of women in the media. As already said it was enjoyable to
> produce and as I'd hoped challenging yet rewarding too.
> ```

Fig. 3.32 An example of a student's work: the conclusion to a report on sexism in the media.

Comment

This conclusion summarises the enquiry well and the range of research techniques employed. It clearly draws attention to difficulties experienced during the interview and the problems of obtaining information. There is an attempt to connect the findings from different research methods and to generalise the conclusions to enable statements to be made on the media and sexism in general. The personal comment provided is useful but the conclusion would have benefited from a clearer restatement of the aims of the research, a more objective assessment of the results in relationship to the aims and comparison with any similar research.

17 ▷ PUTTING YOUR RESEARCH TOGETHER

❝❝ Present your work in a way which makes it easy to understand. ❞❞

Your enquiry must be presented in a manner which helps your teacher to understand what you have done, and helps to prove or disprove your hypothesis or answer your research questions. Avoid presenting your work as an undifferentiated mass. Make sure that it is broken down into separate sections or chapters, with headings which follow each other logically and help readers find their way around your work. Ensure that your information is presented in an appropriate format: for example, that statistics are presented in graphs, pie diagrams, etc. and are included in the relevant sections. (See Chapter 4.)

Your completed work should include the following:

- a contents page, in which you list the chapter/section headings;

- an introduction, in which you set out your hypothesis or research question(s), explain why you chose the topic and outline what you actually did;

- the subsequent chapters, which must be carefully planned and logically ordered. Make sure that the information you include is relevant to each section chapter. Your presentation should be clear and comprehensible, and should make use of, if possible, a variety of forms of presentation where appropriate, such as diagrams, maps, pictures, graphs, etc. Where you quote from any source – book, article, leaflet, etc. – make sure you say where it comes from;

- a conclusion, in which you present your findings, readdress your research question/ hypothesis in the light of your work, and attempt to explain your findings and outline the problems and limitations of your work;

- a log book, in which you record the stages of your work and copies of any letters sent, transcripts of interviews you have made, etc.;

- a bibliography, which is a list of all the books, articles, etc. you have used.

INTERPRETATION AND EVALUATION

GETTING STARTED

In this area of Integrated Humanities the examiner is interested in your ability to *use evidence* to *aid the understanding* of the particular issue or issues you are studying. You must demonstrate *three* main skills in this area:

1 You must show you can interpret, organise, compare and use evidence, making sure the evidence selected is *relevant* to the task set. Does it fit the purpose *for which it is being used?*

2 You must show your understanding about the *unreliability* of evidence and the possibility of bias in the presentation of evidence.

3 You must show you are able to draw a *reasoned conclusion* from the evidence available about the issue or issues under study.

These skills can be demonstrated either in assignments which target *one* particular aspect of the interpretation and evaluation of evidence, or in assignments which can be used to assess a student's ability in *all* aspects of the interpretation and evaluation of evidence.

ESSENTIAL PRINCIPLES

1 DIFFERENT TYPES OF EVIDENCE

It is possible to draw upon evidence from a wide variety of sources; the key is to select what is most appropriate to the issue or issues you are studying. The chart below shows some possible types of evidence available. Before starting your study look carefully through it and choose the types which will help you.

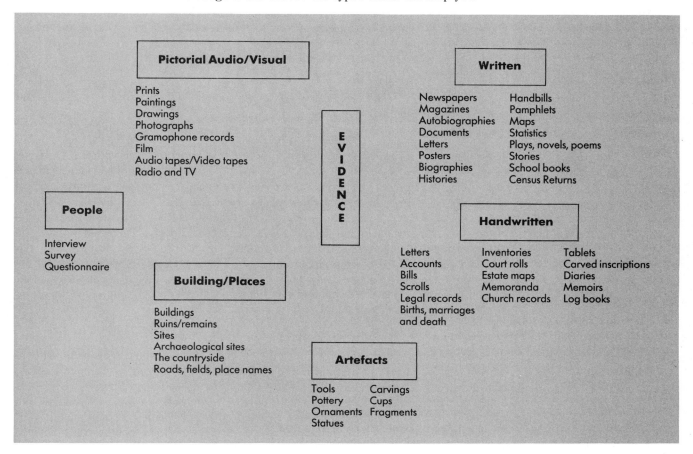

SOME KEY POINTS TO CONSIDER WHEN WORKING WITH EVIDENCE

❝❝ Some advice on working with evidence ❞❞

To assist in making the most of the evidence available for a particular study it is advisable to consider some systematic approach. What follows is a suggestion of how this might be done. It is intended only as a guideline: if another method seems more likely to get results, then obviously use that.

Stage One

Choose the evidence which will help you complete your study. Look at the section on 'Different Types of Evidence' above and decide what you need. Once you have decided, you may then have to work out how to get the evidence you require. This may involve carrying out your own enquiry; see Chapter 3 for guidance on this.

Stage Two

Having collected the evidence you require, question it.

❝❝ Question the evidence. Is it of use? ❞❞

- What does it say/show/present/demonstrate?
- Can I understand it?
- Who presented it?
- Under what circumstances was it presented?
- When was it presented?

At this stage you are attempting to understand the evidence. Before you can use it in the study you must understand it.

Stage Three

Examine *all* the evidence available. It is important not to make any decision without considering everything you can find out about the issue or issues under study. Not to do this will lead to inaccuracies.

Stage Four

Is it always the case that the more often evidence appears the more acceptable it becomes?

Sort the evidence. In many respects this is a continuation of the questioning of the evidence. The evidence available may present different viewpoints or interpretations. For each piece of evidence ask: How is it different from/similar to other evidence looked at? The weight of support for one particular viewpoint may well help you decide on its accuracy.

Stage Five

Judge the evidence. At this stage two main decisions have to be reached:

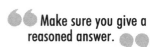

How reliable is the evidence? Can you accept it?

- How reliable is the evidence?
- Can it help me in – that is, is it relevant to – my task?

In assessing the reliability of the evidence a link will have to be made with the questions asked initially. One aspect which needs exploring is the background of the evidence. Has it been presented from any particular standpoint? For example, someone with firm political views is *likely* to present evidence from that perspective. This must obviously be taken into account when judging the evidence. Another point to be considered is the circumstances under which the evidence was presented. More guidance will be given on the assessment of evidence later in this chapter.

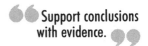

Do people or the mass media make their bias known?

Having examined the reliability of the evidence a decision as to its usefulness must be made. If the evidence examined *does not* help you to understand the issue or issues under study it is *worthless* and should not be used. What you choose to *leave out* can be important in gaining you credit in assessment.

Stage Six

Make sure you give a reasoned answer.

Support conclusions with evidence.

Use the evidence. Having moved through the previous stages it should now be possible to use the evidence to complete your study. It is important to present a reasoned answer. Indicate why you have adopted a particular standpoint or view. Support this with evidence. A balanced and therefore high-quality piece of work will include reasons why you have not only accepted a particular view but also rejected other possibilities. Again, support your conclusion with evidence. In the finished piece of work you must demonstrate that you have given detailed consideration to all the evidence you had access to.

2 ▷ RELIABILITY OF EVIDENCE

This book is biased!

One of the most important questions you will have to ask when working with evidence is whether it is *reliable*. In other words, is it accurate? Can it be accepted? Can it be used to support the answer to the issue under study? A few points have already been made on how you might assess the reliability of evidence; these will be developed in this chapter. Needless to say, all evidence you examine will show a certain bias or one-sidedness. This book is no exception. We have chosen to concentrate on this skill of assessing the reliability of evidence because we think it is important not only in your Integrated Humanities studies but also in everyday life. This is our particular 'bias'!

If you look at the list of types of evidence on page 113 you will realise it is impossible to discuss each one in detail. Therefore, we have chosen to examine types of evidence which are used quite often in Integrated Humanities assignments. However, the points made and the questions raised are applicable to most of the evidence you are likely to look at in your Integrated Humanities course.

3 ▷ USE AND MISUSE OF STATISTICS

Ask questions.

Statistics are widely used, especially in newspapers, on television and by politicians. They can be used to support a point of view; they can add weight to an argument; and they can be used to mislead rather than inform. In your assessment and interpretation of evidence you may be faced with statistics. What follows will help you to evaluate them.

The first stage is to *question* the production and presentation of the statistics. The finished statistical data will be the result of certain decisions made by the *statistician*, the person or persons responsible for putting the statistics together. This may include getting *primary* data from the public and will have involved making decisions such as:

- the design of the research;
- the sample to be investigated/surveyed/questioned;
- the method of research;
- the organisation and presentation of the collected data.

Look back to Chapter 3 at the information on Primary Research.

These points will need evaluating in deciding on the reliability of the data. The setting up of *Primary Research* has been explained in the chapter on enquiry and may be worth reading again at this point as it will help in your evaluation of statistics. Remember, statisticians are human and are capable both of making mistakes and of deliberate bias!

PRESENTATION OF DATA

Your work in maths and design will help here.

The way statisticians *present* the data collected may well affect the message they convey. In your role as the evaluator of the evidence you must be aware of some of the ways presentation can mislead. Here are some examples:

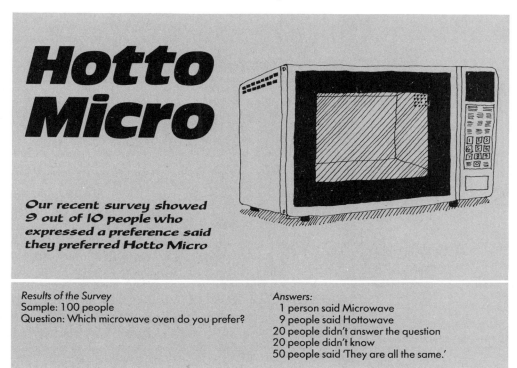

Fig. 4.1 Advertising bill board: Hotto Microwave ovens.

Have the findings in this survey been distorted?

Season 1987–88	Wolverhampton Wanderers	Tottenham Hotspur
League Games Won	27	12
League Games Drawn	9	11
League Games Lost	10	17
League Goals Scored	82	51
Goals Against	43	48
Attendance at Home Matches (compared with previous year)	+41%	+0.15%

Fig. 4.2

Which team was the most successful according to the figures in the table? Would you want any other information before making up your mind?

In both examples you have to consider whether an accurate picture has been presented. Has all the *relevant* information been included? In the case of the football teams, has a comparison been made between *like and like*? For the football team comparison here is

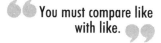

You must compare like with like.

some other information which may influence your decision on which was the most successful team:

- In 1987–8 Wolverhampton Wanderers played 46 games in Division Four of the Football League; Tottenham Hotspur played 40 games in Division One.
- For Tottenham Hotspur average home attendance was 25,921 in 1987–8 (25,851 in the previous season); for Wolverhampton Wanderers average home crowds were 9,854 in 1987–8, compared with 5,754 in the previous year.

Is it relevant to compare football teams from different divisions? Can a Division Four football team be considered 'better' than a First Division team because it has won more league games?

Misleading impressions can be created by comparing things which are not similar. You must be aware of *this possibility* when evaluating statistics as evidence.

Look at this other example:

School leavers GCSE and GCE results		
TYPE OF SCHOOL	% of leavers who got five or more GCSE passes Grades A–C	% of leavers who got two A-levels
Maintained Grammar School	64.5	38.2
Comprehensive Schools	15.5	8.7
Public Schools	69.2	40.3

Fig. 4.3 Table of GCSE and GCE results.

From this set of statistics it seems obvious that the results in comprehensive schools are much worse than those in the other types of school, but is this comparison a fair one? Are the three types of school similar? Has a comparison been made between *like and like*? Faced with a table of statistics like this you would have to *reconstruct the background* to what is being compared. If you did this you would find that grammar schools accept only students who can show an already high level of academic ability; they refuse to take other children into the school. It isn't surprising, therefore, that their results are 'better' than those of comprehensive schools, which must accept students with wide-ranging abilities. Most public schools also exclude children who appear to have little chance of passing GCSE or 'A' levels. They do this by setting an entrance examination.

Consequently, the table above is not comparing like with like. By *reconstructing the background to the evidence*, the apparent clarity of the point made by the statistics is challenged. More will be mentioned later about reconstructing the background to evidence.

So, remember to look out for statistics which *do not* compare *like with like*. They can give results which are unreliable.

Reconstruct the background to the evidence.

VISUAL REPRESENTATION OF STATISTICS

Take care when statistics are presented as graphs.

There are times when statistics are presented as *graphs*. In evaluating this form of presentation you must be aware of how it can mislead. Visual presentation of statistics can lead to many optical illusions! Your work in maths and design will help you here.

Look carefully at the three different presentations of the same sales figures for breakfast cereals. Which graph would you choose to publish if you wanted to show people your company was doing well?

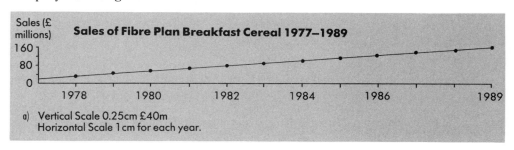

a) Vertical Scale 0.25cm £40m
Horizontal Scale 1cm for each year.

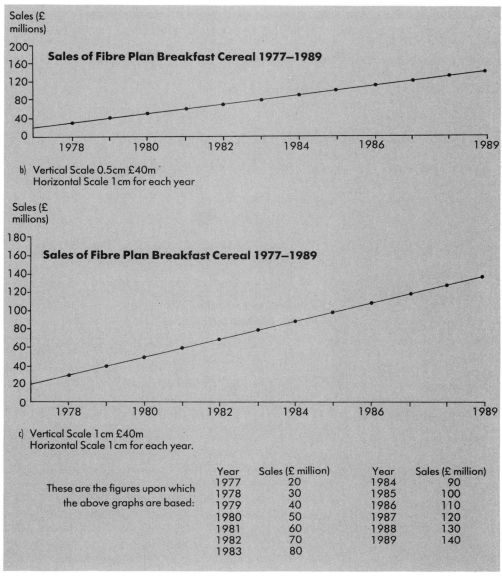

Year	Sales (£ million)	Year	Sales (£ million)
1977	20	1984	90
1978	30	1985	100
1979	40	1986	110
1980	50	1987	120
1981	60	1988	130
1982	70	1989	140
1983	80		

These are the figures upon which the above graphs are based:

Fig. 4.4 Sales of Fibre Plan breakfast cereal 1977–89.

Now look at this example. How successful is the garage at selling cars?

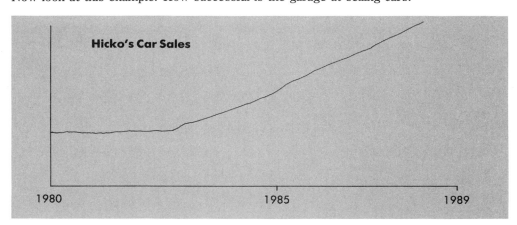

Fig. 4.5 Hicko's car sales.

What do you notice about this example? Well done! You spotted the error; this graph has no *scale*! Consequently, it could represent anything, either a massive increase in car sales over the period of time shown or a much smaller increase.

In the two examples given, the importance of *questioning* the evidence is re-emphasised. When faced with statistics in graph form, questions should be raised about the scale used on the graph. From this, you would go on to question further the evidence before making an assessment as to its usefulness. One such question could be about when the *starting point* or *base year* for the graph was. The decision about which year to start drawing the graph could make a crucial difference to its 'meaning'.

> **Ask questions of the evidence.**

> **What is the base year of the graph?**

The following example illustrates this point:

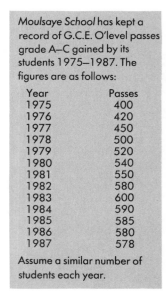

Moulsaye School has kept a record of G.C.E. O'level passes grade A–C gained by its students 1975–1987. The figures are as follows:

Year	Passes
1975	400
1976	420
1977	450
1978	500
1979	520
1980	540
1981	550
1982	580
1983	600
1984	590
1985	585
1986	580
1987	578

Assume a similar number of students each year.

Fig. 4.6 Table of GCE 'O' level results.

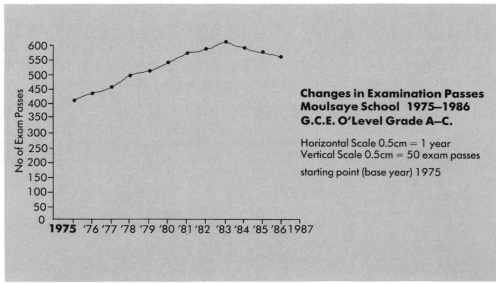

Fig. 4.7 Graph of exam passes 1975–86.

Now look at the graph below produced by a governor of Moulsaye School who wants to show the rest of the school governing body that standards have fallen at the school.

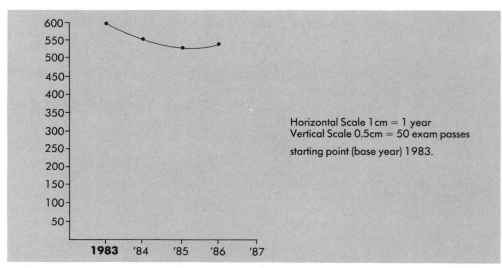

Fig. 4.8 Graph of exam passes 1983–7.

The governor has selected his starting point (*base year*) where it will best support his point of view. This gives quite a different meaning from the overall picture of examination passes at the school as represented in the first graph.

The choice of base year or starting point is also important when statisticians talk about *percentage changes*. The head teacher at Moulsaye School might want to compare students' performances in 1987 and 1975.

66 Your work in maths and design will help again here. 99

$$\frac{\text{Difference between 1975 and 1987 passes } [578 - 400]}{\text{Number of passes in 1975}} = \frac{178}{400} \times \frac{100}{1}$$

$$= \frac{178}{4} = 44.5\%$$

There has been an *increase* of 44.5% in the number of examination passes since 1975.

In choosing a different base year, what is the percentage change in examination passes between 1983 and 1987?

$$\frac{\text{Difference between 1983 and 1987 passes } [578 - 600]}{\text{Number of passes in 1983}} = \frac{-22}{600} \times \frac{100}{1}$$

$$= \frac{-22}{6} = -3.6\%$$

Since 1983 there has been a *decrease* of 3.6% in the number of examination passes. This result is probably the one the governor would use to support his view that standards are falling at Moulsaye School.

Averages can also be misleading and care must be taken when using them as evidence. *As with all evidence, they key is to question them.*

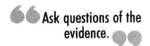 **How are averages worked out?**

Averages are commonly used in discussions of what people earn. Often quoted is the average weekly wage. Recent statistics have suggested that this is £220 per week. This gives the impression that *most people* are comfortably off. Is this a realistic impression? Within this calculation could be workers who earn £100 per week and others who earn in excess of £500 per week. Obviously, the question to ask when faced with an average like this is what were the *lowest* and *highest* wages included in the calculations?

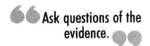 **How accurate are averages?**

When calculating the *mean average* it is an important rule that only similar totals should be used; in this way the mean average will be *representative* of the set of totals.

For example: 7, 8, 9, 8, 8, 7, 9, 9, 7
Mean Average: 8

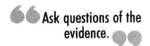 **Again, your work in maths will help here.**

However, if one total is much higher or lower, it could lead to a mean average which is *unrepresentative* of the set of totals.

For example: 3, 4, 5, 3, 4, 4, 15, 3, 4
Mean Average: 5

Percentages (%) can also mislead and need to be used carefully. Look at this example about wage negotiations:

Fig. 4.9

Is this wage increase 'fair and reasonable'?

Look at the figures below. How much money has been gained from the 5% wage increase? What has happened to the gap between the assistant cleaner's wage and that of the managing director?

	Assistant Cleaner	Managing Director	Wage Gap
Present wage per year	£6,000	£30,000	£24,000
New wage with 5% increase	£6,300	£31,500	£25,200

Clearly, it is important to look at the *original figures* before being 'convinced' by percentages.

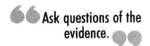 **Ask questions of the evidence.**

It is hoped that this section has raised your awareness of how to use statistics. Like all evidence, they have to be *questioned*. Although we have concentrated so far on the misuse of statistics, it is not our intention to put you off using them. Far from it. Statistics can be invaluable in studying a variety of issues. Our aim is simply to point out some of the pitfalls involved.

USING CENSUS INFORMATION

Gathering facts and figures to find out about the conditions of society has been going on for centuries. The Doomsday Book is an example which immediately springs to mind. In Britain, a survey of the entire population is carried out every ten years by the government. This survey is known as the *census*. Efforts are made to contact all householders in Britain so that information about every person is gathered. The first census was in 1801 and the most recent in 1981. The personal information on the *enumerators' returns* must remain secret for 100 years. The 1981 returns will not be released until after the year 2081. However, the results of the 1981 census are available now in the form of statistics. This means that the answers to all the questions have been collected together; the totals are given in numbers. These results are available for the whole country, for each county, and for small areas.

THE NATIONAL CENSUS

This is a copy of part of a government publicity leaflet about the 1981 Census.

Fig. 4.10 Part of the government publicity leaflet for the 1981 census.

In strict confidence

1981 Census England

H Form for Private Households

A household comprises **either** one person living alone **or** a group of persons (who may or may not be related) living at the same address with common housekeeping. Persons staying temporarily with the household are included.

To the Head or Joint Heads or members of the Household

Please complete this census form and have it ready to be collected by the census enumerator for your area. He or she will call for the form on **Monday 6 April 1981** or soon after. If you are not sure how to complete any of the entries on the form, the enumerator will be glad to help you when he calls. He will also need to check that you have filled in all the entries.

This census is being held in accordance with a decision made by Parliament. The leaflet headed 'Census 1981' describes why it is necessary and how the information will be used. Completion of this form is compulsory under the Census Act 1920. If you refuse to complete it, or if you give false information, you may have to pay a fine of up to £50.

Your replies will be treated in STRICT CONFIDENCE. They will be used to produce statistics but your name and address will NOT be fed into the census computer. After the census, the forms will be locked away for 100 years before they are passed to the Public Record Office.

If any member of the household who is age 16 or over does not wish you or other members of the household to see his or her personal information, then please ask the enumerator for an extra form and an envelope. The enumerator will then explain how to proceed.

When you have completed the form, please sign the declaration in Panel C on the last page.

A R THATCHER
Registrar General

Office of Population Censuses and Surveys
PO Box 200 Portsmouth PO2 8HH
Telephone 0329-42511

Please answer questions H1 - H5 about your household's accommodation, check the answer in Panel A, answer questions 1-16 overleaf and Panel B on the back page. Where boxes are provided please answer by putting a tick against the answer which applies. For example, if the answer to the marital status question is 'Single', tick box 1 thus:

Please use ink or ballpoint pen.   1 ☑ Single

Fig. 4.11 Front cover of 1981 census.

Look at this copy of the front cover of the 1981 census. Great importance is placed on the accurate completion of this survey, to such an extent that fines are imposed if false information is given.

Once information has been gathered it is studied by government civil servants, who are able to detect changes in the condition of the British population. Information is then passed

H3   Amenities

Has your household the use of the following amenities on these premises? Please tick the appropriate boxes.

- A fixed bath or shower permanently connected to a water supply and a waste pipe

1 ☐ YES – for use only by this household

2 ☐ YES – for use also by another household

3 ☐ NO fixed bath or shower

- A flush toilet (WC) with entrance inside the building

1 ☐ YES – for use only by this household

2 ☐ YES – for use also by another household

3 ☐ NO inside flush toilet (WC)

- A flush toilet (WC) with entrance outside the building

1 ☐ YES – for use only by this household

2 ☐ YES – for use also by another household

3 ☐ NO outside flush toilet (WC)

14   Address of place of work

Please give the full address of the person's place of work.

For a person employed on a site for a long period give the address of the site.

For a person not working regularly at one place who reports daily to a depot or other fixed address, give that address.

For a person not reporting daily to a fixed address tick box 1.
For a person working mainly at home tick box 2.

15   Daily journey to work

Please tick the appropriate box to show how the longest part, by distance, of the person's daily journey to work is normally made.

For a person using different means of transport on different days show the means most often used.

Car or van includes three-wheeled cars and motor caravans.

Full address and postcode of workplace
Address (BLOCK CAPITALS please)

....

....

including Postcode ☐☐☐☐▨☐

1 ☐ No fixed place
2 ☐ Mainly at home

1 ☐ British Rail train
2 ☐ Underground, tube, metro, etc
3 ☐ Bus, minibus or coach (public or private)
4 ☐ Motor cycle, scooter, moped
5 ☐ Car or van — pool, sharing driving
6 ☐ Car or van — driver
7 ☐ Car or van — passenger
8 ☐ Pedal cycle
9 ☐ On foot
0 ☐ Other (please specify)

....

0 ☐ Works mainly at home

Fig. 4.12 Questions from the 1981 census.

 Who uses census data? on to local councils, government departments, universities and others who can make use of the information. Books of census material are put together and made available to the public, which means you!

The National Census is the major example of a statistical survey in Britain. The cost of administering the survey, the time taken to formulate the questions and the importance placed on completing it accurately mean the results of the survey are more likely to be reliable and can be used in a variety of ways. As a source of evidence for you, they can be invaluable.

USING ORIGINAL CENSUS DOCUMENTS

One of the difficulties in using original census material from a century ago is that all the enumerators' returns were handwritten, usually in the Victorian 'copperplate' style. This

How to understand census documents

can make them difficult to read. Also, to shorten the task of writing down the required information, the enumerator sometimes used abbreviations, again making understanding difficult.

To help you use original census material here are some guidelines about the information available on the documents and some notes about the most common abbreviations used.

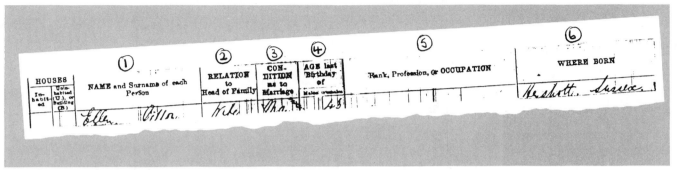

Fig. 4.13 An extract from the 1881 census showing the enumerator's headings.

1   *Name and surname of each person*
This column will contain the names of all the people who took part in the census. The information in this column is most useful when trying to trace family history. It can also be used for a survey of forenames. Which were the most popular at the time of the census?

2   *Relation to head of family*
The title 'head' was usually given to the father or husband of the family. However, an unmarried woman with her own house, or a widow, would be the head of her household. This column gives the relation of each person to the head of the household and can be used to examine family size by counting the number of people in each family. If anyone else was staying in the house then the words 'lodger', 'visitor' or 'servant' may appear in the column.

3   *Condition as to marriage*
This column tells whether the person was married, unmarried, widow or widower.

4   *Age last birthday of males/females*
The ages for males and females are given in two separate columns and are usually given in years only, but in the case of a young baby age may be shown in 'months' or 'days'.

What jobs did people have?

5   *Rank, profession, or occupation*
The word 'rank' means if someone had a title, such as Earl, Lady or Lord, it would be entered in this column. However, the main function of this column is to record the types of jobs or occupations people had at the time of the census. This is very useful and can show the occupational structure of a particular community.

6   *Where born*
This is another useful piece of information for tracing family history. This column shows where people were born and identifies those born in the local area and those who had come from outside the locality. It usually states the village, town or city and the county of birth, though sometimes only the county is given.

This is a list of the most common abbreviations used by the enumerators. They can also be seen in Fig. 4.14.

Watch out for abbreviations.

Daut ⎫
       ⎬ – Daughter
Dau ⎭

Gr. Daut ⎫
          ⎬ – Granddaughter
Gr. Dau ⎭

Serv – Servant

Widr – Widower

Mar – Married

'Do' or '– do –' both mean
'the same as above'

Unm – Unmarried

USING CENSUS MATERIAL

In the explanation of the enumerators' form it was mentioned how an enquiry into family history could be improved by using census material. However, this is not the only usage of such evidence. There are various investigations which would benefit from census information as evidence. Here are a few examples:

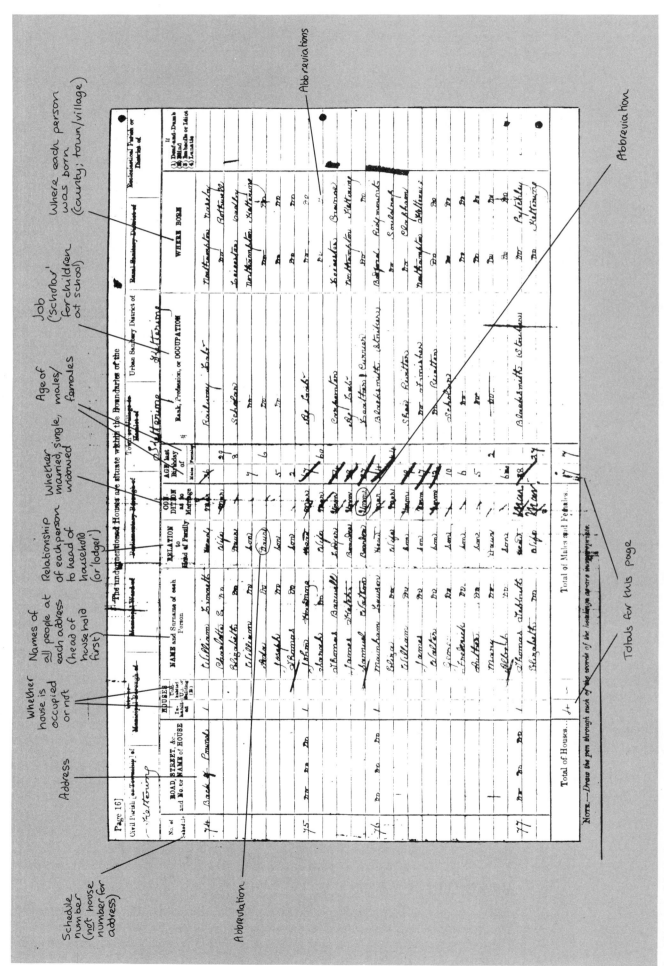

Fig. 4.14 A page of the 1881 census, showing abbreviations.

■ Birthplaces and occupations

The census can be used to investigate the birthplaces of people living in a chosen community. It should be possible to identify from the column titled '*Where born*' those people who were born in the chosen area, in the same county as the chosen area, or in other parts of the country. From this information the extent of *migration* into the chosen area could be identified. By looking at the '*Rank, profession and occupation*' column an explanation for the migration might be suggested. It may be that the chosen area had become associated with a particular industry and people had moved into the area seeking employment.

> **A study of migration in a particular area could use census material.**

■ Family size

The census should provide information about the size of families. A comparison could be made between family size in the nineteenth and twentieth centuries to see whether the size of families had remained the same, increased or decreased. This evidence could be used with other evidence to create a picture of family life in the nineteenth century compared with family life today.

> **Has family size changed?**

■ Children at school or at work?

This investigation involves identifying those children who went to school (indicated as scholars in the '*Occupation*' column) and those who did not. By studying several census returns it may be possible to detect an increase in the number of children going to school. In an attempt to explain these changes further evidence, such as government legislation and the changing attitudes of people towards education, would need examining. Where census returns indicated a great number of children working an analysis of their occupations and their ages could help create a picture of child labour in the nineteenth century. However, to get a more accurate view of child labour during this period an assessment of other relevant evidence is required.

Statistics – key points

This section has hopefully given you some idea of how statistics can be used, or misused. As with all evidence, you must *ask questions* of the statistics you use and evaluate them: will they help you answer the issue or issues under study and are they reliable? Above all else, make sure they are *used* with *all the other* available evidence in the study.

> **Ask questions.**

This checklist may help you when dealing with statistics as evidence:

- Who collected the statistics? When and how were they collected? Are they reliable? Have they been collected accurately? Make sure they are not estimates, guesses, or invented.

- Are the statistics complete or a sample of all the possible statistics available?

- How have the statistics been presented? Why are they presented in this way? Has any crucial information been left out of the presentation? Be careful with visual presentations.

- How have the statistics been used? Are they used only to support the view of the person who selected them? Are the statistics used to support a statement which may be biased?

- If averages or percentages are used, do they mean anything? How were they calculated?

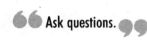

4 ▶ PICTURES AND PHOTOGRAPHS AS EVIDENCE

Pictures can be valuable sources of evidence for many investigations. They can tell a lot about the attitudes of people – how they live or lived, work or worked, enjoyed themselves – and about major events that have taken place, but like all sources of evidence they have to be *evaluated*. The main problem with pictures as evidence is the uncertainty about whether the picture created by the artist actually portrays real things. Sometimes artists sketched pictures to make something look more attractive than it really was. Other artists drew the same topic to make it look more dreadful. Pictures can represent the particular bias of the artist or of the people who had asked for the picture to be drawn. For example, artists who drew battlescenes often did so from the point of view of the participating armies. As a result the drawing would reflect that point of view. Also, we cannot always be certain that the pictures we see were actually drawn or printed on the spot, or even that they were based on sketches made in the field. Some illustrations were based on newspaper reports or eye witness accounts and thus reflected that point of view. Many detailed and life-like pictures were 'imagined' by the artist in the studio.

> **Pictures nowadays usually mean photographs, but before photographs there were only paintings and drawings.**

> **Pictures can be biased.**

Look at the drawings below. All are about factory life in the mid-nineteenth century. Can you spot any differences?

a)

c)

b)

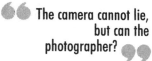

Fig. 4.15

PHOTOGRAPHS

> The camera cannot lie,
> but can the
> photographer?

It is sometimes said, 'The camera cannot lie', but how far does a photograph accurately represent reality? Most photographers carefully select the best viewpoints for their photographs. It is the photographer not the camera who decides what to photograph, so the scenes captured on film may reflect the bias of the photographer and support preconceived ideas. The *camera* cannot lie, but the photographer can. Photographs can be altered to improve the appearance of the people shown in the picture, or to black out something which spoils the view.

Pictures and photographs – key points

As with the section on statistics, the intention here is to point out some of the problems involved in using pictures and photographs as evidence. Being aware of these could act as a starting point for the evaluation of the type of evidence. These checklists may also help:

Pictures

- Is the picture realistic or is it a cartoon or caricature?
- What does the picture show?
- When was the picture drawn?

- Why was the picture drawn or printed? Is it part of a news item? Is it an illustration for a book or pamphlet? Has it been drawn or painted to make you want to protest? Is it designed to raise emotions (anger, pity, sadness, patriotism, etc.)?
- Is there any indication that this is a picture from the imagination of the artist?
- If it is a cartoon, what is it about? What does it tell about the point of view of the artist or where it was published?

Photographs

- What does the photograph show?
- When and where was the photograph taken?
- Why was the photograph taken? Is the photograph designed to portray a point of view about the subject?
- Is it a *posed photograph?* If it is, does this affect the value of the photograph as evidence?
- Does the photograph reflect the reality of the situation? Has it been *altered?* Has a particular scene been chosen to reflect a preconceived view?

EXAMPLES OF STUDENT ASSIGNMENTS

❝❝ Selecting the right evidence is the key. ❞❞

As already stated on page 113 there is a wide variety of evidence available. The key to a successful assignment in this area of Integrated Humanities is to *select* the appropriate evidence for the issue under study.

Rather than continue to analyse individual types of evidence, a task which would take many more pages, we propose to look at some popular topics of study chosen by students for assessment in this area. Needless to say, many of the principles already highlighted in the evaluation of statistics, pictures and photographs are applicable to the other types of evidence.

❝❝ Be original in your choice of issues to study. You could get credit for this. ❞❞

It is impossible to include every topic of study requiring the evaluation and interpretation of evidence. What follows are some examples of common topics selected by students for assessment in this area. However, these are not the only topics acceptable to the examination boards. Don't be afraid to come up with your own original topics; you may get credit simply for being 'original'.

Historical 'Mysteries'

❝❝ Historical mysteries are popular assignment topics for students. ❞❞

A study of the past will undoubtedly lead to differences of opinion about the reasons for events and actions that occurred. The very nature of historical investigation encourages the evaluation and interpretation of evidence. This has led to many controversies, with people holding different opinions about what really happened. Virtually any study of a particular period will uncover such differences in viewpoint. Some of these have captured the pubic imagination and have consequently become very well known. These popular historical 'mysteries' have proved a good area of study for students wishing to demonstrate their interpretation and evaluation skills.

Examples of these mysteries are:

- the mystery of the *Mary Celeste*;
- What happened to the Romanovs?;
- the curse of Tutankhamen;
- the Gunpowder Plot – a plot to kill or a plan to catch?;
- the mystery of the two Princes in the Tower.

As an indication of how students might approach these mysteries, what follows is a detailed look at the *mystery of the two Princes in the Tower.*

Background to the Mystery

On the 9 April 1483 King Edward IV died, leaving a widow, several daughters and two sons, Prince Edward, aged twelve, and Prince Richard, aged ten. Prince Edward, as the eldest son, should have succeeded his father as King. However, because Edward was young, his father had stated in his will that Richard, Duke of Gloucester, the boys' uncle, should become the Protector of Prince Edward and help him to govern until he was old enough to rule alone. On July 6 1483 the Duke of Gloucester was crowned King Richard III and after this date the two Princes were never seen again. What happened to them? This is the question students have to try and answer. Over the years, as this mystery became popular, a wealth of evidence was uncovered concerning the events. This is one such piece of evidence:

What happened to the two Princes?

After his coronation in July 1483, King Richard went to Gloucester and there he decided that he must kill his nephews, for as long as they were alive, people would not think him the true King. So he sent a letter to Sir Robert Brackenbury, Constable of the Tower, asking him to put the Princes to death. Robert refused and Richard was angry, wondering who on earth he could trust to do this murder. His Page suggested Sir James Tyrell who agreed. Brackenbury was ordered to hand over the keys of the Tower. Tyrell decided to murder the Princes in their beds and chose two men, Miles Forest and John Dighton to do the job. About midnight they entered the Princes chamber and they pressed the feather bed and pillows hard on the children's faces until they had stopped breathing. Tyrell was fetched and he had them buried at the foot of the stairs. Later, Richard had them re-buried at a secret place. This story is well known to be true, because when Tyrell was imprisoned in the Tower in 1502 for treason, he confessed that it was done as I have described.

Fig. 4.16 Sir Thomas More's evidence.

More has solved the mystery – or has he?

At first sight it seems that the mystery has been solved. According to Thomas More, in 1502 Sir James Tyrell confessed that:

- the Princes were suffocated by himself, Miles Forest and John Dighton, acting on the orders of Richard III, who wanted the Princes *murdered*;
- The motive was power, for while the Princes were alive the people of England would not accept Richard III as the true King.

What a good piece of evidence. The mystery is solved – or is it?

Question the evidence.

Remember, one of the first things to do when working with evidence is to *question it*. Don't take it on face value. What questions could be asked about this evidence? What about these:

- Who was Thomas More?
- What is the background to the evidence?
- What is *fact* and what is *opinion* in the evidence?
- Why did Tyrell confess in 1502, nineteen years after the event?

You may be able to think of more questions to ask.

Who had a motive to murder the Princes?

Thomas More gives a motive for the murder. Is this fact? Did Richard III confess and give this as his motive? Or is this motive only More's *opinion*? Here is some information about Thomas More. After reading this, how valuable is More's evidence?

Sir Thomas More (1478-1535)

At 13 years of age Thomas More went to live with John Morton, who was then Archbishop of Canterbury. Thomas liked John and came under his influence. Morton disliked Richard III and had been his enemy. Richard had imprisoned Morton in 1483. Whilst a prisoner Morton had plotted against Richard. He supported Henry Tudor's claim to the throne and was rewarded by being made Chancellor (Prime Minister) of England.

Sir Thomas More wrote a book about Richard in 1513 and a lot of his information came from Morton. When Richard became King, More was only 5 years old.

Fig. 4.17 Information on Sir Thomas More.

This is how one student explained More's evidence.

Sir Thomas More, another writer, also wrote an account of what happened, although his story is more believable. In his evidence he says that Richard was jealous of the Princes and so they were murdered. He employed Sir James Tyrell, (an English soldier and later, Governor of Guisnes Castle which guarded the English held part of Calais), to find two men to carry out the murder and, according to More, they did this successfully.

After the death of Richard, 19 years later in 1502, Tyrell confessed to having been an accomplice to the murder. Shortly after the confession, Tyrell was executed for treason on 6th May. This account was long accepted at face value, but when examined closely certain problems emerged: First of all no written confession was produced by the government. It is difficult to see why, whether guilty or not, Tyrell decided to talk, so long after the event. Sir Thomas More somehow discovered where Tyrell had the bodies buried, but other sources of evidence who have written anything about Tyrell do not confirm it, and from this I cannot understand how More knew that.

Perhaps, if Tyrell ever did confess, it was because he knew that he'd be killed so he started to ask forgiveness for all the bad things he'd done so that when he died he'd go to heaven (as they were all very religious at the time).

This rumour of his confession was spread by King Henry VII so as to stop possible rivals thinking the Princes were still alive. Perhaps Henry had something to hide . . .

Sir Thomas More's evidence contained a detailed study of the events; more detailed than anyone of that time. He was also an enemy of Richard. Most of his evidence was received from John Morton, with whom he stayed with as a younger boy. Morton also disliked Richard as he had been imprisoned by him in 1483. He supported Henry Tudor's claim to the throne and was later rewarded by being made chancellor (Prime Minister) of England.

How Morton knew what was said in the confession is a mystery because details of the evidence were not made public and so More's account was inaccurate in some places and pure fantasy in others.

Maybe some of the events were forgotten or twisted as More was only five years old when it happened but he wrote the book at the age of 35.

Fig. 4.18 A student's response to Sir Thomas More's evidence.

66 Who heard Tyrell confess? 99

66 Had Henry VII a motive for murder? 99

In the student's account More's evidence is questioned, concerns are expressed and an explanation for some of these concerns is offered. For example, the fact that Tyrell confessed so long after the event is said to be a result of his impending death and his desire to repent his sins in order to get to heaven. Not all of the questions raised by the student are answered in this extract. Doubt is cast on Henry VII, who was the only one to have heard Tyrell's confession. Why was it not written down? From here the student has a lead in the investigation which needs to be pursued. Is Henry VII involved in the disappearance of the Princes? Would he have a motive?

Student assessment

The student has shown developed skills of evaluation in her assessment of this evidence. She has explained in some detail why the information should be treated with caution. For example, there is no written confession from Tyrell, the age of More at the time of the event and his age when his book was written. She has also indicated More may have been influenced in his view of Richard III by John Morton, a known enemy of Richard III. In this way the information may be unreliable as it presents the views of someone unlikely to give a balanced opinion of Richard.

To improve, the student could have developed further the points made. Some are mentioned or hinted at, but they are not explained or linked together. Also, the argument between fact and opinion could be emphasised.

When considering written evidence, bear the following checklist in mind:

Written Evidence

- What does the piece of evidence say? What is its origin? What type of written evidence is it – for example, letter, article, diary? Is it likely to be reliable?

- Why was it written? When was it written? Does the answer to these questions affect the accuracy of the evidence?

- Is the writer presenting an argument, or writing about something they witnessed or were told about? Can the writer be trusted?

- Which parts of the evidence are opinions and not fact? What language is used to convey the point of evidence? Does the choice of language suggest anything about the reliability of the evidence? Is it exaggerated?

- Are there signs of bias or prejudice in the evidence? Has the writer taken sides?

- When comparing this evidence with other evidence does it show any errors of fact? Is a distorted view given? Are things missed out in order to support the view presented in the evidence?

5 > NEWSPAPERS AS EVIDENCE

Another common assignment topic for this area of Integrated Humanities is an investigation into the reliability of newspaper articles. This is achieved by analysing certain articles and the newspapers in which they appear. This is not only an ideal way to assess students' interpretation and evaluation skills; it also allows them to demonstrate an understanding of how newspaper articles can influence people's views.

As an indication of how two newspapers can report the same story differently, look at the two articles in Fig. 4.19 a) and b). Which is the most reliable?

The article from the *Guardian* appeared on page two of the paper, but in the *Sun* it was the main front-page headline. Does this suggest anything about the importance placed on the article by each newspaper? Can you identify from each account the major cause of the problems at the school? Are they the same? What attitude or view of the issue is the *Sun* trying to develop? Is this the same in the *Guardian*? In what ways has the *Sun* attempted to create a particular view of the incident?

This is how one student attempted to explain the way newspapers present unreliable stories.

66 Look at headline differences. 99

66 Look at the use of language in the two articles. 99

BIAS IN THE PRESS

In newspaper reporting there are many ways of showing bias. It can be subtle and very gentle or it can be bold, like a special advert showing their bias. Bias can be represented in news stories where the wording is tilted so it makes their bias look good. Different newspapers will print different stories based on their own opinion

---

Teachers act over 'racial tension'

Teachers in Liverpool last night suggested that a racially tense school should be closed 'from time to time' to allow talks between staff and officials to sort out organisation and discipline problems.

The call from the National Union of Teachers' branch came after seven white senior pupils at University Community Comprehensive said that they would boycott lessons unless they had pledges of safety from the headmaster.

One pupil is alleged to have said: 'There is one rule for the whites and another for the blacks. The teachers are frightened to do anything in case they are called racist.'

The pupils allege that attempts to create racial harmony have failed, even though, like the city's other new comprehensives, the school has a teacher with a brief to tackle race relations. They say that a blackboard must be called a chalkboard, discos must become reggae parties, the school held two minutes silence for a man hanged in South Africa, and that library books have been racially censored.

The pupils have complained to the headmaster, Mr Peter Fowler, about racial tension and lack of discipline in the school, which was formed last September when three schools merged as part of the city's education reorganisation.

Education officials and union leaders, while admitting that there has been tension in recent weeks, said that most of it is the inevitable inter-school rivalry after the merger.

Fifteen pupils, aged about 15, yesterday put their case at a 75 minute meeting with Mr Kenneth Antcliffe, director of education. Also present were the chairman of the education committee, Mr Dominic Brady, the chairman of the school governors, Mr Tony Hood, and other governors, parents and members of the Merseyside Community Relations Council.

Mr Antcliffe said afterwards that the incidents raised by the pupils were 'minor' and should not be got out of proportion.

Traditional rivalries between the schools had been heightened by their merger to produce a compre-

hensive of about 700 pupils, based on the old Paddington school, which drew pupils from the ethnic community of Liverpool 8 and had a racially troubled past. Linked with it were the Liverpool Institutes for boys and for girls, while there were also said to be rivalries with a nearby Catholic girls' school.

The branch secretary of the NUT, Mr Jim Ferguson, which represents most of the school's teaching staff of over 60, said that pupils and parents had been told they would be able to continue courses, but there were not enough specialist teachers to go round.

'It has not been an easy merger but it is unfair to widen it in racial terms,' he said.

Earlier Mrs Josephine Campbell, a governor and chair of the parent-teachers' association, said: 'We had a parents' meeting and agreed that there is a lack of discipline. Black parents felt that staff were biased towards white children and white parents felt the opposite.'

Fig. 4.19 a) An extract from the *Guardian*, 13 February 1986.

School of race hate

- Seven white kids quit over bullying
- The blackboard is called a chalkboard
- Two minutes silence for a hanged African

Seven white boys quit their race-hate school yesterday because of bullying by black pupils.

They accused white teachers of turning a blind eye to the bullies for fear of being branded racist.

The boys claimed headmaster Peter Fowler told them he could not guarantee their safety — so they walked out.

Four of the seven are prefects at Liverpool's Community County Comprehensive.

Worried education chiefs summoned the boys — all aged 15 and 16 — to a top-level meeting.

The boys claimed that at the troubled schools:

BLACKBOARDS have been banned — they are now known as chalkboards.

DISCOS are out — they are called reggae parties.

A TWO MINUTE silence was observed for a man hanged in South Africa.

AFRAID

One boy said 'it's like two different schools.

'There is one set of rules for the whites and another for the blacks.

'The teachers are frightened to do anything in case they are called racist.'

The seven boys were so afraid of being attacked that they sought protection in the girls' section of the school.

They claimed 45 other children have quit the school because of racial tension.

The seven spelled out their complaints at talks with the school governors and Liverpool's education director Kenneth Antcliffe.

A PUPIL was disciplined for drawing Greenland bigger than Africa.

There are 700 boys and girls aged between 11 and 16 at the school. More than 250 of them are black.

The boys who quit used to belong to Liverpool Boys Institute High School, where Beatles George Harrison and Paul McCartney were educated.

They said the bullies came from the predominantly black Paddington School, which merged with the Institute last year.

A council spokesman said last night: 'The director said there is no evidence of a black-white dimension.'

But Tony Hodd, chairman of the school governors said: 'Anyone who has watched Grange Hill on TV will know the friction generated by merging schools.'

And Pat Brookes, leader of Liverpool's parent action committee, said: 'There has been an awful lot of racial tension bubbling for months — and it's only just under control.'

Fig. 4.19 b) An extract from the *Sun*, 13 February 1986.

of what is most important. This is evident in the Daily Express about the Falklands war, where the emphasis is on the people who thought Neil Kinnock was cruel and tactless. This showed us that the Daily Express's opinion is a right wing one because they were biased against Neil Kinnock, who is left wing.

The opposite front page heading of what's inside is from the Daily Mirror, and it is typical of the kind of story to be used where a famous person has had a secret lover who is going to reveal all about it.

I was Geoff Boycott's secret lover . . . . by the girl he called his POCKET BATTLESHIP

Newspapers will not always print the same stories in the same places. A good example of this is between the Daily Express and the Guardian. We can see the Guardian, which is a left wing paper, only mentions the 'Dennis Healey TV Row' in a 4½ cm square box to the left of a large broadsheet newspaper on the Daily Express, which is a right wing newspapers, uses, on the same story, nearly a whole page. This shows their bias against Dennis Healey who a left wing representative.

Newspapers can show their bias on the government by printing a statement from the government and then printing a new story next to it, which contradicts it. An example of this could be that the government release a statement on how good prison security is and the newspaper prints a story about drugs in prisons or of prison riots.

Headlines can be biased by certain words. An example of this could be :-

Two sets of Young People Congregate in a Pub

Two Gangs Involved in Pub Brawl

Another real life example of this, between the Daily Express and the Guardian is:-

Healey in TV Row

Healey The Hypocrite

Different newspapers will print different headlines depending on what their bias is. The next four examples are all on the same story, but are put across differently by newspapers.

'Headmaster who insists on corporal punishment asked to leave' — The Guardian (left wing)

'Dismissal of Head in Caning Row' — The Independent (independent)

'Flogging Head Sacked' — Daily Mirror (left wing)

'Head Forced To Resign To Appease 'do-gooders' ' — The Telegraph (right wing). This implies the 'do-gooders' are left wing parents.

All of these newspapers used different words to make a headline for the story depending on their bias. Words can be very emotive and in one paper they may be good but in another paper it may be the opposite and be bad. Here are some examples:-

Thrifty could be used in one and miserly in another paper or firm could be used in one and stubborn in another paper. This shows us that the stories may be the same but the opposite words are used, depending on their bias and what their viewpoint is.

Pictures have a major effect on bias, even though we don't think a picture could show bias. A picture can show an attractive or an unattractive image. A right wing newspaper, like the Daily Mail, could print a glowing picture of Margaret Thatcher and a really nasty picture of Neil Kinnock.

We can see from this that bias can be represented in a number of ways that are often very subtle and people never think about it being biased, so it does get its message across sometimes.

Your examples are excellent

Fig. 4.20 A student's work on bias in the press.

Student assessment

The student is evaluating the reliability of newspaper articles. He has gone into some detail about the possible reasons why an article should be regarded with caution. These include the political background of the paper, the use of language and pictures, the positioning of articles, and the conflicting nature of articles.

To improve, the student could have included relevant extracts from newspapers to support the statements made. For example, the article from the *Express* about Neil Kinnock and the Falklands War, and the two articles about Denis Healey. The view that the *Guardian* is a left-wing paper is questionable; 'does not tend to support the Conservatives' would have been more accurate. The headline about Geoff Boycott could have been explained and used more.

Testing the student's analysis

Fig. 4.21 An extract from the *Daily Mirror*, 2 November 1988.

Using the points raised in the previous example of a student's work, study this article from the *Daily Mirror*. How reliable is it?

Angry angels accuse Thatcher

SHE'S ROBBED NURSES

SNATCHER: Thatcher under fire

CHEATED: A conned angel

Hospitals hit by walk-out chaos

By JILL PALMER AND CHRISTIAN GYSIN

THOUSANDS of angry nurses protested yesterday that they've been conned and cheated over their long-awaited pay shake-up.

Some staged walk-outs at hospitals — and more action is threatened all over the country.

The nurses are outraged at being downgraded so that they will receive far less than the 15.3 per cent increase promised by Premier Margaret Thatcher.

● In the North-East, two hospitals at South Tyneside were shut down and operations at two others cancelled because of a work-to-rule by nurses.

● In the North-West, midwives staged a two-hour walk-out at North Manchester General Hospital and 50 psychiatric nurses there will start a strike today.

● In London, nurses at a VD unit at Charing Cross Hospital are threatening to strike for two hours tomorrow — their second protest this week.

Did you notice:

- the headline;
- the use of language:
  - nurses described as angels
  - aggressive language towards the government and Mrs Thatcher in particular. Look at the words under each photograph: 'SNATCHER: Thatcher under fire' and 'CHEATED: a conned angel'.
- Photographs:
  - Does Mrs Thatcher look concerned about the plight of the nurses in this photograph?
  - Does the nurse look cheated and angelic?

> **Question the evidence.**

The general theme of the article is that the nurses have been cheated and let down by Mrs Thatcher and the government, who have broken promises. What is missing in this article?

- Has the government or Mrs Thatcher been given the opportunity to answer the charge that they cheated the nurses?
- Has any nurse who has *benefited* from the regrading been interviewed?
- What political party does this newspaper tend to support?
- What was actually *promised* in April when the agreement regarding the nurses was announced?

Can you think of anything else? Can you present an account as to why this article may be unreliable, supporting your comments with evidence? If you can, this would be an acceptable piece of work for assessment in this area of Integrated Humanities.

This is an example of the kind of task which could be set for this area of study. What follows is a student's attempt at the task.

Fig. 4.22 The task for a study of bias in the news.

Select a series of articles from any newspaper and assess the reliability of the report.

This task is designed especially to test how well you assess the reliability of evidence.

You have to show, and explain, why the reports you have chosen may be unreliable. They may display bias, they may be unreliable because of who wrote them, or in which newspaper they appeared, or during the time they were written, or for many other reasons.

It may be best to select a news story and see how it is presented in two different newspapers, each one with a _different_ political bias.

Remember full explanation as to why and where the report shows bias is needed.

Task 1.
Introduction

For this task a series of articles have been selected from various newspapers being conservative, labour and independent. With these cuttings assessments will be made to show the reliability of the report, compared to others.

The main aim is to state whether bias is present in the reports, closely connected to the papers own personal political views and preferences.

Other details that will provide evidence are:

a) The size of the article – the amount of page space and the number of columns given to the story, maybe to show it's importance.

b) Where in the paper the article is placed – the page that the article is placed in and where about on the page it can be read.

c) The size of the title and the use of colour – does the title draw your attention, does it strike out.

d) The wording of the title – does it attract and urge the reader to continue examining the article. Is it scandalous or informative?

e) The content and vocabulary of the article — does the wording change dramatically from newspaper to newspaper? Are the stories different, in anyway onesided? Which is the correct article?

f) Any pictures given — do they show happiness — do they coincide with the report — do the pictures reflect anything of the papers own opinions on the article.

With these factors in mind I shall be looking at the following sets of articles based upon a) the red cross campaign.

ARTICLES 1   The first group of articles have been taken from the 'Daily Mail' — a conservative paper and 'The Mirror' — a labour paper.

The articles are centred upon the story of a labour representative named Larry Whitty and how he has used the Red Cross emblem for one of his campaigns.

Daily Mail — Conservative Newspaper
This article can be referred to overleaf

The article has been given a large area of space and is alot bigger than the article in the labour paper. The headline is bold, and heavily printed in definite black lettering. Because of this the readers attention is captured and motivated to read the entire report. The headline also introduces and informs the reader of the general outline to the story. In this case the title is almost scandalous and shows a very biased opinion of the man concerned.

   Being a conservative paper they have taken the opportunity to reflect Larry Whitty in a bad and malicious way. The reason for the exaggerated article is due to the fact that the character in the report is labour and the conservative group like to criticise, comdemn and ridicule their opposition by publicising small, unimportant events into full scale reports. They portray the article in a dramatic and extended way with the addition of the reporters personal views and opinions on behalf of the conservative members.

   The content of the paper in aspect of the language and vocabulary is clear and simple and can be easily understood. Although it is apparent that the article has been over-reported and blown out of proportion, there is no slang involved or over theatrical quotations. The use of language portrays a seemingly accurate report to the Daily Mail readers, and reflects the meaning of the story.

   Photographs are used to add an amount of realism and supportive dimension to the account, yet reflect a grim and embarrassing Mr. Larry Whitty and a positively angry Phillip Kelly.

   The report however, has included and applied more topics into the account concerning the Geneva Convention. I feel that this was unnecessary and is not involved with the main core of the report. This addition shows the conservative aspect and views of the Labour party, obviously needing to emphasise and show themselves to be greater, depicting the dissappointing and unapproved of areas of their opposition, being labour.

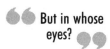

   The construction of the report and overall appearance is good and well laid out, it is easy to follow and is appealing to the readers. It includes all the necessary information concerning the report and gives a thorough account of the story.

The Mirror — Labour newspaper
Article below

The initial factor recognisable is the size of the article for this particular report. The event was taken from well in the paper from the bottom half of the page. This reflects the embarrassment that the Labour party feels with the knowledge that one of their members has made a mistake, and the coverage it has been given. The positioning of the article also portrays the unimportance of the report and the attempt of camouflaging the entire account.

Labour's cross boss

LABOUR Party general secretary Larry Whitty hit out yesterday after being found guilty of using a Red Cross-style symbol as a campaign emblem.

He claimed the case had been politically motivated.

"It was instigated by Government departments," he said.

At London's Horseferry Road court he was given a 12-month conditional discharge and ordered to pay prosecution costs of £200.

GUILTY: Whitty

The headline is very small and weak, it does not attract the reader or show any sign of appeal, compared to the Daily Mails article. The headline is uninformative and shows a different view of the story stating 'Labours cross boss'. It indicates that they believe the story to be over publicised and the anger that they feel about the cherade.

Being a Labour paper, the article has been cut down and is very brief. It gets to the point of the story immediately and is very direct, staying strictly on the story and only covering the essential necessities.

The language used is short and does not elaborate. However it can be detected that slang is used very slightly using the words 'hit out' When reading the report the use of this form of vocabulary appears to create the emotions that the reporter feels. He is solely biased about the story and happenings, anger covering the true account of the report. The report has been written in a way that states the misbelief felt by the labour party, taking the attention and stirring the readers feelings, making them feel angry and furious too.

Whitty in a disturbed and angry posture, his facial expression being understandably angry, covering any embarrassment he feels.

The article has obviously been written directed at the labour follower and supporter. It has been accounted for in such a way that labour members will not be lost, but will feel bitter about the event. The report has almost been accounted for by the writers own opinions and views of the story which the labour readers would depend upon.

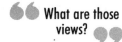

The 'Party' have been wrongly accused.

What are those views?

Fig. 4.23 A student's work on bias in the news.

BUDGET LEAFLET USED WORLD-FAMOUS LOGO

Labour man guilty in Red Cross row

LABOUR Party General Secretary Larry Whitty was **convicted** yesterday of illegally using the international emblem of the Red Cross in a political campaign.

He was given a conditional discharge and ordered to pay £200 costs over a party pamphlet calling for more health spending which featured a red cross symbol.

Mr Whitty had denied the offence of using a design 'so nearly resembling' the emblem in contravention of the 1957 Geneva Convention.

Tribune's Philip Kelly

The Red Cross symbol

In a second case at London's Horseferry Road court, Philip Kelly, editor of the Left-wing weekly Tribune, was conditionally discharged with £50 costs after a last-minute change of plea to admit a similar offence. His publication had featured a red cross on its front page.

Mr Roy Amlot, prosecuting Mr Whitty, said the movement was rightly jealous of its emblem — a red cross on white background — which was recognised throughout the world as a sign of its neutrality and impartiality.

It was considered of vital importance by the British Red Cross Society, with 52 branches in England and Wales, and the International Red Cross, which provides aid to the sick and wounded in wartime and works for better health and disease prevention throughout the world.

The emblem was especially important where the Red Cross acted in areas of conflict, Mr. Amlot told the court, so was protected from misuse not just by commonsense but by the law.

Withdrawn

Before the Budget in March this year the Labour Party made use of the sign in a campaign designed to put pressure on the Chancellor to spend extra money on the Health Service instead of making tax cuts.

It distributed a leaflet to constituencies which featured a red cross inside a £ sign. Underneath the slogan 'Make Budget Day NHS Day' was a caption and the words 'Labour' and a picture of the party's red rose logo.

The British Red Cross found the use of the emblem for political purposes totally unacceptable, said Mr Amlot, and

NHS campaign broke the Geneva Convention

By FRANK THOMPSON

its Director General, Mr John Burke-Gaffney, wrote to Mr Whitty asking that it be withdrawn.

If Labour had done so that might have been the end of the matter. But Mr Whitty replied to the letter, saying that while he regretted any embarrassment to the Red Cross, he had taken legal advice that the material did not contravene the Geneva Act.

Mr Anthony Arlidge, QC, for Mr Whitty, claimed the fact that the logo appeared on a £ sign meant it was not on a white background and did not 'nearly resemble' the official emblem.

Its arms were of marginally different lengths whereas those on the official sign were all the same, he added.

Outside the court an angry Mr Whitty claimed the prosecution was 'politically motivated'.

'This case should never have been taken,' he said.

'No one in their right mind could confuse the Labour publication for an official publication of the Red Cross.'

The party said in a statement that the prosecution was initiated by the Defence Ministry and the Department of Trade 'clearly under political direction.'

Important

It went on: 'They have stretched to breaking point an obscure but important piece of legislation designed to protect the integrity of the Red Cross in a war zone — an essential protection — to try to inflict petty embarrassment and expense on the Labour Party.'

Philip Kelly claimed: 'This serves to show that the Red Cross in this country is closely connected with the establishment and the Tory Party.'

Mr Burke-Gaffney said after the case: 'I'm sad about the whole thing but glad the court feels the emblem should be protected.'

Larry Whitty: 'Case was politically-motivated'

This article is taken from the Daily Mail. It is a conservative paper.

Student assessment

In the introduction the student suggested a clear understanding of the points to look for when assessing the reliability of newspaper articles. However, in the analysis of the chosen articles she does not develop this understanding in the points and comments made. Opportunities are missed to present a detailed evaluation of the articles. Nonetheless, she has gone into some detail about the possible reasons why accounts should be regarded with caution, particularly with regard to the political bias of newspapers.

The student's introduction shows a sound understanding of the features involved in assessing the reliability of a newspaper article. She could have developed point (e) (on page 135) and given some examples of the language used by newspapers to present a particular view; language to show favour or opposition to an issue, etc. Point (f) is a good one, and is clearly explained. She has set out the terms of reference for her task, leaving the reader in no doubt as to the purpose of the exercise.

The student deals with the political bias of the first article but could have elaborated on this by comparing Whitty's case with other crimes, such as murder or rape. What has caused it to make the front page: the seriousness of the crime or the fact that it involves the Labour Party Secretary? A reason for the position of the article has been suggested but it could have been emphasised more. When assessing the language in the *Daily Mail* article, the student's comments are not supported with evidence. In fact, several unsupported statements are made. For example, how does 'the use of language portray a seemingly accurate report'? Is this the student's own bias showing? More could have been made of the use of language and the choice of photographs in evaluating the reliability of the account.

The conclusion of the *Mail*'s account needs attention. From whose point of view does it give a 'thorough account of the story'?

In the assessment of the article which appeared in the *Daily Mirror* the student could have highlighted the difference between the *tone* here and in the *Daily Mail*. Why was this? According to the *Mirror*, who was responsible for the case coming to court? Why should the newspaper take this stance? These are questions the student could have tackled.

Suggestions have been made for improvement in these general comments about the assignment. These should be looked at especially with reference to the analysis of the article in the *Daily Mirror*, which lacks depth. Also the choice of language and use of photographs in the *Daily Mirror* article required more comment.

6 ▷ CONCLUSION

❝❝ Have you identified all these points? ❞❞

❝❝ The North–South Divide – only one of many topics ❞❞

As already stated earlier in this section, it is impossible to include all the areas of study which could be used to assess *interpretation and evaluation* skills. What we hope we have achieved in this section is to:

■ indicate what the examiner is looking for in this area of Integrated Humanities;

■ provide a system by which you can begin to interpret and evaluate evidence;

■ provide examples of the type of evidence available

■ give guidance about using specific types of evidence, particularly statistics, pictures, photographs and written evidence;

■ provide examples of *some* assignments, with comments, which students have completed for this area of assessment.

To end this chapter a possible coursework assignment which could be used for assessment in this area of Integrated Humanities will be outlined. This will include a task, a sample of resources which could be used to complete the task and a student's response to the task.

This particular task is not chosen because we think it is a especially 'good'. It is simply an example of *one* topic students have studied for assessment in this area of the course.

A SAMPLE COURSEWORK ASSIGNMENT – THE NORTH–SOUTH DIVIDE IN BRITAIN

NORTH versus SOUTH – THE BRITISH EXPERIENCE

This piece of work is concerned with the arguments related to the distribution of wealth in this country. In particular it centres upon whether there is a difference in the QUALITY OF LIFE between the NORTH and the SOUTH of Great Britain. The 'quality of life' is assessed by a huge number of factors. These are just a few examples:

    employment/unemployment
    average wage
    provision of services
    education
    type/quality of housing
    health

You will undoubtedly come across others.

Assignment

Your task is to produce a major article for a foreign magazine/newspaper using <u>one</u> of the following headlines as your starting point.

a) NORTH/SOUTH DIVIDE – THE ANSWER IS IN THE PAST.

b) NORTH/SOUTH DIVIDE – THE FACTS.

c) NORTH/SOUTH DIVIDE – IT'S A MYTH!

d) POVERTY – IT'S NOT JUST IN THE NORTH

Important points:-

1) Make it interesting.

2) Include relevant maps/charts/tables/diagrams

3) Assume that your readers know nothing about this subject.

4) Plan carefully – the finished article must *not cover more than four sides* of standard file paper. You may use these four sides as you wish. Try to be imaginative.

5) Ensure the article has sufficient depth.

Fig. 4.24 Brief for a study on the North–South divide.

The resources used are by no means the only ones now available for this topic. In fact, the statistics and articles are out of date. However, we have included this sample of resources because they were the ones used by the student whose work is included. This makes it possible to identify the evidence used in the student's assignment. To study this topic today more up-to-date evidence would have to be collected – a good exercise for your enquiry skills!

> **A sound introduction. The purpose of the assignment is clear and the North–South divide is defined.**

NORTH–SOUTH DIVIDE ... THE FACTS...

In Britain a North–South Divide is often talked of where the population in the North usually have less job opportunities, worse health, less annual income, a worse crime rate and a bad rate of economic growth.

In this article I will put forward the facts in relation to this problem.

The Divide is an imaginary line drawn from the mouth of the River Severn to the Wash. The main cause of the difference in the standards is unemployment. Since 1979 (when the present Conservative Government came to power) 94% of all job losses in Britain were North

of the Divide. From June 1979 to June 1986 356,000 jobs were created
in the South, while in the same period the North lost 1,101,000.
Since 1979 the North has lost 547,000 manufacturing jobs and gained
548,000 service jobs.

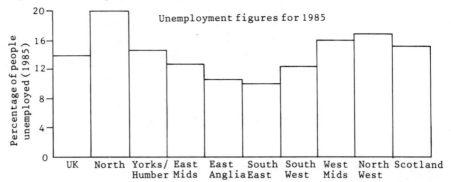

Unemployment figures for 1985

Poor health and crime appear to be connected with unemployment. Most
people agree that unemployment is associated with ill-health but
disagree as to whether unemployment causes ill-health. It is very
difficult to separate fact from fiction.

Two Cambridge economists; Rowthorn and Ward, used Professor Harvey
Brenner's research model. He recently investigated the link between
unemployment and ill-health. They estimated that:

*'A sustained rise in unemployment of one million over the next five
  years could be associated with 50,000 additional deaths and over
  60,000 cases of mental illness.[EQ]

Some other findings from various sources state that:

*i The unemployed suffer greater mental stress, as shown from
    research in Bradford and Sheffield.
*ii The NSPCC states that child abuse has increased sharply in the
     past two years.
iii Suicide and depression cases have increased
*iv In high unemployment areas doctors reported a large increase in
    the numbers of prescriptions of anti-depressants, a rise in
    alcoholism and domestic violence and additional problems
    associated with high blood pressure.
*v Psychological changes take place in unemployed people that can
   affect their families.

These findings appear to indicate that unemployed people are less
healthy generally than employed people.

Death rates are also higher in the North of Britain. The U.K. average
is 1,141 deaths per 100,000 people. The areas in the North (except
the East Midlands) are above average. The following figures confirm
this

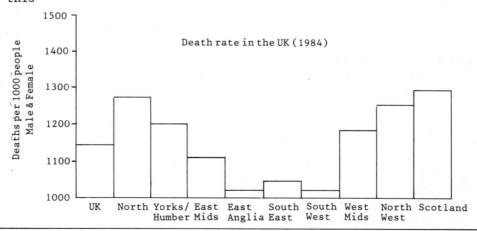

Death rate in the UK (1984)

> Evidence is used to make the link between ill health and unemployment. The South is healthier than the North, which shows another sort of inequality.

1984 figures show that the S.M.R. (Standardised Mortality Ratio) is also higher in the North than in the South.

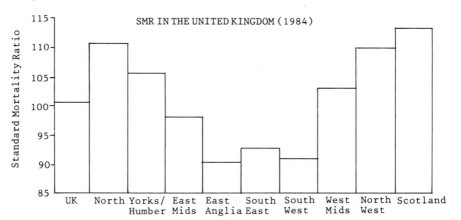

G. Melvyn Howe (who is Emeritus Professor of Geography at the University of Strathclyde) backs up these figures in an article in which he asks "Where would you go to live longer?" In the article he states that one man in eleven can expect a fatal heart attack before the age of 65. Areas that have high S.M.R.'s have high rates of fatal heart attacks.

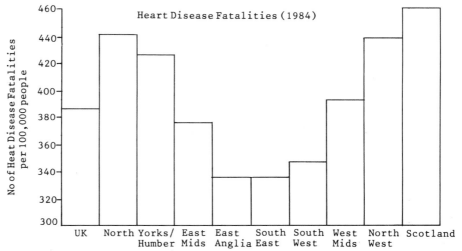

In 1984 the Northern five counties of England had the highest mortality rate from cancer. The figures were 344 per 100,000 males and 275 per 100,00 females.

> The information about household budgets could have been linked more to unemployment, the price of food, especially healthy food, and health problems. Some attempt has been made to do this, but it could have been developed further.

Generally speaking, people from the deprived areas, as opposed to people from the more affluent parts of the country have quite different ideas about budgeting their incomes- be it from their work place (or more often in the North money from the Dole etc.) The importance of feeding themselves with health giving food does not often occur to them. The result is usually a diet of fattening and filling food and badly balanced meals helped on their way with alcoholic drinks and cigarettes. It is not surprising that their health suffers eventually.

A possible reason for the populations of the South East being healthier than that of the North is that in the South only 23% of expenditure went on fattening food alcoholic drink and tobacco, this being a lower proportion than elsewhere.

> Is the statement about why people turn to crime one of fact or opinion? Could this have been supported with evidence?

People who are out of work are more likely to turn to crime out of envy and desperation to get property they cannot afford, or to get money to pay off their ever mounting and never ending debts... (mortgages h.p. etc.)

Figures from 1984 show that the crime rate is highest in the North of Britain. The North, North West and Scotland are the worst black-spots with 7,727, 7,775 and 8,421 offences respectively notified to the police. The rest of the nation have about 6,500 offences notified to the police. While East Anglia had just 4,689 offences.

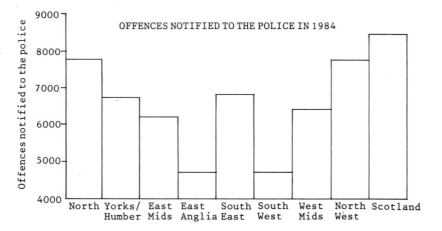

In 1984 the average weekly income was £191.90. Only one area had an average higher that that, and that was the South East with a staggering £230.00 and East Anglia surprisingly on just £181.30. The East Midlands was on £188.30. The North had just £167.90. The average income in Southern areas was £201.00 while north of the Divide it was £175.60.

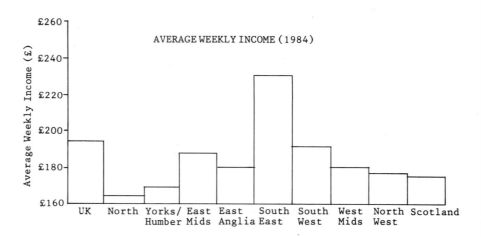

When the cost of living rises this usually starts a chain reaction with salaries and wages also increasing. In 1984 the average cost of a house in the North was £22,600 while in Greater London it was £39,300. This difference in house prices is reflected in the incomes. The higher incomes in the Greater London areas meant that people could afford to pay more for their homes than people living in the North. The sellers of the properites in London simply kept putting their prices up. The buyers then demanded more salary from their employers and so the chain reaction of rising prices kept going on and on.

As most young people in the North are unemployed they are unable to obtain loans to buy their own homes. One of their alternatives is to live in a Council House. In some cases the local authorities do not spend too much money on improving these homes and so there is a greater chance of these young people living in low standard accommodation.

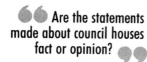 The section on house prices could be used to illustrate why it is difficult for people from the north to move south, thus emphasising the divide.

Are the statements made about council houses fact or opinion?

Children at school, say Fourth and Fifth Years, in the high
unemployment areas would probably think that their job
opportunities are minimal and because of that would think that
school education was not relevant or worthwhile.
During the last General Election the various political parties drew
attention to the so called "North-South Divide". They drew attention in
in the media to the differences between the North and the South
especially in the areas of inadequate police protection, low
standard of education, overstretched Health Service, and
insufficient investment. The elected Government has promised to
carry out it's Manifesto Pledge to try to find a solution to this
unacceptable imbalance. Their stated policy is to re-vitalise the
Northern inner cities. Government and commercial investment is to be
massive in these areas. Education and the Health Service is to be
greatly improved. This is coupled with the desperate attempts to
help schoolleavers to learn a relevant trade in the Youth Training
Scheme.

The problems are massive and have been there for far too long. I
cannot see how they can be solved overnight, but with willingness on
everyones part a positive advance can and must be made.

66 **Clear conclusion which illustrates the government's acknowledgement of the Divide by including strategies for improvement in their election manifesto.** 99

Fig. 4.25 A student's work on the North-South divide.

Student assessment

The choice of title in this work requires the student to present facts which illustrate there is a North–South divide. In so doing, he must show he can interpret, organise, compare, and use relevant evidence to present a case. In this example, the student has shown a high-level understanding of the evidence available and has put this to use to support the title of the work. The meaning of the evidence is explained competently and an attempt is made to discuss the implications of the evidence. The evidence chosen fits the purpose of the task; it illustrates the facts about the North–South divide as defined in the introduction to the assignment. It is the interpretation and use, rather than the evaluation of the evidence, which has been assessed in this assignment.

The general comments made about the work have included some suggestions for improvement. These should be looked at again. The main concern is identifying fact and opinion. Certain statements made – attitudes towards education and council house spending, for example – are unsupported. Are these fact or opinion?

Before starting your own assignments you must make sure you know what your teacher will be looking for in the assessment of your work. Once this has been identified and is clear in your mind, you can structure and present your work in a way which will give you access to the assessment objectives laid down in the course you are following. *It is vital for you to seek guidance from your teacher as to what is required from you in the work.* Make sure you know *how you can achieve your maximum* in the assignment you are completing.

Key points of the chapter

1 Before completing assignments in this area make sure you are clear what your teacher will be looking for when assessing the work.
2 Use all the evidence available in making a reasoned conclusion.
3 Remember, the examiner is looking for the following:

- the ability to interpret, organise, compare and use relevant evidence to answer the task set;
- understanding of the unreliability of evidence, including awareness of bias.
- the ability to present reasoned conclusions from the evidence available about the area of study.

CHAPTER 5

COMMUNICATION

WRITING

TYPES OF WRITING

TYPES OF TASK

DRAWINGS AND PICTURES

USING VIDEO/AUDIO RECORDINGS

GETTING STARTED

Being able to communicate, transmit or present effectively your understanding, findings, etc. is a skill which you will require in all your assessment tasks. However, some may be specifically designed to assess your ability to communicate.

Communicating means conveying your ideas, etc. to other people. Many methods can be used:

■ **Written work**

This will, for practical reasons, be your main approach. It will include different types of writing and writing for different purposes and audiences. Your writing may also be in different formats – for example, essays, reports, etc. – and in response to a particular stimulus.

■ **Script/dialogue**

This is writing which is intended to be spoken, or is an exact record of what has been said. Examples could include scripts intended for radio programmes, an imagined conversation between two or more people, a prepared public speech, etc.

■ **Audio-visual presentation**

These might include audio tapes, 'radio' programmes you have produced, video tape recordings of dramas or documentaries which you have produced, or records of a piece of investigation; or it might be a tape-slide production which presents information, draws attention to certain issues, etc.

■ **Pictures and displays**

These might be representations of objects, places, etc. which you are discussing, or advertising posters, cartoons, etc. which convey particular ideas or messages.

■ **Graphs, charts, diagrams**

These can be used to convey statistical or other forms of information in a manner which makes them concise and easily understandable.

■ **Oral communication**

Discussions, debates, interviews with your teachers, role-plays, etc. are acceptable as long as enough information is provided to enable assessment by examiners to take place.

Other means of communication for assessment could include models, photographs, games and computer software, etc.

ESSENTIAL PRINCIPLES

Whatever means of communication you select, it must:

- be suitable and relevant to the subject-matter which you wish to communicate;
- be capable of being stored, so that it is available for assessment and moderation;
- provide enough evidence for your own individual work or contribution to be assessed and meet the particular requirements of the examination boards.

Key points

- You should be able to communicate clearly, using a variety of methods as appropriate.
- Your work should be organised so that it is logical, coherent and easily understood.
- There should be sufficient relevant detail in your work to give a clear picture of what you wish to convey.
- You should be aware of who you are communicating to ('audience') and should adopt an appropriate method, style, etc.

1 ▷ WRITING

Obviously, the form of communication which you will use most frequently in meeting assessment tasks will be writing. There are many different forms of writing – these will be explored later – and your work will involve you in writing of different lengths and for different purposes. These are some important points to bear in mind for all types of writing:

❝ Plan your writing. ❞

- **Be prepared**
  Written work requires careful planning. Planning your work will help you to make sure you understand what you are writing about. Start with the title of your work:
  - What are the key words in the title of the task? Do you understand what they mean? Are there any specialist terms, concepts, etc.?
  - Are there any 'command' terms or phrases in the title which tell you what is expected of you – for example, are there terms which ask you to give more than one point of view, such as 'discuss', 'give the advantages and disadvantages', 'to what extent is it true that', etc.?
  - Are there any limiting terms and phrases which instruct you to restrict yourself to a particular area or information source – for example, 'according to the passage', 'from the figures given in the table', etc.?
  - Is any guidance given with the title? Questions sometimes tell you to include certain areas or subjects in your answer – for example, 'What are the main factors which influence how people vote in general elections? In your essay, comment on the following: the importance of the family; social class; the mass media; the policies of political parties; party leaders; tactical voting.'

Planning your work will help you to identify areas which you need to find out about. Begin with what you already know, then consider, what are the gaps in your knowledge? Where will you find the information you need?

❝ Make sure you know what should go where. ❞

- **Be organised**
  You should be clear about what you are going to say and where you are going to say it. Most pieces of continuous writing (essays, descriptions, etc.) require a clear structure. Make sure that you organise your work in paragraphs. Each paragraph should be clearly directed towards a particular point or key idea, or group of related points or ideas. You will probably be expected to produce an introduction, establishing what you are going to be writing about, demonstrating that you understand your task, setting the scene, etc.; the main body of your work – the discussion of the subject, account of events, etc.; the conclusion, summing up what you have said, reconsidering the question you started with, reflecting on what you have written about, etc.

- **Be logical**
  Each paragraph/section should follow easily from the previous one. Make sure you give some thought as to how you can link your paragraphs.

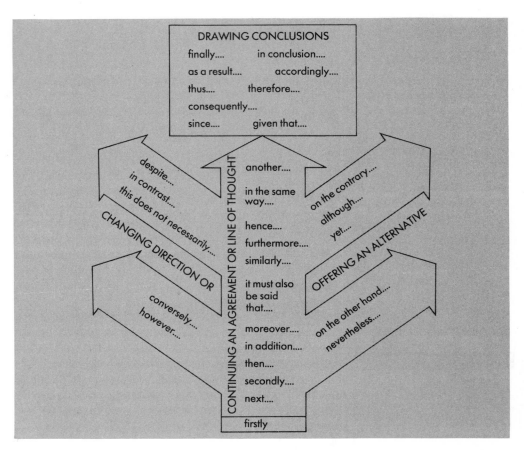

Fig. 5.1 Linking paragraphs.

Each paragraph should only include points which are relevant to your work and give sufficient details to help whoever reads your work to form a clear picture of the subject.

- **Be aware of the style of writing required of you**

  Who is your writing intended to be for? For example, is it a report for the police, social services etc., a letter to a particular person, or a standard essay or account which is asking you to demonstrate your understanding of a particular issue, theme or event? What is the purpose of your writing? Are you being asked to convince, persuade, explain, etc.?

- **Remember to review your work.**

  If you started out with a question, have you really answered it, or attempted to answer it? Is your work relevant to the subject you were writing about, or have you allowed yourself to become sidetracked into other areas? Does your work develop logically? Have you missed out any words, etc.?

CHOOSING/EXAMINING THE TITLE:

Have I identified the key words in the title? ☐

RESEARCHING:

Have I done all the research necessary? .... ☐

PLANNING:

Have I made a plan for the essay? .... ☐

WRITING THE ESSAY:

Have I used an appropriate style? .... ☐

Is what I've written relevant to the title? ...... ☐

Does it develop logically, and have a conclusion? .... ☐

Are the facts and quotations accurate? ...... ☐

PRESENTATION:

Have I written enough/too much? .... ☐

Have I quoted the sources I used? .... ☐

Do I need a bibliography – have I listed the books I read? .... ☐

CHECKING:

Is each main idea in a separate paragraph? .... ☐

Have I missed out any words? .... ☐

Have I punctuated my work properly? .... ☐

Fig. 5.2 An essay checklist.

TYPES OF WRITING

66 Make sure you are clear about the type of writing which is appropriate for your task. 99

Even within a particular writing format or task type, such as an essay, there can be different types of writing. The 'type' depends on what you are being asked to do: for example, whether you are being asked to describe something, to recount a story, etc.

NARRATIVE

Narration means, basically, saying what happened. It can mean telling a story or giving an account of the different stages involved in a particular course of events. For your Integrated Humanities work, the sorts of task in which you may be required to use narrative writing could include:

- writing an account of how you devised and carried out part of your enquiry;
- explaining what happened during your work experience or on a particular visit, etc.;
- relating a series of events – for example, the course of a local industrial dispute – where you may not have been directly involved;
- writing an imaginative piece in which you are required to put yourself in a different situation, or see yourself as a different person, so that you can show your ability to empathise.

66 What you include should always be relevant. 99

In narrative writing you must always ensure that what you write is relevant, providing enough details, but not including irrelevant information which only confuses the reader or has little to do with the focus of your task. Be selective. Choose the essential details which help the reader to understand your account.

You may also need to be careful that events are sequenced. This approach will be important in an account of the course of a particular conflict (such as a study of the events leading up to the defeat of the miners in the strike of 1984–5). It may also be required if you have been collecting oral histories, where sequencing will require careful thought if the interviewee recalled events and situations in no particular order (see Chapter 3).

DESCRIPTIVE

Description means being able to convey to the reader what something/someone is like, and can make use of a wide range of information such as general appearance, colour, height, width, condition, texture, age, etc., or can draw on other senses such as taste, smell and sound. Selecting and combining the relevant details can help to build up a clear picture for the reader.

The main use of descriptive writing in your Integrated Humanities work will be for accounts of observations you have carried out (see Chapter 3). Some examples are:

- descriptions of a particular locality, observed in, for example, a village study, a survey of a shopping centre, or a description of different zones of a town or a rural landscape;
- descriptions of a particular building, such as a leisure centre or day nursery, where the internal layout and facilities provided might be detailed;
- descriptions of a particular aspect of human behaviour, such as in pedestrian counts, or surveys of how people make use of a local country park.

As well as giving descriptive accounts based on your own observations, you may also need to describe places/people from studies you have done in class, using notes you have made, textbooks and other sources of information. When you are describing something remember to make sure you ask yourself if the description you are giving is relevant; is it necessary to the task you are completing? When you have decided that your description is appropriate, you should then ask yourself if you have given enough detail for the reader to be able to picture what you are trying to convey.

DISCURSIVE

Discursive writing is used to discuss and analyse an issue, theme, etc. It could involve examining why things happen – considering the advantages and disadvantages, weighing up a number of different points of view on a subject – or trying to establish to what extent something may be true. In Integrated Humanities many essay questions and research questions require discursive writing: for example, as you develop skills of interpretation and evaluation.

Make sure that you plan your work carefully, so that you give yourself the opportunity to consider the different arguments, features and points of view involved. You must be able to present these in a coherent and well-organised way, making use of appropriate evidence wherever possible.

IMAGINATIVE

Imaginative writing usually means creating a story or description of something that is fictitious with the main aim of entertaining the reader. For the purposes of your Integrated Humanities work, this is unlikely to be sufficient. Imaginative writing may not be required very often in your course, but it can be an aspect of tasks which are designed for you to show your ability to empathise. Where you have to imagine that you are someone else or are in a different situation, location or culture, you will be able to write what is essentially fiction; but you should always remember that the task you are engaged in also requires you to show in your writing that you have understood factual information, issues and problems relating to the topic for which the imaginative writing has been set. Your writing must show an awareness of the environment, the living conditions, the lifestyle, beliefs and values of the person, place or time you are writing about, together with a concern for the issues and controversies of the time. The account which you produce must illustrate this awareness consistently. Make sure you do not get 'carried away' with the story.

PERSONAL

Personal writing includes such writing formats as letters to friends and relatives, entries in diaries and accounts of personal experiences. It provides the opportuniy for you to express feelings and emotions and to convey your reactions and responses to things. This may be required in some Integrated Humanities tasks where your reactions and attitudes are important: for example, where you have designed and carried out enquiry and discovered evidence which has made you change your mind about the issue. You may also be required to write down your reactions and emotions to a particular event or visit: for example, to record how you felt during a visit to a day-care centre or during a community placement. You may be set a task which involves writing letters and diary entries in which you are invited to give your own views on an issue, or inviting you to show your ability to empathise. Remember that personal writing is characterised by the expression of feelings, opinions and attitudes.

DRAMATIC

> Don't get carried away.

Drama is, of course, associated with stage, radio and television plays, and with films. In all these media, the actual presentation to the public is audio-visual; dramatic writing is the script used. Remember, therefore, that 'dramatic' does not necessarily mean 'thrilling'. It does not refer to the content but rather to the format, and can be the script for a piece of comedy, tragedy, soap opera, drama-documentary, etc.

The key feature of dramatic writing, then, is that it is a written version of what is intended to be spoken. The sorts of tasks you may be required to do which involve dramatic writing can be very varied, from short dialogues to scripts for a video production which might include consideration of filming techniques, etc. Remember, however, that the task is likely to have been set to assess more than just communication, so don't get carried away with the medium/style.

When writing any kind of script or dialogue, it is important to be aware of the differences between speech and writing. If a piece of dialogue you are writing is to be convincing, it should sound natural when read out loud. In speech we often don't bother to complete sentences, we repeat ourselves, hesitate, etc. We make use of 'slang' and are able to convey meaning by tone, using exclamations, etc. For example, consider this sentence: *When Debbie suggested that they should go to join the demonstration, Rob agreed.*

Now think of all the ways Rob might have expressed his agreement with Debbie's suggestion. He may, of course, have said, 'I agree.' The possibilities, however, are almost endless, ranging in length from 'OK' to, 'Go to the demonstration? That's a really good idea!'. His words could have expressed his actual feelings about the idea, such as reluctance . 'Well, I'm not sure. . . er. . . oh, all right' – or resignation – 'I suppose so' – or excitement – 'Yeah, great!' – etc.

When you are writing dialogue, think of how the characters would normally speak, the sort of language they would use and the way they would express their feelings and attitudes, but don't forget the other aims of your writing, what you are trying to convey, etc.

3 ⟩ TYPES OF TASK   ### USING ARGUMENTS

This will involve you in taking on an argument, making a case for it and putting forward a point of view: for example, in essays on controversial subjects such as 'Discuss the case for and against capital punishment', 'Do developed countries help or hinder developing countries?', etc. This type of task can also be used to test other assessment objectives, such as:

■ enquiry – if you have demonstrated research skills in the way in which you have identified, collected and selected evidence which is relevant to your work;

■ interpretation and evaluation – in your ability to weigh up and analyse the arguments you consider;

■ understanding – in your ability to demonstrate your knowledge of terms and concepts which are relevant to the subject you are discussing.

Key points to remember

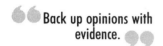
Back up opinions with evidence.

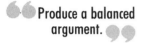
Produce a balanced argument.

Fig. 5.3 A student's response to a question on the arguments for and against capital punishment.

■ You must ensure that what you say is backed up by evidence, so that the points you make are supported. Don't rely merely on giving your own opinion; you should also provide evidence to demonstrate why you hold that opinion or view. Use examples to back up your arguments whenever possible. Always ensure that the examples or evidence you provide are relevant to the points you are making.

■ Be prepared to consider different points of view or arguments which are relevant to the subject you are discussing. This will enable you to demonstrate that you have given the subject some thought and have developed a reasoned and logical piece of work. When considering different arguments, try to include the pros and cons – the advantages and disadvantages – which you consider appropriate.

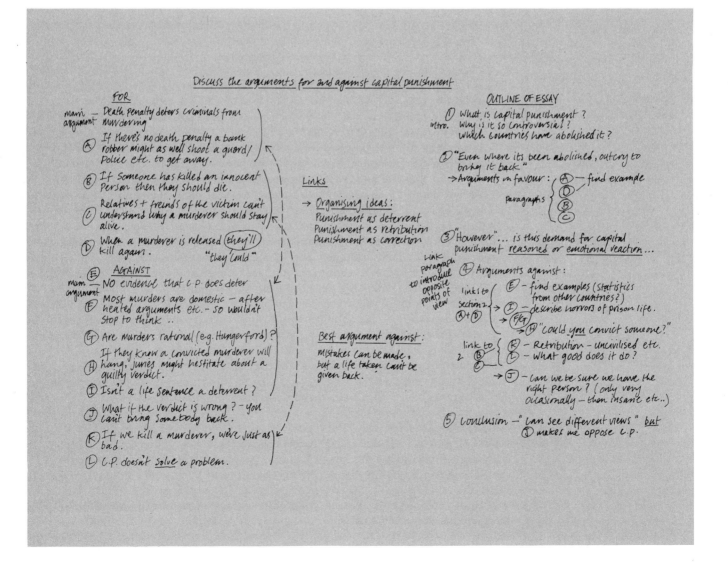

- When presenting different arguments, attempt to summarise them. To do this you will need to identify the key ideas or points associated with them. Include enough detail to be able to convey clearly what the central points are, but not so much that you produce a cluttered effect, distracting the reader and drawing attention away from your main point.

- Make sure that before you begin writing your final draft your work is planned and organised. Planning enables you to think forward, assemble your ideas and information, think about how your work will develop and what you are going to say and where. There are many approaches that you can adopt to plan and organise what you are going to write. What is important is that the method you use is useful to you, helps you to think about what you are going to write and provides you with a guide, giving you a route through the subject you are going to discuss.

- The conclusion to your work can be particularly important to you. Make sure that it reflects the arguments which have been discussed and developed throughout your work. Use it for summing up and make sure that any personal comment which you introduce is directed towards the ideas and points which you have covered in your work.

> 66 Make use of your conclusion. 99

> 66 A good introduction, which sets the schene 99

State what David Alton is trying to achieve with his abortion bill, what will the consequences be of this bill if it becomes law? What opposition does this bill face and state your own personal view on the bill.

David Alton, a Roman Catholic Liberal MP for East Molesley, Liverpool, had tried to pass an Abortion Bill 20 years 1 day after David Steel introduced a Private Members Bill in Parliament which was to become the 1967 Abortion Act. The 30 year old's bill was to limit the present Bill which is 28 weeks to 18 weeks but if it does go in to made law a few questions will be needed before he puts the bill to law. But first the 1967 Act was to have passed a law stating that it was no longer an offence for a pregnancy to be terminated by a doctor, if 2 doctors agreed on two points. The first is that to carry on with the pregnancy would involve a greater risk to the life or the physical or mental health of the mother, or of her existing children, than if she had it terminated. The second is that there was a substantial risk that if the child were born it would suffer serious physical or mental handicap.

Some people are trying to forget the most serious questions that need to be answered and they are if the bill does become law obviously Back-Street abortion will rise again. People don't realise that Back-Street abortion is very dangerous as if the abortion is done at home or similar areas, it will often lead to scars and also infection and possible death. This is was what Steel was trying to abolish in the first place. Another of these questions is that is Abortion wrong another is that any member of Parliament have any right to do such issue that affect women? However the question is the foetus a baby while in the mother or is it a baby when it's born? and if is a baby in the mother then what week is it classifed as a baby?

Doctors' leaders say that it would condemn shcoolgirl rape and incest victims and mentally handicapped women to unwanted motherhood. The BMA (British Medical Association) are also against the abortion bill and complaining that the bill was not tried to be beaten, medically it is not even logical. They are also say if the bill succeeds, it will mean that women who are expecting serously handicapped babies are soon to learn the bad news when it's too late.

One of the BMA members Dr Michael Pane the chairman of the association also disagrees about the idea of Alton's bill. He says that he will not support a bill that will make subnormal girls, who may be incest or rape victims having to have babies.

One of the organisations which is supporting Alton's bill is the LIFE organisation which is helping women who have been abandoned by their partner. Most women there have thought about wiether to abort it but most of these are having the babies. The Catholic Church is also support Alton's Bill as they regard that abortion is a 'Sin in all cases'.

Alton says that every child has the right to live and that includes handicapped children. He also says that handicapped children doesn't have to live in a life of misery and they are just as good anybody else. That might be the case but what he doesn't know is that he doesn't know what it's like to be handicapped and doesn't know how they feel.

Rosie Barnes, an SDP MP from Greenwich, is a mother to 3 children but she had her doubts about having the children. Her eldest son Danny was one the the children Mrs. Barnes was worried about. She had German Measles while she was carrying Danny, and she went to the doctors straight away. The doctor said she would have a child with a small handicap, about 10% or so. Dann was born with partial hearing and is finding school life hard as the children at his school call him 'Daniel Deafo'. He, of course, gets really upset about it and hates going to school every morning and his mother explains how he has had an unhappy childhood.

Mrs. Barnes says that if she knew she had a handicapped child she was carrying she would abort it immediately. She explains how unhappy she was about carrying her third child, Joseph. She was so sad and worried that Joseph would be handicapped. Doctors couldn't tell her until she was 20 weeks pregnant and up and till then it was hell for her. She had the test and it showed that Joseph would be a perfect baby.

On a survery done in 1986 after 24 weeks 'private clinics' where 88% of all late abortions are performed, 24 weeks is already the upper gestational limit. However Alton's bill deals with only 4.8% of all abortions but only 8% of abortions are performed on grounds of Handicaps.

Alton says by 18 weeks the foetus is not a 'blob of jelly', it can feel pain, it reacts to light, it has a complete skeleton and reflexes and it's heart can pump 50 pints of blood daily. This goes back to one of the questions mentioned before. Is it a baby when it's in the women or is it a baby when it's born?

In my own personnel view it's somethink that needs to be thought about seriously on with time and to see there is no right or wrong answer. I do agree with abortions especially if the child is going to be handicapped. This is because a handicapped child theres no life or fun, they can not enjoy life like we can. I feel sorry for handicapped children especially the ones who aren't allowed outside their own homes. But saying that I do feel that abortions, are so they call it, 'sinful' because if the chiled is going to be alright then there is no need to destroy it. I used destroy because I feel that a foetus can not be killed as it, in my own view, isn't a baby but until it is born.

"States both sides of the argument "

"Conclusion sums up argument and personal comment refers back to points discussed in the essay "

Fig. 5.4 A student's response to a question on David Alton's abortion bill.

Comment

This essay clearly explains its subject-matter in the introduction and outlines what is going to be discussed. It develops the argument well, giving a clear and logical account. It is well organised, making good use of linked paragraphs, and enables the reader to move easily through the arguments. It examines different points of view, giving adequate summaries of their main points. The conclusion is connected to the main body of the work and is related to the arguments which have been developed throughout.

WRITING REPORTS

Writing a report on something involves conveying a body of information. You may have to report the findings of your enquiry into a particular subject, making a report from information and evidence which you have been provided with, or making a specialist report from the point of view of a person in a particular job or position – for example, a police report, a social work report, etc.

Key points to remember

- You will be concerned mainly with the presentation of factual information. It is important that the information is ordered, using headings and subheadings where appropriate. These should be logically connected and enable your work to develop. It may be appropriate to number the points you are making.

- The aim of a report is to give a clear picture of the subject under discussion. If you assume that your reader has no previous knowledge, this will help you to ensure that you have included all the relevant information.

  Where you have a lot of information to convey, make each point concisely, being brief and to the point.

- Where the report is aimed at a particular audience, make sure that you adopt an appropriate style of format. For example, if you are producing a newspaper report you will need to engage the reader's attention, so shorter sentences and paragraphs, eyecatching headlines and subheadings, will be appropriate. Consider the appropriate language needed to convey the key facts and think about what is the most concise way to convey the relevant information. Newspaper articles usually try to interest the reader immediately by including in their opening paragraph a reference to the key points of the article. They do this by answering the questions: Who? Where? When? What? (See Fig. 5.5).

- Find out about the style of newspaper reporting through your own reading. Note the main features of the language which are typical of popular journalistic style, the way in which quotations are used, the use of emotive language, and the ways in which often irrelevant personal details about individuals are included in the articles. Remember that newspaper accounts of events seek to give a particular view or impression. Study the ways in which language is used to achieve this (see Chapter 4).

- Other reports will require a more formal style, with a more precise and accurate use of vocabularly and presentation. This may involve you in writing to a particular format – for example, completing a form, or compiling a report for shareholders of a company/mini-enterprise, where information, written and statistical, is expected to appear under particular headings: profit and loss, marketing strategy, etc.

- Where you are asked to write a report from a particular point of view – for example, a social worker or police report on someone – try to think of what sort of information would be relevant and important, and what the purpose of the report would be. This will involve consideration of what particular professionals look for to explain events or behaviour and how an adequate account can be given with the minimum of personal comment or opinion.

Baby food jars banned at store

by staff reporters

But tins declared safe after blackmail scare

SUPERMARKET giant Tesco has returned tins of baby food to its shelves in Northampton after checking them over the weekend.

But all Heinz and Cow and Gate jars will not reappear until tamper-proof jars are available.

The decision to withdraw baby food was made at the weekend after jars spiked with glass and metal had been bought at several of the chain's 375 stores, said company spokesman Peter Stephens.

He welcomed the plans by Cow and Gate and Heinz to destroy existing stocks of baby food and to introduce plastic shrink wrappers to ensure the food is tamper proof.

Mr Stevens said that it was impractical to serve baby food over the counter, so the shelves will remain empty until tamper-proof jars are available.

who   where   when   what

Alan's donkey work down on the farm

JASON the donkey is now living a life of luxury at Cottons Farm House, near Cogenhoe, after being rescued from a London Gar-den Centre. He's one of the lucky ones.

For every year thousands of loveable pets like Jason are abandoned by their owners. And only the odd handful ever find new homes.

This was the message emphasised by Lena Davis for National Pet Week which began a few days ago.

Lena who is one of the trustees of the farm said: "When people buy an animal they must realise it is for life. Animals are a lot of hard work, but they are definitely worth having around.

"It has even been proved that stroking animals is physically and psychologically beneficial for the owner and the pet!"

But the caring farm is not a dumping ground for unwanted pets. It already has its hands full with 25 animals roaming around!

Fig. 5.5 Two newspaper articles (Source: *Northampton Mercury*, 5 May 1989).

COURT REPORT

POLICE REPORT - CONFIDENTIAL

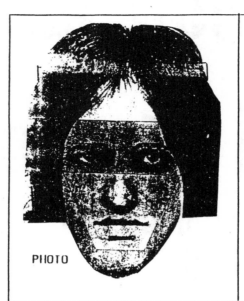

PHOTO

DESCRIPTION

HEIGHT : 6' 0"

EYES : BROWN.

HAIR : DARK BROWN
          FAIRLY LONG.

DRESS : CASUAL
           FAIRLY UNTIDY

HIGH FOREHEAD.

MUSCULAR FRAME.

NAME SCOTT. D. ROBINSON.	D.O.B. 4/10/69	AGE 18

ADDRESS	STATUS
42A BILLINGTON FLATS LIVERPOOL. MERSEYSIDE.	SINGLE **OCCUPATION** UNEMPLOYED.

PREVIOUS CONVICTIONS

        SHOPLIFTING - LIVERPOOL 1983

        SHOPLIFTING - LIVERPOOL 1985

        SHOPLIFTING - LIVERPOOL 1986.

FAMILY BACKGROUND

        PARENTS SEPARATED WHEN HE WAS TEN.
        FATHER REPORTED TO BE VIOLENT - HAVING
SEVERAL OFFENCES OF HIS OWN.

Name... Scott Robinson............................   Form... 5EAG.................

Date ...9/9/1986....................   Absent ...7.1... out of 146... half-days

General Comments

   Scott's rather poor and unsatisfactory work is in no way a measure
of his capabilities or intelligence — more of his attitude to the
subject and the discipline of the classroom. He is easily distracted
and has a disturbing influence on his peers. His work would
definitely improve if he only tried to concentrate more.

   He does have considerable ability and it seems a waste for him not
to use it to his advantage.

   Scott could easily gain a grade D or above if only he worked more
conscientiously and participated more in the oral discussions, for
the rest of the course.

EFFORT

Makes some effort with pressure and close supervision.			Sometimes makes an effort without undue pressure and supervision.			Usually makes an effort to work and improve.			Always works to the best of his/her ability.		
	✓										

CONDUCT

Behaviour is tolerable only with pressure and close supervision.			Behaviour is usually appropriate with pressure from staff.			Behaviour is usually appropriate to the task.			Behaviour is always appropriate to the task.		
✓											

HOMEWORK

Homework is rarely attempted.			Homework is usually attempted.			Homework is adequately done.			Great care and attention is given to homework.		
✓											

PRESENTATION

Rarely produces neat, clear work.			Has produced some neat, clear work.			Usually produces neat, clear work.			Always presents work neatly and clearly.		
		✓									

Estimated G.C.S.E. Grade on Current Performance .....F/G..............

Suggested Targets

   Scott could easily gain a grade D or above
if only he worked more conscientiously and part
icipated more in the oral discussions, for the rest
of the course .

Signed .L.Marshall........
Subject Teacher.

SOCIAL WORKER'S REPORT ON SCOTT ROBINSON

Scott David Robinson, aged eighteen and in residence at 42A Billington Flats, Liverpool, comitted the crime of theft on the 22nd October 1987, at a semi-detached house within a mile of his own flat. This is the first burglary he is known to be connected with although he has been caught shoplifting on several occasions, for which he has been attending a Probation Officer.

 **More details needed**

After an interview with Scott I estimated a total score of around 295 marks on the Prediction Table, which shows he has not had an easy childhood and that of others like him between 63.5% and 89.2% have become delinquents. I also noticed that he felt no regret for his crimes, but appeared bored.

From the age of five to the age of ten he had to contend with fighting from his parents, who were going through a difficult stage in their marriage, which did not only involve verbal abuse, but also that of a physical nature. His father apparently blamed Scott for the arguments, and so took to using violence with him. His mother was the complete opposite and when his father eventually left, she neglected to discipline him to compensate for the upset of the previous years.

These experiences have left him in a very confused state, as neither of them have shown any particular affection for him and has had the result of making him rebel against all authoritative figures — including teachers, as shown on his Fifth Year School Report (1986) and policepersons.

Scott's environment and his poor financial affairs have also been thought to be factors which have turned juveniles to crime. He lives in a block of high-rise council flats in the inner-city area of Liverpool, where there is high unemployment and high criminality. Living in such an area has obviously affected him because he and his peers haven't enough money to go out with, because like Scott they only live on the benefit from the state and there are no free amenities, such as youth clubs. This gives them little to do apart from walking the streets, which leads to vandalism and stealing from others because they can not afford the things themselves.

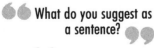 **What do you suggest as a sentence?**

Good use made of environmental factors

Scott's problem has been building up steadily from an early age and, in my opinion, a sentence of any kind would cause more harm than good as his rebellious attitude, described in his school report, would affect other inmates. I think he would benefit more from attending sessions where someone can listen sympathetically to his problems and advise him, showing him someone cares about his welfare.

PSYCHOLOGIST'S REPORT ON SCOTT ROBINSON

Scott David Robinson, an eighteen year old male from the county of Merseyside shows many classic psychological theories in explanation for his apparent criminality, in his background and personality.

The parents, most psychologists will agree, have a very large effect on their children's personality especially during the first five years of their lives, as they are solely dependant on them, and are mostly influenced by their attitudes and actions.

The conditioning of Scott is a very confusing area for him, especially that of discipline because his mother neglected it altogether, and his father applied very strict rules. Scott has rebelled against this for one of two reasons, either due to the confusion he feels because he does not know what is expected of him, or in opposition to his father, who forced it upon him.

A bit confused

His attitude has also been affected by 'learning theories' and the fact that he was constantly approached by violence from his father, taught him that this type of behaviour was acceptable in the society.

Scotts parents did not give any impression of love to their son and at home, they were always to busy arguing between each other, as the Social Worker has explained to give Scott any of the attention he needed. This may possibly have been the factor which led him to crime, as it is one of Freud's theories that when a need is denied individuals give it to themselves. In Scott's case he showed affection for himself by giving himself gifts and demanding attending by his rebellious behaviour, often using violence, for reasons I have explained previously. Some of these incidents are referred to in Scott's last School Report.

Another theory which the unaffectionate family group show exceptionally well is that of the failure for the 'superego' to develop. This is not only shown by the fact that he steals in the first place, but mainly because he feels no guilt after the crime, which again was noted by the social worker, which definitely shows only the selfish levels of personality the 'Id' and 'Ego'.

All these explanations centre around his early childhood but he has 'learnt' or been 'conditioned' since, by his peers and environment. They have conditioned him to crime, as it is a relatively common occurrence in inner city areas — firstly petty crime, shoplifting and becoming more serious.

The only recommendation I would like to make is not to send this individual to prison or a detention centre of any kind because he would probably learn to be a better criminal, by discovering new methods from other inmates.

An attempt made to explain behaviour in terms of theories

Fig. 5.6 A student's work: a court report.

Comment

A very good attempt. The reports are clearly ordered, with relevant information contained within particular paragraphs, which allow for a full picture to be built up. The style of the reports is adequately matched to their task. The candidate makes an attempt to identify the types of knowledge which the authors of the report may see as being important and has tried to relate it to the theories and concerns likely to be held by them.

PERSUASIVE WRITING

This involves you in not just expressing a point of view, belief, idea or body of information but also in trying to convince other people of its importance or relevance to them. This sort of writing could be in the form of:

- producing an advertisement to promote a particular product or service;
- trying to attract people to join an organisation or take up a particular career;
- writing a pamphlet to promote a cause or idea;
- encouraging people to give money to, or support for, something, or to behave in a particular way: for example, vote for a certain political party, change their attitude towards the environment, etc.

Key features of persuasive writing

- **Omission**

  Selecting and emphasising particular facts which promote your case, and leaving out or playing down others: for example, in a political leaflet, pointing out your successes and not your failures, etc.

- **Exaggeration**
  Overstating your case and presenting it in the best possible light: for example, claiming your product is the best on the market, giving the impression that things are worse (or better) than they are, etc.

- **Repetition**
  Hammering home a point by repeating the same key word or phrase: for example, in a leaflet warning about the effects of pollution, listing a number of statements of examples, beginning with the word 'danger'.

- **Persuader words**
  These are words or phrases that make the reader feel that she or he must agree with you: for example, 'of course', 'it's obvious that', 'everyone knows that', 'certainly', 'definitely', 'it's a fact that', etc.

- **Rhetorical questions**
  These are questions which do not call for an answer and are used to make the reader feel involved: for example, 'You are not going to let them get away with this, are you?', 'How on earth did you manage without this?', etc.

4 ▷ DRAWINGS AND PICTURES

❝❝ You don't have to be a great artist to communicate in pictures. ❞❞

Pictures can sometimes convey ideas, drawing attention to things in a more vivid and relevant way than words. To produce your own pictures you do not need to possess any great artistic ability. Try to think of your drawing ability in the same way you treat handwriting in your written work. Handwriting is obviously important for communication, but as long as your work is legible it will be assessed on how it conveys information and meets assessment objectives rather than how attractive it is. In the same way, pictures will not be assessed just on your ability to draw accurately but on your ability to use the medium to convey information. You can produce pictures to back up, illustrate or reinforce what you are writing about. Make sure that what you produce is relevant to your writing and that it is part of the argument you are making or the information you are trying to convey.

Pictures can be used as your main method of communication. They can be especially relevant when you are conveying certain messages to particular audiences. For example

- As part of an advertising campaign, you could produce a poster to advertise your product. A drawing can be more persuasive and a more concise way of getting your information across. The images you create can often sum up more effectively than words the feelings, attitudes and associations which you are trying to convey.

- Putting across ideas or events in a comic format can transmit information simply and could be used, for example, to design a piece of communication to inform a wide audience or communicate with other pupils.

- Pictures can be used to demonstrate a sequence of events. This will involve selecting and designing scenes and pictures which most clearly represent the process that is taking place.

- Pictures can also help you to describe how you could convey something in a different medium: for example, to accompany a script and set of directions to show how you could produce a film sequence, or to describe particular events. This does not require any great artistic ability; it simply means that you need to convey what a scene will look like, what characters should be in it and where they are located. Your illustrations here are similar to notes to assist with direction.

Fig. 5.7 A student's work in comic format.

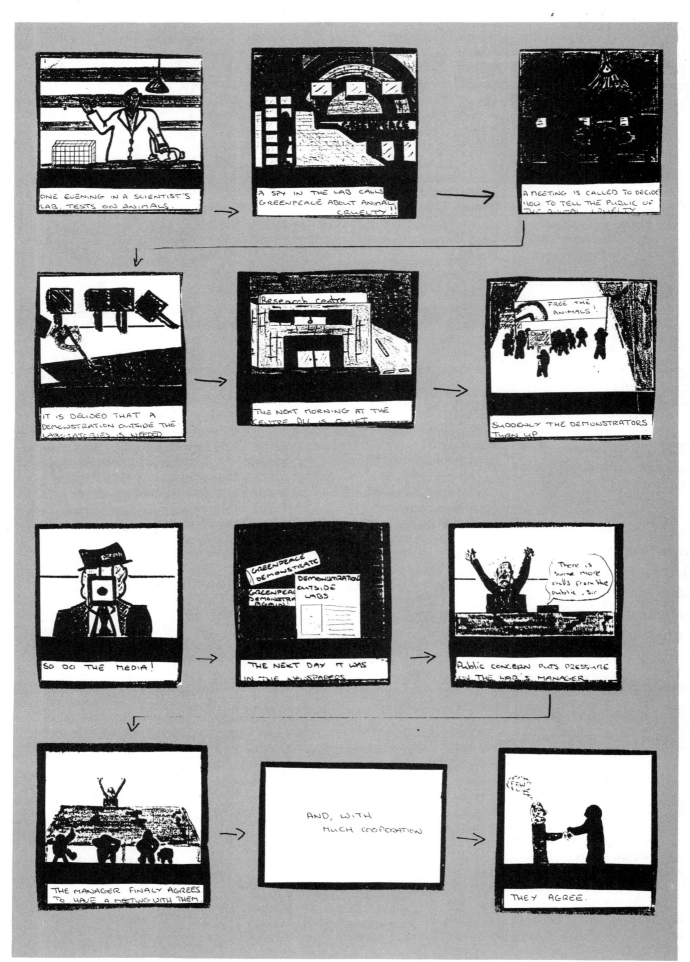

Fig. 5.8 Information transmitted in comic format.

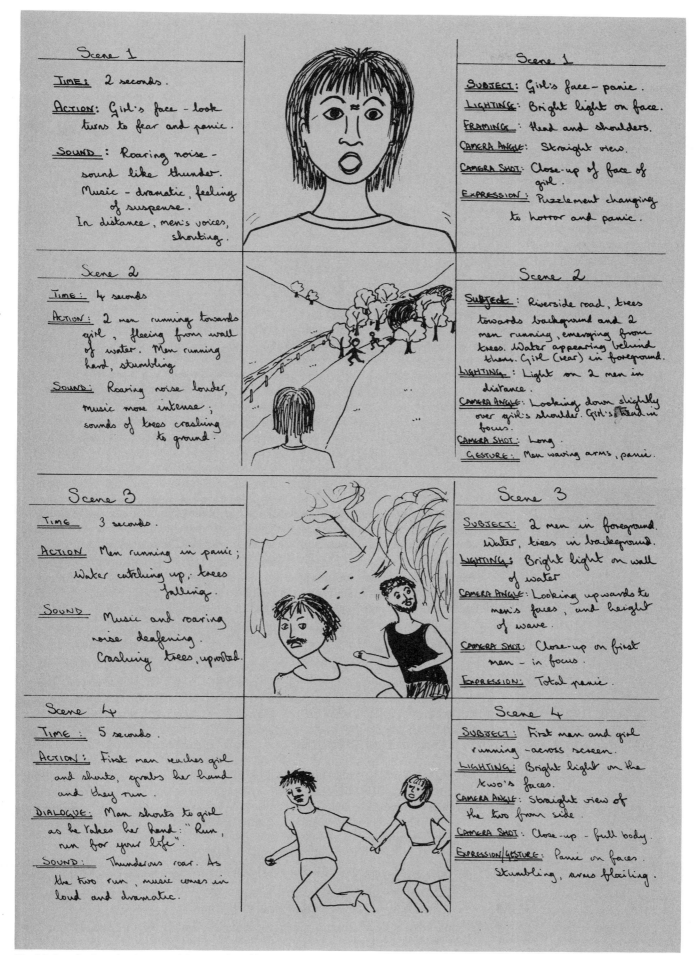

Fig. 5.9 A student's work: pictures and directions for a film.

Scene 5

TIME: 5 seconds

ACTION: Wave overtakes the two people and sweeps them off their feet. Unable to hold on to each other.

SOUND: Thunderous roar deafening. Screams as they're swept over. Music increases to climax

Scene 6

TIME: 6 seconds

ACTION: Water flow slackens off into fast-flowing 'river' flood. First man and girl catch hold of tree floating past. Second man (drowned) appears again.

SOUND: Roaring noise slackens off and music calms as two people reach floating tree. Sad music as second man's body floats into view.

Scene 5

SUBJECT: Mainly water – man and girl in foreground. Trees and debris in water.

LIGHTING: Light on water.

CAMERA ANGLE: Looking down slightly

CAMERA SHOT: Long-medium

EXPRESSION/GESTURE: Panic, helpless.

Scene 6

SUBJECT: Man and girl holding on to tree. Second man's body floating into view.

LIGHTING: Bright light glinting on water.

CAMERA ANGLE: Looking down.

CAMERA SHOT: Long medium, view straight across 'river', backing off to take in floating body.

GESTURE: Reaching out to tree; shoulders relax, heads drop forward with relief.

5 > USING VIDEO/AUDIO RECORDINGS

Recordings can be used:

- to support your written work – for example, an audio tape of an interview you have conducted as part of an enquiry, or a video tape you have made which draws attention to, or provides evidence for, an evaluation of television advertisements;

- as a different medium to present your assessment task in its entirety – for example, an audio tape you have produced of a radio broadcast of 1960s music and news to demonstrate your understanding of the period, or a video recording you have made to enquire into how accessible your school is to a disabled person;

- as a record of your work or performance – for example, an audio tape made of an interview between you and your teacher on a topic you have been researching, or a video tape made of your performance with others in a role-play.

If you are making the recordings yourself you must ensure that you plan your use of recordings. If you are making a video recording, remember that, for example, films and recordings which you may see on the television are produced with very careful planning during which every shot and angle is thought about. Although you are unlikely to have access to sophisticated editing equipment, you should at least be able to demonstrate that you have thought about what you are going to record and how.

Make sure that you understand how to operate any equipment you are going to use and always ensure, for example, that the sound level is adequate and that you are recording what you think you are recording.

Whatever the purpose of your recording, it should conform to the requirements made of any form of communication:

- it is suitable and relevant for the assessment task;

- it provides your teacher with enough evidence to be able to assess your own individual work and effort;

- it is organised, logical and coherent in its final form;

- it gives enough detail to provide a clear understanding of the subject you are discussing or researching;

- it is appropriate for your audience.

GETTING STARTED

Many areas of study within your Integrated Humanities course will require you to work *independently*. You will be expected to find, use, and present material by yourself. You will be working to *deadlines* laid down by your teacher. Some students find it very difficult to work in this way; the quality of their work suffers and with it their eventual GCSE grade. You might be one of these students! To help you become *more effective*, we have included some guidelines on how to *cope* with the demands of your Integrated Humanities course. You need to consider the following principles:

- *organise* and *plan* your work and time;
- *ask questions* and be an *active* learner;
- *get information* in many different ways;
- *sort out* ideas by *discussing* them with friends, teachers, and other adults;
- get the most out of *reading*, which means reading in different ways, depending on what you want;
- *make notes* which make sense so you can use them later;
- understand *how* you learn best: everyone learns differently, but there are some basic ideas about learning which you ought to consider.

CHAPTER 6

MANAGING YOUR LEARNING

GET ORGANISED

UNDERSTANDING YOURSELF

ASKING QUESTIONS

FINDING INFORMATION: READING, NOTE-TAKING

GROUP WORK

TRYING TO IMPROVE

SHARING A PROBLEM

ESSENTIAL PRINCIPLES

1 ▷ **GET ORGANISED**

❝Avoid stress and don't panic.❞

❝Don't waste classtime and so increase your homework.❞

❝You have to plan carefully to meet your deadlines.❞

❝Get into the routine of setting realistic targets.❞

It is more difficult to work at your full potential if you are stressed. Stress often occurs when students cannot keep up with the tasks set. This must be avoided, as the tendency is to *panic* and so underachieve in this situation. To avoid this you must *plan your time*. This includes *classtime* and *homework*. How often do you waste classtime? This wasted classtime increases the work to be done at home, which in turn causes a clash with the other things you wish to do 'in your time', like jobs, household chores and relaxation. Better *organisation* of your time would prevent this from happening.

One way to achieve this is by keeping a *list or diary* of all the things you have to achieve each week. You could do this for your other subjects as well as Integrated Humanities. It may be that in your Integrated Humanities course you have been given a *deadline* of two weeks to complete a piece of work. At the beginning of this period you may think you have plenty of time. This leads you into a false sense of security and before you know it, the deadline has arrived and you have done little towards completing your task. At this point you are likely to rush your work and produce something which does not reflect your true ability.

To avoid this situation you must *plan* carefully what you have to do. Once this has been established, set yourself *targets* for achieving the things which you have identified as necessary for the completion of your work. In this way, you are working continuously, rather than leaving everything until the last minute. Remember, make the most of classtime and do not leave too much to be done at home.

This is an example of a coursework planner which may be of use.

Planning sheet for intergrated Humanities

TASK :–   Assess the reasons for an increase in Nuclear Power
DATE SET: May 10th
DATE TO BE COMPLETED :   May 24th
CLASSTIME AVAILABLE :   6 Hours
AREAS TO BE ASSESSED: Evaluation and Interpretation of Evidence

Things to do to achieve set task   Targets for completion

① Read booklets and resource sheets provided by school and make notes on: By 17th May mainly using classtime (max. 3 hours)

     What is the energy problem ?
     What is nuclear power ?
     What are the problems, if any, of nuclear power ?
     What are the financial costs of nuclear power ?
     What are the human costs of nuclear power ?
     What are the environmental costs of nuclear power ?
     What are the alternatives to nuclear power ?

② Research (visit Library / phone up / get leaflets / use school resource bank)   By 17th May Mainly using homework (max. 3 hours)

     What are the views of Environmental groups about nuclear power ?
     For example : Greenpeace, Friends of the Earth.
     What are the views of the C.E.G.B. ?
Make notes from these sources on the questions stated above.

③ Assess the reliability of these views – including bias.   By 20th May

④ Present answer to the task set – seek advice from teacher if necessary.   20th – 24th May 2 hours of classtime + homework.

Fig. 6.1 A planning sheet for Integrated Humanities.

2 UNDERSTANDING YOURSELF

> 66 How do you learn best? 99

Linked to the successful planning of your work is the ability to understand the *circumstances in which you learn best.* Everyone is different and so learns in different ways. It takes some people longer to understand things than others. How do you work best? The following points might help you to answer these questions:

- **When are you awake?**
  This may sound a silly question but some people work best in the mornings, some in the afternoons and some late at night. To make the most of your time, especially at home, you need to identify the part of the day when you operate best as a student.

- **How often do you need a break?**
  It is suggested by many that learning occurs best in short, concentrated periods. Long periods of study should be avoided. Try a bit of research yourself. How long can you work well and how often do you need a break?

- **Do you work better in silence?**
  Some people can work in a noisy environment, which may be music playing or the television switched on. Others need silence to achieve their best. When do you do your best work?

> 66 How and when do you learn best? 99

It is important for you to try and understand how you learn effectively. This will help you make the best of your time and so improve your chances of gaining a good GCSE grade. To sum up:

- Plan your work. Break down a big task into separate activities. *Set yourself short-term targets which can be achieved.*

- Decide when, and for how long, you are going to work.

- Organise a space for work (somewhere at home or school) and make sure you have all the materials you need.

- When you have finished your work session *review* your progress. Cross the completed task off your list of things to do.

3 ASKING QUESTIONS

> 66 Ask questions. 99

Good learners always ask questions. There could be a wide variety of questions you wish to ask concerning the issue under study. Some of these may be common to all the tasks set in your Integrated Humanities course; others may be directly related to a specific task. Some common questions are:

- What is it I have to do?
- What does my task involve?
- What do I have to understand?
- How am I going to get the necessary information to complete the task?
- How am I going to communicate my answer?
- How am I going to be assessed?
- What have I learned?

The need to ask questions about your work is a theme which occurs throughout Integrated Humanities courses. You will already have seen this emphasised in Chapters 3 and 4.

4 FINDING INFORMATION: READING, NOTE-TAKING

These vital parts of effective learning have already been discussed in Chapter 3 as part of the stages of an enquiry. It would be as well to refer to this section now and refresh your memory about how to approach these issues. They certainly play a key role in completing good pieces of work.

5 GROUP WORK

> 66 Emotive and controversial issues are studied in Integrated Humanities courses. 99

Many Integrated Humanities courses allow you to study relevant and current *issues*. These can be very emotive and controversial, which means that people tend to have firm views about them. Before you can fully appreciate and understand the issues, you must be aware of these different viewpoints. One way of achieving this is through group work.

Working in groups is a good way to improve your learning and to develop the important skills of *discussion* and *listening*. Being able to work and discuss in groups is invaluable because:

- You can learn from others and sort out your own ideas.

- When you are trying to understand a new idea, it helps to think it through and try to explain it in your own words.

- Others in the group can show you ways of looking at things you had not thought of for yourself.

- *Listening and talking* skills are valuable outside school. You can gain a great deal from discussions with friends and adults. When you go to work you will have to listen and talk to other people in order to do your job.

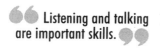
Listening and talking are important skills.

SUCCESSFUL GROUP WORK

The following points are worth considering if you want to try group work as a way to help your learning:

1 All members of the group must understand clearly what they are supposed to be doing and have enough information to complete the task set. The decision to work in a group may be yours or your teacher's, but whoever it is, *clear goals* for the group are essential.

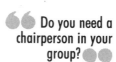
Do you need a chairperson in your group?

2 There may be the need to select a chairperson for the group who would ensure that discussion is kept to the matter in hand, and that everyone in the group is given the opportunity to speak. There must be some order to the discussion, otherwise a situation could develop where the loudest voice has the longest say; if this occurs, the full potential of group work as a learning tool is not going to be reached.

3 You may also need to select a secretary, whose job it would be to take notes so that an accurate record is kept of the discussion which takes place. This could provide the basis for a report to other groups or to your teacher about the state of your discussions. The secretary might also be responsible for setting time limits for the group discussion. This may help the group to concentrate on the issue under discussion and increase the sense of purpose in the group.

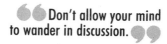
Don't allow your mind to wander in discussion.

4 If you are going to learn from group discussion you must be prepared to *listen* and change your mind. Listening is a difficult skill. How many times has your teacher told you about not listening? When listening to someone talking it is very easy to let your mind wander and to lose concentration. To try and avoid this, keep active during the discussion. You may wish to take notes or ask questions in your head about the things you have heard.

5 During the discussion be *polite*. Don't interrupt when someone is in the middle of explaining something. If you disagree, don't just say 'rubbish' or 'I don't agree.' When it is your turn to speak, explain *why* you disagree.

GROUP WORK, DISCUSSION AND INTEGRATED HUMANITIES

One way to get the most out of discussion is for people in the group to take on particular roles and present views from this standpoint. For the benefit of the discussion they '*get in role*'. It has already been mentioned how Integrated Humanities deals with relevant and controversial issues. It is therefore possible to set up group work in such a way that members of the group each take on a role which allows them to put forward the differing viewpoints held about the issue under study. By adopting one standpoint not only are you helped to empathise with that view (see Chapter 2) but, when adding it to the views expressed by other group members, your overall understanding of the issue benefits.

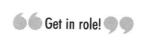
Get in role!

There are many areas of study which would benefit from role-play exercises. However, one issue which is particularly relevant at the time of writing concerns the destruction of the Amazon rainforests. You could arrange a group discussion for four, each member taking on one of the following roles:

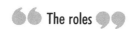
The roles

1	Amazonian Indian	He/she is concerned about the effect the destruction of the rainforest will have on his/her tribe, whose lifestyle would be greatly affected: they may be forced to move, run the risk of disease from people moving into the area, their livelihood could be lost.
2	Brazilian Government Official	This person looks at the issue only in terms of the effect it will have on the economy of Brazil. Brazil has a large national debt. They owe millions of pounds to other countries. The destruction of the rainforest will aid the

country by making the mineral deposits in Amazonia more accessible. Also, a quick profit could be made on the sale of timber.

3 Environmentalist | This person views the issue purely in environmental terms. What effect will it have on animal, plant and human life? What about the 'greenhouse effect' and the impact this would have on the world's climate?

4 Poor Resident of Sao Paulo | This person has been taken in by government propaganda, which promises a better life in Amazonia. They see the development of this area as a way to escape the slums of Sao Paulo and improve their lives.

66 Role-play helps understanding. 99

Each member of the group has to be sufficiently briefed about their role. They will need detailed information about the viewpoint they are to put forward and must be able to identify with the role. If this happens, the subsequent discussion could be lively and enlightening, giving a great understanding of all the views involved in the issue. This will enable you to form your *own* view concerning the destruction of the rainforest.

AN EXAMPLE OF A STUDENT'S WORK

This assignment was the end result of several weeks' work concerning the problems of developing Amazonia. It included some role-play group work. The actual task set was to design a development plan for Amazonia. The student was given 100 units of money and had to decide how to spend this on the development, justifying all the decisions.

DEVELOPING AMAZONIA

AREA FOR DEVELOPMENT	UNITS
AGRICULTURE	8
FUEL AND POWER	15
SMALL–SCALE INDUSTRIES USING LOCAL MATERIALS	10
LARGE–SCALE INDUSTRIES USING LOCAL MATERIALS	19
MINERALS AND RAW MATERIALS	16
TRANSPORT AND COMMUNICATIONS	12
SOCIAL SERVICES, EDUCATION, HEALTH CENTRES	10
ENCOURAGEMENT OF SETTLEMENT	10

66 The government official's argument showing here 99

Agriculture is probably the most single important area for development. Without it a country cannot survive. Therefore, for a settlement to be successful there must be a good access of food and water. There are three such areas in Amazonia: the Varzea Zone along the River Amazon, the extreme northern coast of Brazil and the area that borders Venezuala and Guyana. I decided that I would develop all three areas for settlement as there are deposits of minerals and raw materials nearby all of them than can be exported or used to help the running of Amazonia. In the Varzea Zone I would have the cultivation of cocoa, bananas, jute, maize and manioc. On the plantations to the western end of the Varzea Zone I would have sugar. On the coastal region I would have tobacco on the plantations. Finally on the plantation in the north of Amazonia I would put cocoa. I would increase the rice production as it is a very saleable product overseas and very good base food for the population as it is cheap and easy to cook. I decided that I would use the cattle rearing in the north to provide food for the population of Amazonia and the cattle rearing on the coast for exporting. I decided I would spend eight units on agriculture.

Government official's view again

If Brazil wants to become more developed the minerals and raw materials must be exploited. I decided that I would mine the bauxite on the banks of the Amazon as well as the manganese further downstream. I would mine the manganese, gold and iron near Pôrto Velho on the Madeira. Finally I would keep the nest of the minerals for further refining. As far as the new materials go I decided I would extract rubber and gum from the trees (the rubber would come from western Amazonia and the gum from northwestern Amazonia. I decided I would spend fifteen units on minerals and new materials.

I would then have to decide what small and large scale industries I would set up. I decided the large scale industries that I would set up would be an aluminium smelter, an iron smelter and a factory for producing goods from rubber ie. coats, car and bike tyres, hoses, tubing, inflatable boats, washing up and surgical gloves, rubber band, elastic, sealing, latex, tennis and golf balls and car bumpers. Amazonia has the main components for making steel making- iron and manganese- but it could be a bit over optimistic thinking that I could have a forth large scale industry in an unskilled workforce.

Not much concern expressed about the Amazonian Indian so far

The small scale industries I decided to set up clothes making and paper making industries using fibre, sweet making using the gum, fishing and ranching.

Map to show where the minerals are mined and refined.

The student provided a map to illustrate his development plan. This is shown on page 170.

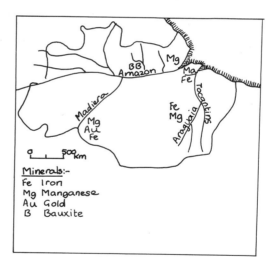

However, before these industries can commence they need to be able to be powered. Probably the most obvious and best way to do this is hydroelectric power. However if I were to do this I would severe the main lines of communication – the rivers – and have to rely on less than adequate roads. But without the power the country does not develop. So what I would do would be to set up the HEP stations carry on relying on the roads for a couple of years, then after the profits have started to come in tar-mac the roads. I would set up four HEP stations; one on the Madiera, one on the river near the bauxite, one on the Araguaia and one on the Tocantins. These HEP stations should be able to cope with the expected new settlements as well. Other forms of power that I would explore would be tidal energy, solar power and biofuels – an example of biofuel is alcohol which is used to power cars. I would spend fifteen units on fuel and power.

What about the Indians?

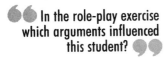 The slum dwellers in Sao Paulo will be interested in this.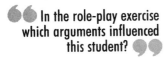

Before any of these can begin there must be people to run the factories. There need to be T.V. and radio campaigns, letters through doors and posters advertising Amazonia. This campaign would include job expectations, social services and other good points about life in Amazonia.

When they reach Amazonia they would need to be assured of good social services. As the greater part of the population will be unskilled. I would set up two technical colleges — one at Manaus and one at Porto Velho. There, those that go to them will be taught how to operate machinery in the factories, mines and power stations. Health could be a real problem — expecially malaria — so I would set aside enough money to build hospitals and health centres. I would start government grants to encourage businesses to Amazonia. There also need to be long term as well as short term schemes. These would be pension and unemployment benefit schemes. I would spend ten units on social services.

Finally comes transport and communications. The roads in Amazonia very nearly all gravel tracks. These tracks become extremely hazzardous during and after rainstorms and are littered with pot holes, As I do not want to deter people coming to Amazonia I would tar-mac the Trans Amazonian Highway and the Marshal Rondon Highway. Another reason for doing this is that the constant flow of traffic expected would need good roads to prevent excessive accidents.

What about the Indians?

Limitations

With agriculture the main problem is deforestation which could quite easily occur if over indulgence takes place.

The problem with fuel and power is that the HEP stations cut off the main line of transport and communications leaving the only route the roads.

The trouble with large and small scale industries is finding skilled workers and getting the minerals and raw materials.

At last — some concern expressed about environmental issues

Mass mining and extraction will cause the minerals and raw materials to be used up quickly. If that happens (as they are the basis of Amazonian life) industry will go, so will the jobs and then the people. This will also cause limited deforestation.

The transport and communications looks very costly. The maintenance of thousands of miles of roads will be virtually impossible and at the moment the gravel tracks are hardly used — and do not look like changing in the near future.

There looks to be no problem with most of the social services except education. That will be a long process as most people can not read or write. There is the added problem of who is going to teach them.

The encouragement of settlement looks to be disasterous. The campaign is mainly aimed at poor people wanting to get away from poverty. As they are poor, though, they will not be able to afford a TV or radio, and probably can not read so the posters and letters are useless to them.

Conclusion

In conclusion I would say that Amazonia is a region of Brazil that needs to be developed slowly as the profits can be spread out over a long period of time giving a good income also spreading out the costs as well.

In the role-play exercise which arguments influenced this student?

Fig. 6.2 A student's work on Amazonian development.

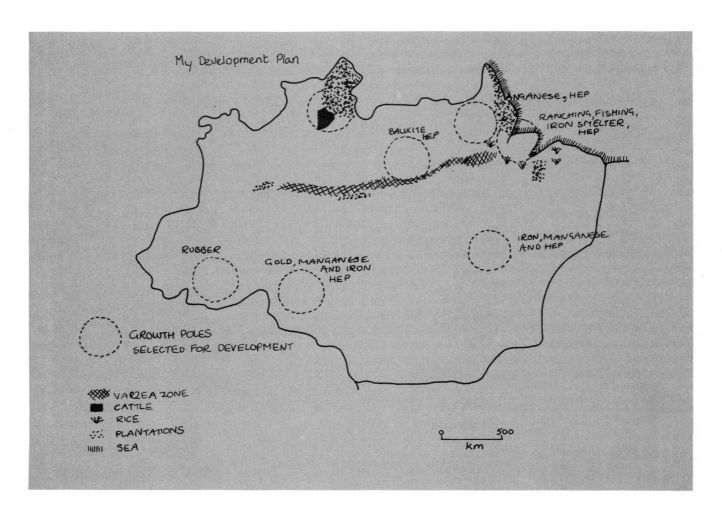

My Development Plan

MANGANESE, HEP

RANCHING, FISHING,
IRON SMELTER,
HEP

BAUXITE
HEP

IRON, MANGANESE
AND HEP

RUBBER

GOLD, MANGANESE
AND IRON
HEP

GROWTH POLES
SELECTED FOR DEVELOPMENT

⊠ VARZEA ZONE
■ CATTLE
Ⅴ RICE
⁘ PLANTATIONS
‖‖‖‖ SEA

0   500
km

6 > TRYING TO IMPROVE

❝❝ Use your marked work to improve. ❞❞

❝❝ Make sure you understand the assessment for the course. ❞❞

❝❝ Act on advice. ❞❞

One of the aims in following an Integrated Humanities course is to gain your maximum at GCSE. Consequently, you are always looking to improve your performance. However, before you can improve, you need to know how well you are doing. You get important feedback about your performance when your teacher marks your work. Although marks, grades and levels are important, they are of little use unless you understand what they mean. You should *ask your teacher* for as much information as possible about the criteria used to assess your work and about what he/she is looking for in each of the grade boundaries for GCSE. Chapter 1 has attempted to explain the assessment procedures for the three examination boards who offer Integrated Humanities. Look back at this. Does it help you to understand what is required? If not, ask your teacher to explain. You will not win the game unless you know what the rules are!

Don't overlook the teacher's comments in your work. This is one way in which your teacher communicates with you and the comments will be useful. Try and act on the advice given. If you do not understand any comments made, ask for clarification. *Ask questions.*

To understand further what it is your teacher and the examiner are looking for in student work you could offer to mark the work of a classmate. You may want them to comment on your work. Not only would this help your understanding; it would also give you an idea of other people's thinking. Here is a marked piece of coursework. Look at the comments made by the teacher. Do they give advice about how to improve? Are the good parts of the work identified?

7 > SHARING A PROBLEM

❝❝ Discuss your problems. ❞❞

There are bound to be occasions when you face problems with your Integrated Humanities work. This is quite natural. What you mustn't do is allow this problem to magnify and affect your success. Although your parents or guardians are unlikely to have experienced courses like Integrated Humanities in their schooling, it is important for you to discuss your problem with them. They may be able to help. Explain the course to them. Tell them what is required of you, how you will be assessed and the fact you have to keep to deadlines. They may well be able to help you achieve these. If they understand the nature of your work they are more likely to appreciate the types of activities you have to

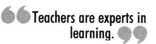
Teachers are experts in learning.

complete: for example, visiting libraries, completing questionnaires, interviews, surveys and assessing public opinion. If your parents or guardians are aware that the course involves you *actively* in your learning, they will be able to help.

Don't forget, your teachers are experts in learning. Do not be afraid to ask them for help and advice. Make sure you ask for help as soon as you think you may have a problem. Don't wait until the problem becomes a crisis! Friends could also be used to discuss problems and concerns with. Share ideas and help each other to plan work. In this way you will have a better chance of coping with *stress* caused by your studies.

To conclude, your Integrated Humanities course is likely to be structured in a way which demands a lot of *independent* study. You must *plan* and *organise* your time to cope with this. Make sure you meet *deadlines*, seek *help* when it is needed, *ask* questions and *use classtime* profitably. In this way you have a better chance of achieving your maximum and of getting a good grade at GCSE.

INDEX